EXAMKRACKERS MCAT®

REASONING SKILLS:
VERBAL, RESEARCH & MATH

9TH EDITION

JONATHAN ORSAY

OSOTE
PUBLISHING

Major Contributors:
Joshua Albrecht, M.D., Ph.D.
Jennifer Birk-Goldschmidt, M.S.
Stephanie Blatch, M.A.
North de Pencier
Lauren Nadler
Colleen Moran Shannon

Contributors
Max Blodgett
David Collins
Ari Cuperfain
Ashley Feldman, Esq.
Darby Festa
Amanda Horowitz
Mohan Natrajan
Laura Neubauer
Steven Tersigni, M.D., M.P.H.

Advisors:
Mark Pedersen, M.D.
Ahmed Sandhu
Morgan Sellers, M.D.
Arielle Sullum
Sara Thorp, D.O.
Charles Yoo

Art Director:
Erin Daniel

Designers:
Dana Kelley
Charles Yuen

Layout & composition:
Nick Williams

Illustrators:
Stephen Halker
Kellie Holoski

ISBN 10: 1-893858-71-5 (Volume 1)
ISBN 13: 978-1-893858-70-1 (6 Volume Set)
9th Edition

To purchase additional copies of this book or the rest of the 6 volume set, call 1-888-572-2536 or fax orders to 1-859-255-0109.

Examkrackers.com
Osote.com

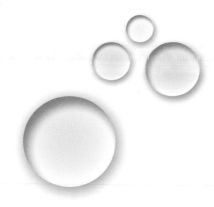

PHOTOCOPYING & DISTRIBUTION POLICY

Acknowledgements

The hard work and expertise of many individuals contributed to this book. The idea of writing in two voices, a science voice and an MCAT® voice, was the creative brainchild of my imaginative friend Jordan Zaretsky. I would like to thank Scott Calvin for lending his exceptional science talent and pedagogic skills to this project. I also must thank seventeen years worth of Examkrackers students for doggedly questioning every explanation, every sentence, every diagram, and every punctuation mark in the book, and for providing the creative inspiration that helped me find new ways to approach and teach biology. Finally, I wish to thank my wife, Silvia, for her support during the difficult times in the past and those that lie ahead.

Introduction to the Reasoning Skills Manual

The Examkrackers books are designed to give you exactly the information you need to do well on the MCAT®. This manual provides six lectures that will prepare you to master the MCAT®. The first two lectures of the Reasoning Skills Manual will orient you to the MCAT® and will teach you the skills necessary for all sections of the test. The first lecture provides an in-depth introduction to the MCAT® and instruction on the math skills necessary to perform well on the exam. The second lecture provides the research skills needed for 50% of MCAT® questions across three sections, including instruction on how best to read a research-based passage and interpret the results. The next four lectures of this book focus on the Critical Analysis and Reasoning Skills section of the MCAT®. With step-by-step instructions, this manual will help you to strengthen your verbal and reasoning skills. This manual teaches the best techniques for reading MCAT® passages and identifying correct answers with speed and accuracy. Use this manual to develop both the verbal and reasoning skills needed for a high score on the MCAT®.

How to Use This Manual

The Examkrackers books include features to help you retain and integrate information for the MCAT®. Take advantage of these features to get the most out of your study time.

- **The 3 Keys** – The keys unlock the material and the MCAT®. Each lecture begins with 3 keys that organize by highlighting the most important things to remember from each chapter. Examine the 3 Keys before and after reading each lecture to make sure you have absorbed the most important messages. As you read, continue to develop your own key concepts that will guide your studying and performance.

- **The thirty minute exams** are designed to simulate and educate. They are similar to an MCAT® section, but are shortened with most of the easy questions removed. We believe that you can answer most of the easy questions without too much help from us, so the best way to raise your score is to focus on the more difficult questions. This method is one of the reasons for the rapid and celebrated success of the Examkrackers prep course and products. Do not be discouraged by poor performance on these exams; it is not meant to predict your performance on the real MCAT®.

The questions that you get wrong and even those you guess correctly are most important. They represent your potential score increase. When you get a question wrong or have to guess, determine why and identify what you will do differently to improve your score.

Study diligently, trust this book to guide you, and you will reach your MCAT® goals.

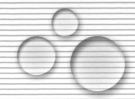

Table of Contents

Introduction to the MCAT® and Math

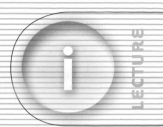

i.1 Welcome to the Examkrackers MCAT® Manuals

These manuals will give you what you need to master the MCAT®. The best way to gain a high score on the MCAT® is to have a deep understanding of both its content and its testing methods. This lecture will begin with a general overview to acquaint you with the nuts and bolts of the exam. Then it will discuss how the MCAT® tests and why it tests this way.

Understanding how the MCAT® works will allow you to study efficiently. Knowing what to expect on test day will prepare you to get the most out of the Examkrackers manuals and out of your studying.

THE 3 KEYS

1. The MCAT® rewards flexibility and connections. Study concepts in order to simplify, understand, and organize content.

2. Remove the disguise of complexity from MCAT® passages and questions to reveal the simple science tested.

3. Keep MCAT® math simple: use proportionality, rounding, units, and scientific notation.

i.2 The Medical College Admission Test

The MCAT® is one measure that medical schools use to judge a student's readiness for medical education. It is a test of your skills in applying what you know. Because it is standardized, the MCAT® tests a finite amount of material in a predictable way. This means that the ability to get a good score on the MCAT® is a skill that can be developed like any other. These manuals will first teach you what to expect from the MCAT® and will then describe the skills and information you need to succeed.

Format

The MCAT® consists of 4 distinct sections: Biological and Biochemical Foundations of Living Systems; Chemical and Physical Foundations of Biological Systems; Psychological, Social, and Biological Foundations of Behavior; and Critical Analysis and Reasoning Skills.

The MCAT® emphasizes biomolecular life processes, interpretation of scientific research, and connections between topics in the basic sciences. It tests psychology and sociology as they relate to human health and biology. Tested topics in physics and organic chemistry have been reduced to make way for this new material. Each section contains passages followed by questions. Passages are usually derived from published articles and essays. There are also stand alone questions between passages in all sections except the CARS section.

The Biological and Biochemical Foundations of Living Systems section contains 59 questions with a time limit of 95 minutes. It covers the biological and biochemical mechanisms that underlie the processes of living organisms. Questions ask you to connect the levels of molecular, biochemical, cellular, organ, and system functions. Developing your ability to move between levels of biological organization will allow you to succeed in this section.

The Chemical and Physical Foundations of Biological Systems section contains 59 questions with a time limit of 95 minutes. It covers basic concepts in physics and chemistry, particularly related to medicine and processes in the human body. This section will reward your comfort in making connections between the chemical, physical, and biological sciences.

The Psychological, Social, and Biological Foundations of Behavior section contains 59 questions with a time limit of 95 minutes. It will require you to consider psychological, sociological, and biological factors relating to phenomena such as formation of identity, personal behavior, and group dynamics. Such topics will be tested in the context of health, illness, and healthcare.

The Critical Analysis and Reasoning Skills (CARS) section contains 53 questions with a time limit of 90 minutes. The CARS section includes passages on a variety of medically-related topics, including public health, medical ethics, and cultural studies, as well as other topics in the humanities, social sciences and the arts. The CARS section tests narrative skills, such as analytic thinking and logic, rather than testing a specific base of knowledge.

Scoring

Each section is scored on a scale of 15 points. The scale is then shifted such that the minimum score for each section is 118 while the maximum is 132. Among all MCAT® test-takers, the midpoint in the score distribution for each section is 125. You might be wondering why the Association of American Medical Colleges (AAMC) seemingly complicated scoring in this way. The AAMC has arranged MCAT® scoring so that it is most easily interpreted by medical schools. The midpoint for the combined score of all four sections is a round number: 500 (125 x 4 = 500). The median score is 500 with a maximum score of 528 and a minimum score of 472. Very few test takers will earn scores close to the maximum or

Hey there, fancy pants. Don't worry about the complex section names. The MCAT® tests the basic sciences. So let's stick with simple names:
1. Biological section
2. Physical section
3. Pyschosocial section
4. CARS section

The new MCAT® has been made approximately 45% longer to make the scoring for each section more accurate. To prepare for the increased length, practice focus and stamina.

I will train, understand, practice and connect.

minimum so these numbers are less important for interpretation. Most medical school applicants will earn scores near the median of 500, which, therefore, can be compared easily to this round number. Since medical schools are looking for above average students, aim to score as far above 500 as possible. The Examkrackers manuals will help you do just that.

i.3 | How the MCAT® Tests

Knowing how the MCAT® tests will allow you to study accordingly. The MCAT® is a test of how well you understand and apply the basics of what you know, not how many facts you can memorize. Although some amount of rote memorization is necessary for the MCAT®, it is not sufficient to do well. The MCAT® invites you to bring an understanding of the simple science and to apply what you have learned in one discipline to problems in another discipline. Each section of the MCAT® integrates aspects across the biological, physical, and social sciences in its passages and questions. The MCAT® asks you to make connections between topics and to apply what you know in new circumstances. The MCAT® can be challenging even for excellent pre-medical students. Exams in introductory science courses reward memorization and the "click" of one correct answer to every question. The MCAT® rewards a deeper understanding of why the simple science makes sense, as well as the ability to solve problems when the answer is not clear-cut. Thinking flexibly, using underlying concepts rather than relying on memorization, and integrating what you have learned across disciplines are key MCAT® skills.

The AAMC deliberately makes both passages and questions seem more complex than what is tested. They use terminology and topics in passages and questions that are not commonly taught in introductory courses. The MCAT® invites you to organize, simplify, and stay oriented in the face of unfamiliar material or seemingly complex terminology. The MCAT® tests your confidence in applying the basic science that is necessary to find the best answer. Learn to recognize the disguise of complexity and do not let it intimidate you.

Some passages in the CARS section will seem to be disorganized, written poorly, or written in a disjointed way. CARS passages may be missing introductory or transitional sentences that normally would be orienting. The passage may jump back and forth between two points of view. This disorganized writing is intentional. It tests how you organize the information you receive and whether you can follow the author's argument while reading for the author's opinion.

The MCAT® rewards flexibility in thinking about the material and applying what you know. It differs from other tests in the type of answer choices provided. Frequently you will find more than one answer that seem to work; sometimes no answer choice seems quite right. Identifying the answer to an MCAT® question means choosing the best answer rather than one that "clicks" but does not answer the question as well. The MCAT® rewards students who develop a tolerance for uncertainty and the ability to discern nuance.

The new MCAT® emphasizes research skills, both in its passages and in 50% of the questions asked across three sections of the test. The MCAT® asks you to interpret articles and studies, follow experiments, understand research techniques, critique methods, and interpret findings.

The Examkrackers method will help you develop the habits and skills that you need to succeed on test day.

A physician carries the most important underlying concepts in hand and is ready with a sense of how systems and physiology are connected. Details can be double checked or referenced as needed. MCAT® practice is medical practice.

Physicians must organize the narrative they receive from a patient to best understand the patient and the patient's needs. CARS practice is medical practice.

A physician is flexible in applying medical knowledge, as medicine rarely offers simple answers. Looking for the "best" answer among imperfect choices rather than the single "correct" one will help you do well on the MCAT®. MCAT® question practice is medical practice.

Recommended medical treatments constantly change as research progresses. Strong research and reasoning skills are critical for the best practice of evidence-based medicine. MCAT® research practice is medical practice.

How to Study for the MCAT®

The Examkrackers method was developed by individuals who achieved very high MCAT® scores through study and practice. Significant experience and thorough research inform every page of the manuals. The Examkrackers manuals are carefully organized to best prepare you for success on the MCAT®. They teach content conceptually, encourage the skills necessary for MCAT® success, and are designed to help you develop mental connections.

As you review the basic science, stay in touch with MCAT® passages and questions. Many students make the mistake of focusing on details of the tested scientific topics without simultaneously building the problem-solving skills that the MCAT® primarily tests. Your preparation of the material should go hand in hand with the unique ways that the MCAT® will ask you to apply that material. Stay in touch with the style of the MCAT® by taking regular practice tests as you review.

The Examkrackers method is a four part approach designed to strengthen your MCAT® skills:

1. Refresh: Preparation & Exposure

2. Remember: Concept Building

3. Relate: Practice, Practice, and More Practice

4. Repeat: Repetition for Success

Refresh is the first part of the Examkrackers method. Re-exposure to basic scientific topics is accomplished by a thorough review of the material and terminology tested on the MCAT®. Examkrackers manuals cover all of the topics necessary for your success on the MCAT®. It does not make sense to waste time studying material that the MCAT® does not test unless that material helps you understand the material that IS tested. The Examkrackers manuals let you know what to study by putting tested topics in bold.

Remember is the concept-building step of the Examkrackers method. Most important to your review of content is how you organize the information, both in your notes and mentally. Make your knowledge base easily accessible on MCAT® day – that is, organized, conceptual, connected, and portable - so that your mind is uncluttered and fully available to attend to the passage or question at hand.

This step will move you beyond the habit of memorization. The Examkrackers manuals emphasize connected, conceptual thinking. The Three Keys, Signposts, and Salty will offer help in the form of portable concepts, connections, mnemonics and occasionally some comic relief. Preparing concepts rather than content will allow you to apply your knowledge to any MCAT® question that you encounter. Each lecture contains 24 practice questions to reinforce your understanding as you read.

Relate is the practice piece of the Examkrackers approach. It is arguably the most valuable in raising your MCAT® score. Ample practice is the best way to learn how to improve your performance and relate your knowledge base to the MCAT® itself. Getting accustomed to the MCAT®'s style is essential to success. Our manuals include In-Class Exams, each with 3 passages and 23 questions, that allow you to apply what you've learned to a simulated MCAT®.

Take full length practice exams regularly. This will give you a baseline score from which to improve as well as regular, specific clues to changing your score. Every question you get wrong represents a potential score increase. Examine the questions that you get wrong to determine how you were led astray and what habits you will change on your next practice test. Use the questions you guess on or get wrong as a guide to subject areas that require extra review.

Repeat is the reinforcement step of the Examkrackers approach. Repetition allows you to strengthen skills and topic areas that need attention. Once you identify a skill that you need to improve to get MCAT® questions right the first

MCAT® passages will often deliberately include new information that is not itself being tested. Your job is to bring and apply the simple science you know to these new situations.

MCAT® practice is medical practice. Be fully present, both mentally and physically, to each MCAT® passage and question you solve. Attend fully to the MCAT® just as you will attend wholly to each patient you encounter.

time, practice, practice, practice! Repeat it each time you take practice questions. Be careful here, because repeating a bad habit can reinforce it. When you review practice tests, be aware of what kind of thinking brings you to the best answer and what habits lead you astray. Only repeat what works!

As you prepare for MCAT® success, make friends with the test. Think of it as a game or a puzzle to solve. Rather than a mountain in your way, a mountain fun to climb. Be confident in your preparation, in your MCAT® knowledge, and in yourself. You are more likely to see improvement if you have a great MCAT® attitude!

i.5 | Preparing for MCAT® Day

Three months is the ideal time frame for MCAT® preparation. Stretching out intensive studying makes retaining all of the information more difficult. Many students make the mistake of first reviewing the material for many weeks before beginning practice questions and exams. Reviewing science by itself does not increase MCAT® scores. Taking MCAT®-style exams is the best way to boost your score. Plan to take one regular, full-length MCAT® exam per week. It is critically important to spend time evaluating the questions you got wrong to learn what to do differently. When you miss a question, review the science, then work on your own to solve the question before looking at the answer explanation, which denies you the opportunity to learn to solve the question yourself. This process builds reliable MCAT® logic, skills, and confidence. Once you have solved the question, read the answer explanation to supplement your approach.

Complete the majority of your review at least thirty days before your MCAT® date. Then switch to a schedule of less review and far more practice. Your comfort with MCAT®-style passages and questions will increase dramatically in these weeks of intense practice and repetition.

One week before the MCAT®, significantly decrease the intensity of your study schedule. The last week before taking the MCAT® should consist of very light studying and revisiting remaining areas that need reinforcement. The decreased workload will help you avoid burnout before MCAT® day and will mentally refresh you for your real MCAT®. During this time, don't overdo it. Trust in what you know and the studying you have completed.

Below are tips for the last week before the MCAT®. Follow our advice in order to be at your best on MCAT® day.

Physical Preparation

Familiarity – Visit your test center, traveling by the same route and method that you will use on test day. Investigate parking, places to get food, and, if you can, the seating situation in the room.

Sleeping patterns – Leading up to the MCAT®, plan the timing of your peak activity to coincide with the time of your MCAT®. If you have scheduled an 8 am test, make sure you are actively studying and taking practice tests at 8 am in the weeks leading up to the MCAT®. Go to sleep and wake up at the same time that you will on the day of the exam. Sleep at least 8 hours every night the week before the MCAT®. Leave plenty of time to wake up before the start of the test. Have an MCAT® friend call you to make sure your alarm worked.

Exercise – Exercise moderately this week. Don't exercise too strenuously in the day or two leading up to the exam.

Food – Eat healthily to keep your energy levels high. Healthy eating will also help you sleep better. Think ahead about what you will eat and drink during breaks on test day.

The fear of the unknown...oh, wait, no unknowns here. The more you know about the MCAT®, the better you can use our materials to KRACK the MCAT®!

Ah yes, the MCAT® muscle is located right next to the Criticalus Thinkae and Problemas Solveras.

Mental Preparation

Studying – You cannot review everything on the MCAT® in one week. Instead, choose your weakest remaining subject and become an expert at it. Then move on to your next weakest subject. Study less each day until the day before the exam, and take that day off. Do not study the night before the MCAT®, no matter what.

Visualization – Visualize MCAT® day. There will be distractions everywhere, but you will be unaffected, remaining focused on the test.

Confidence – Approach the MCAT® with confidence. Don't second guess yourself.

The day before the MCAT®, don't study. Rest and do something fun! A positive mood and a refill of energy and motivation will help you succeed on test day.

On the day of the MCAT®, it is normal to have a highly stimulated sympathetic nervous system. For many students, this results in greater awareness of distractions. People seem more intense, and lights may seem brighter or sounds louder. Practice the skill of focus leading up to the MCAT® so that you can choose not to be misled by distractions, whether internal or external. Instead trust that your adrenaline and sharpened senses are powerful tools that will help you do well on the MCAT®. Attuned senses and a stimulated nervous system will increase your performance abilities. Trust in your studying, your skills, and the time you have invested. Enter the MCAT® with confidence, knowing that you are ready.

On the day before the MCAT®, take some time off and relax! Trust that you have studied hard and are ready. Go into the MCAT® refreshed and confident.

Keep your friends close and the MCAT® closer.

Concepts on the MCAT® are like my trusted wrench. If I know how to use it, it doesn't matter how complicated the problem is, I can fix it!

i.6 | MCAT® Math

The MCAT® will not test your math skills beyond the contents of this book. The MCAT® does require knowledge of the following up to a second year high school algebra level: ratios, proportions, square roots, exponents and logarithms, scientific notation, quadratic and simultaneous equations, and graphs. In addition, the MCAT® tests: vector addition, subtraction; basic trigonometry; very basic probabilities (seen in the context of genetics problems). The MCAT® does not test dot product, cross product or calculus.

Calculators are not allowed on the MCAT®, nor would they be helpful. From this moment until MCAT® day, do all math problems in your head whenever possible. Do not use a calculator, and use your pencil as seldom as possible when you do any math.

If you find yourself doing a lot of calculations on the MCAT®, it's a good indication that you are doing something wrong. Most problems can be solved using simple reasoning about proportions or elimination of unreasonable answers rather than lengthy calculations. As a rule of thumb, **spend no more than 3 minutes on any MCAT® physics question**. Once you have spent 3 minutes on a question without being able to resolve it, stop what you're doing and read the question again for a simple answer. If you don't see a simple answer, make your best guess and move to the next question.

Practice doing MCAT® math quickly in your head.

i.7 | Rounding

Exact numbers are rarely useful on the MCAT®. In order to save time and avoid errors when making calculations on the test, use round numbers. For instance, the gravitational constant g should be rounded up to 10 m/s^2 for the purpose of calculations, even when instructed by the MCAT® to do otherwise. Calculations like 23.4×9.8 should be thought of as "something less than 23.4×10, which equals something less than 234 or less than 2.34×10^2." Thus, if you see a question requiring the calculation of 23.4×9.8 followed by these answer choices:

    A. 1.24×10^2
    B. 1.81×10^2
    C. 2.29×10^2
    D. 2.35×10^2

Wrong way

Answer is something less than $23.4 \times 10 = 234$.

Right way

then answer choice C is the closest answer under 2.34×10^2, and C should be chosen quickly without resorting to complicated calculations. Rarely will there be two possible answer choices close enough to prevent a correct selection after rounding. If two answer choices on the MCAT® are so close that you find you have to write down the math, it's probably because you've made a mistake. If you find yourself in that situation, look again at the question for a simple solution. If you don't see it, guess and go on.

This is me after I hurt myself with complicated calculations on my first practice test.

Remain aware of the direction in which you have rounded. In the example just given, since answer choice D is closer to 234 than answer choice C, you may have been tempted to choose it. However, a quick check on the direction of rounding would confirm that 9.8 was rounded upward, so the answer should be less than 234. Again, assuming the calculations were necessary to arrive at the answer, an answer choice which would prevent the use of rounding, such as 2.32×10^2, simply would not appear as an answer choice on a real MCAT®. It would not appear for the very reason that such an answer choice would force the test taker to spend time making complicated calculations, and those aren't the skills that the MCAT® is designed to test.

If rounding is used in each calculation in a series of calculations, the rounding errors can be compounded and the resulting answer can be useless. For instance, we may be required to take the above example and further divide "23.4 × 9.8" by 4.4. We might round 4.4 down to 4, and divide 240 by 4 to get 60; however, each of our roundings would have increased our result, compounding the error. Instead, it is better to round 4.4 up to 5, dividing 235 by 5 to get 47. This is closer to the exact answer of 52.1182. To increase the accuracy of multiple estimations, **try to compensate for upward rounding with downward rounding.**

Notice, in the example above, that when we increase the denominator, we decrease the quotient (overall term). For instance:

$$\frac{625}{24} = 26.042 \qquad \frac{625}{25} = 25$$

Rounding the denominator of 24 up to 25 results in a decrease in the quotient.

When rounding squares, remember that you are really rounding twice. $(2.2)^2$ is really 2.2 × 2.2, so when we say that the answer is something greater than 4 we need to keep in mind that it is significantly greater because we have rounded down twice. One way to increase your accuracy is to round just one of the factors, leaving you with something greater than 4.4. This is much closer to the exact answer of 4.84.

Another strategy for rounding an exponential term is to remember that difficult-to-solve exponential terms must lie between two easy-to-solve exponential terms. Thus 2.22 is between 2^2 and 3^2, closer to 2^2. This strategy is especially helpful for square roots. The square root of 21 must be between the square root of 16 and the square root of 25. Thus, the MCAT® square root of 21 must be between 4 and 5, or about 4.6.

$$\sqrt{25} = 5$$
$$\sqrt{21} = ?$$
$$\sqrt{16} = 4$$

For more complicated roots, recall that any root is simply a fractional exponent. For instance, the square root of 9 is the same as $9^{1/2}$. This means that the fourth root of 4 is $4^{1/4}$. This is the same as $(4^{1/2})^{1/2}$ or $\sqrt{2}$. We can combine these techniques to solve even more complicated roots:

It's worth your time to memorize:

$$\sqrt[3]{27} = 3$$
$$4^{\frac{2}{3}} = \sqrt[3]{4^2} = \sqrt[3]{16} = ? \approx 2.5$$
$$\sqrt[3]{8} = 2$$
$$\sqrt{2} \approx 1.4 \; and \; \sqrt{3} \approx 1.7$$

You are most likely to see these roots in the context of trigonometric functions. The MCAT® will probably give you any values that you need for trigonometric functions; however, since the MCAT® typically uses common angles, it is a good idea to be familiar with trigonometric values for common angles. Use the paradigm below to remember the values of common angles. Notice that the sine values are the reverse of the cosine values. Also notice that the numbers under the radical are 0, 1, 2, 3 and 4 from top to bottom for the sine function and bottom to top for the cosine function, and all are divided by 2.

TABLE I.1 > Sines and Cosines of Common Angles

θ	Sine	Cosine
0°	$\frac{\sqrt{0}}{2}$	$\frac{\sqrt{4}}{2}$
30°	$\frac{\sqrt{1}}{2}$	$\frac{\sqrt{3}}{2}$
45°	$\frac{\sqrt{2}}{2}$	$\frac{\sqrt{2}}{2}$
60°	$\frac{\sqrt{3}}{2}$	$\frac{\sqrt{1}}{2}$
90°	$\frac{\sqrt{4}}{2}$	$\frac{\sqrt{0}}{2}$

Rounding is an effective tool for solving MCAT® math. Practice it.

Less practiced test takers may perceive a rounding strategy as risky. On the contrary, the test makers actually design their answers with a rounding strategy in mind. Complicated numbers can be intimidating to anyone not comfortable with a rounding strategy.

Practice Problems

Solve the following problems by rounding. Do not use a pencil or a calculator.

1. $\dfrac{5.4 \times 7.1 \times 3.2}{4.6^2}$ ≈ 5

    A.   2.2
    B.   3.8
    C.   5.8
    D.   7.9

2. $\dfrac{\sqrt{360 \times 9.8}}{6.2}$ ≈ 10

    A.   9.6
    B.   13.2
    C.   17.3
    D.   20.2

3. $\dfrac{\sqrt{2} \times 23}{50}$ $\approx \dfrac{1.5 \times 20}{50} = \dfrac{30}{50} \approx 0.6$

    A.   0.12
    B.   0.49
    C.   0.65
    D.   1.1

4. $\dfrac{(2 \times 45)^2}{9.8 \times 21}$ $\approx \dfrac{100^2}{200} = \dfrac{10,000}{200} \approx 50$

    A.   11
    B.   39
    C.   86
    D.   450

5. $\sqrt{\dfrac{2 \times 9.8^2}{49}}$ $\approx \dfrac{\sqrt{2 \cdot 100}}{7} \approx \dfrac{1.4 \cdot 10}{7} \approx \dfrac{14}{7} \approx 2$

    A.   0.3
    B.   0.8
    C.   1.2
    D.   2

Answers

1. C is correct. The exact answer is 5.7981.

2. A is correct. The exact answer is 9.5802.

3. C is correct. The exact answer is 0.65054.

4. B is correct. The exact answer is 39,359.

5. D is correct. The exact answer is 1.9799.

i.8 | Scientific Notation

One important math skill tested rigorously by the MCAT® is your ability to use scientific notation. Scientific notation is used to express values that are either very large or very small. Think of the mass of the Earth relative to a one kilogram bag of flour. Now think of the mass of a single atom relative to the same one kilogram bag of flour. The mass of the Earth in kilograms is approximately 6 with 24 zeroes at the end of it. Written out:

Mass of Earth = 6,000,000,000,000,000,000,000,000 kg.

On the opposite end of the spectrum, the mass of a carbon atom in kilograms is: 0.000,000,000,000,000,000,000,000,001,66 kg. That's 26 zeroes after the decimal place and before the one.

Scientific notation allows us compress these values so that they are more easy to visualize and compare with other values at a glance. In scientific notation, all values are written as the product of exactly two terms. The first term consists of one non-zero digit followed by a decimal place, and then by any number of digits after the decimal place. The second term is an exponential term and will always be of base 10 with the exponent taking on any possible value. This manual will define the terms in scientific notation as follows:

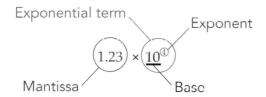

Writing values in this way can make analyzing data much simpler. For instance, if we wanted to know how much heavier the Earth is compared to a single carbon atom, we would have a tough time setting up our calculation and counting all of the zeroes. But with scientific notation, it is easy. Let's illustrate how to construct a value in scientific notation with the following example.

One mile is equal to 1609 meters. Let's think of this as 1609.0 instead. In order to get 1609.0 to the form in the caption above, we must move the decimal point over three spaces to the left, as in 1.6090. Mathematically, moving three spaces to the left corresponds to dividing by 10^3. To keep the equality, we must multiply our result by 10^3. So taking these two operations together, we end up with:

$$1609.0 = 1.6090 \times 10^3.$$

Here's another way of thinking about it: 1609.0 is equivalent to writing 1609.0 multiplied by 1000 and divided by 1000 because $\frac{1000}{1000}$ =1. In other words,

$$1609.0 = 1609.0 \times \frac{1000}{1000} = \frac{1609}{1000} \times 1000$$

The term on the left becomes 1.609, and the second term, 1000, can be rewritten as 10^3. So we get our scientific notation value, 1.609×10^3.

We can go the other way as well to work with smaller numbers. One inch is equal to 0.0254 meters. To get 0.0254 in the form we need — namely 2.54 — we must move the decimal to the right two times. This is equivalent to multiplying by 10^2. Once again, to keep everything equal, we must divide our result by 10^2. Dividing by 10^2 is the same as multiplying by 10^{-2}. So,

$$0.0254 = 2.54 \times 10^{-2}.$$

In order to maximize your MCAT® score, familiarize yourself with the techniques and shortcuts of scientific notation. Although it may not seem so, scientific notation was designed to make math easier, and it does. Practice the following techniques until you come to view scientific notation as a valuable ally.

MAGNITUDE: It is important that you gain a feel for the exponential aspect of scientific notation. 10^{-8} is much greater than 10^{-12}. It is 10,000 times greater! Thus, when comparing one solution whose concentration of particles is 3.2×10^{-11} mol/L with a second solution whose concentration of particles is 4.1×10^{-9} mol/L, visualize the second solution as hundreds of times more concentrated than the first.

Pay special attention to magnitudes when adding. For example, try solving:

$$\begin{array}{r} 3.74 \times 10^{-15} \\ + \ 6.43 \times 10^{-3} \\ \hline \end{array}$$

On the MCAT®, the answer is simply 6.43×10^{-3}. This is true because 6.43×10^{-3} is so much greater than 3.74×10^{-15} that 3.74×10^{-15} is negligible. Thus you can round off the answer to 6.43×10^{-3}. After all, the exact answer is 0.00643000000000374.

Try solving:

$$\begin{array}{r} 5.32 \times 10^{-4} \\ \times \ 1.12 \times 10^{-13} \\ \hline \end{array}$$

> Paying attention to the difference in magnitudes when adding is particularly important in the context of acid-base chemistry, as you will see in the chemistry manual.

The MCAT® answer is something greater than 5.3×10^{-17}. We cannot ignore the smaller number in this case because we are multiplying. **In addition or subtraction, a number at least 100 times smaller can be considered negligible. This is not true in multiplication or division.**

The fastest way to add or subtract numbers in scientific notation is to make the exponents match. For instance:

$$\begin{array}{r} 2.76 \times 10^{4} \\ + \ 6.91 \times 10^{5} \\ \hline \end{array}$$

The MCAT® answer is something less than 7.2×10^5. To get this answer quickly we match the exponents and rewrite the equation as follows:

$$\begin{array}{r} 2.76 \times 10^{4} \\ + \ 69.10 \times 10^{4} \\ \hline \end{array}$$

This is similar to the algebraic equation:

$$\begin{array}{r} 2.76y \\ + \ 69.10y \\ \hline \end{array}$$

where $y = 10^4$. We simply add the coefficients of y. Rounding, we have $3y + 69y = 72y$. Thus 72×10^4, or 7.2×10^5, is the answer.

When rearranging 6.91×10^5 to 69.1×10^4, we simply multiply by 10/10 (a form of 1). In other words, we multiply 6.91 by 10 and divide 10^5 by 10.

$$\begin{array}{c} \times\ 10 \\ \nearrow \\ 6.91 \times 10^5 = 69.1 \times 10^4 \\ \searrow \\ \div\ 10 \end{array}$$

A useful mnemonic for remembering which way to move the decimal point when we add or subtract from the exponent is to use the acronym LARS:

$$\textsf{L}_\text{eft} \ \textsf{A}_\text{dd}, \ \textsf{R}_\text{ight} \ \textsf{S}_\text{ubtract}$$

Multiplication and Division

When multiplying similar bases with exponents, add the exponents; when dividing, subtract the exponents. $10^4 \times 10^5 = 10^9$. $10^4/10^{-6} = 10^{10}$.

When multiplying or dividing with scientific notation, we deal with the exponential terms and mantissa separately, *regardless of the number of terms*. For instance:

$$\frac{\left(3.2 \times 10^4\right) \times \left(4.9 \times 10^{-8}\right)}{\left(2.8 \times 10^{-7}\right)}$$

should be rearranged to:

$$\frac{3 \times 5}{3} \times \frac{10^4 \times 10^{-8}}{10^{-7}}$$

giving us an MCAT® answer of something greater than 5×10^3. (The exact answer, 5.6×10^3, is greater than our estimate because we decreased one term in the numerator by more than we increased the other, which results in a low estimate; and because we increased the term in the denominator, which also results in a low estimate.)

When taking a term written in scientific notation to some power (such as squaring or cubing it), we also deal with the decimal and exponent separately. The MCAT® answer to:

$$(3.1 \times 10^7)^2$$

is something greater than 9×10^{14}. Recall that when taking an exponential term to a power, we multiply the exponents. The first step in taking the square root of a term in scientific notation is to make the exponent even. Then we take the square root of the mantissa and exponential term separately.

$$\sqrt{8.1 \times 10^5}$$

Make the exponent even.

$$\sqrt{81 \times 10^4}$$

Take the square root of the mantissa and exponential term separately.

$$\sqrt{81} \times \sqrt{10^4} = 9 \times 10^2$$

Notice how much more efficient this method is. What is the square root of 49,000? Most students start thinking about 700, or 70, or something with a 7 in it. By using the scientific notation method, we quickly see that there is no 7 involved at all.

$$\sqrt{49,000} = \sqrt{4.9 \times 10^4} \approx 2.2 \times 10^2$$

Try finding the square root of 300 and the square root of 200.

$$\sqrt{300} = \sqrt{3 \times 10^2} \approx 1.7 \times 10^1$$

$$\sqrt{200} = \sqrt{2 \times 10^2} \approx 1.4 \times 10^1$$

Practice Problems

Solve the following problems without a calculator. Try not to use a pencil.

1. $\dfrac{2.3 \times 10^7 \times 5.2 \times 10^{-5}}{4.3 \times 10^2}$

   A. 1.2×10^{-1}
   B. 2.8
   C. 3.1×10
   D. 5.6×10^2

2. $(2.5 \times 10^{-7} \times 3.7 \times 10^{-6}) + 4.2 \times 10^2$

   A. 1.3×10^{-11}
   B. 5.1×10^{-10}
   C. 4.2×10^2
   D. 1.3×10^{15}

3. $[(1.1 \times 10^{-4}) + (8.9 \times 10^{-5})]^{\frac{1}{2}}$ $\sqrt{2 \times 10^{-4}} \approx 1.4 \times 10^{-2}$

   A. 1.1×10^{-2}
   B. 1.4×10^{-2}
   C. 1.8×10^{-2}
   D. 2.0×10^{-2}

4. $\frac{1}{2}(3.4 \times 10^2)(2.9 \times 10^8)^2$ $0.5(3)(9) \times 10^{2+16}$ $LARS$
   $\approx 14.5 \times 10^{18}$
   $\approx 1.45 \times 10^{19}$

   A. 1.5×10^{18}
   B. 3.1×10^{18}
   C. 1.4×10^{19}
   D. 3.1×10^{19}

5. $\dfrac{1.6 \times 10^{-19} \times 15}{36^2}$ $\dfrac{30 \cdot 10^{-19}}{(3.6 \times 10^1)^2} = \dfrac{30}{16} \cdot \dfrac{10^{-19}}{10^2} = 2 \cdot 10^{-21}$

   A. 1.9×10^{-21}
   B. 2.3×10^{-17}
   C. 1.2×10^{-9}
   D. 3.2×10^{-9}

Answers

1. B is correct. The exact answer is 2.7814.

2. C is correct. The other numbers are insignificant.

3. B is correct. The exact answer is 1.4107×10^{-2}.

4. C is correct. The exact answer is 1.4297×10^{19}.

5. A is correct. The exact answer is 1.8519×10^{-21}.

Logarithms

An order of magnitude means a ten times difference. 500 is one order of magnitude greater than 50; 4×10^7 is five orders of magnitude greater than 4×10^2. It is also correct to say that 3×10^7 is five orders of magnitude greater than 4×10^2 even though it is not exactly 100,000 times greater.

It is important to be able to handle problems involving logarithms, especially in the natural sciences. Logarithms are typically used when a certain physical property can have any value ranging across multiple orders of magnitude. These include the concentrations of dilute solutes in solution (the pH scale) and the intensity of sound waves (as in the decibel scale).

The logarithmic scale is used to compress very large or very small numbers into more manageable values. In this respect, it is similar to scientific notation. Questions involving logarithms will be written as follows:

$$\log_b x = y$$

The subscript b is called the base. This equation can be read as saying that "b raised to the y power is equal to x." Mathematically, this is expressed as

$$b^y = x$$

Logarithms can be tricky since the base is not always the same. However, for the MCAT® the base will usually be ten. So suppose we wanted to find the log of 1000. We would set up the problem as follows:

$$\log_{10} 1000 = y \rightarrow 10^y = 1000$$

We can see that we need to multiply 10 by itself three times to reach 1000 ($10 \times 10 \times 10 = 1000$). This means that the base 10 log of 1000 is 3. Similarly, since

$$10^{-y} = \frac{1}{10^y}$$

We have $\log_{10} 0.001 = y \rightarrow 10^y = 0.001$, and the base 10 log of 0.001 is -3.

It is also important to be able to round with logarithms. Consider the following example:

$$\log 88 = ?$$

We know that $\log 10 = 1$ and $\log 100 = 2$. We can predict that $\log 88$ will fall somewhere between 1 and 2, and indeed, $\log 88 = 1.94$. In general, we can round by first writing the equation in scientific notation and then using the method that follows. Suppose we needed to find the logarithm of 67,000. We would first write this as:

$$\log (6.7 \times 10^4)$$

We can rewrite this equation by splitting up the two terms and adding them together:

$$\log (6.7 \times 10^4) = \log (6.7) + \log (10^4)$$

The second term is equal to exactly 4, and the first term will be somewhere between 0 and 1. This means that we would expect our answer to be greater than 4 but less than 5. Actually, $\log(67,000) = 4.83$. For the logarithm of a number smaller than 1, such as 0.054, we would again convert to scientific notation and use the same process:

This will be helpful on the MCAT® if you need to solve an equation with log fractions, such as or Nernst (electrochemistry).

$$\log(0.054) = \log(5.4 \times 10^{(-2)}) = \log (5.4) + \log(10^{(-2)}) = \log(5.4) + (-2)$$

We can then predict that the solution will be between -1 and -2. The actual value of $\log(0.054)$ is -1.27.

The method we used on the previous page is based on a rule that all logarithms follow. If the product of two terms is contained within a logarithm, the solution will be equal to the sum of the individual logarithms. In other words,

$$\log(A \times B) = \log(A) + \log(B)$$

Similarly,

$$\log\left(\frac{A}{B}\right) = \log(A) - \log(B)$$

Let's take this one step further. Consider the logarithm of a number squared, for example, $\log(A^2)$. This can be rewritten by expanding A^2 to $A \times A$.

$$\log A^2 = \log(A \times A) = \log(A) + \log(A) = 2\log(A)$$

This can be extended to any exponent, so a general formula is,

$$\log(A^n) = n\log(A)$$

Most of the logarithms you encounter on the MCAT® will be base 10 logarithms of the form we have seen above. However, you may also come across logarithms using base e. Logarithms of base e are referred to as 'natural logs' and are written as $\ln(x)$. The mathematical constant e has a value of approximately 2.72, but for the MCAT®, we will approximate it as 3. Whereas for base 10, the log of 100 (10×10) is 2, for base e, the ln of 9 (3×3) is around 2. Natural logs appear in a handful of thermodynamics equations, but it is unlikely that you will be required to compute complicated base e logarithms.

i.10 | Equations and Proportionality

Much of the natural science content on the MCAT® involves relating properties to one another. Questions will commonly ask you to predict how a change in one property affects another property. Some of these relationships are more straightforward than others, but every relationship on the MCAT® can be expressed in the form of an equation, where the combination of terms on the left side is equal to the combination of terms on the right side. There are many different ways to visualize equations, but we will focus on two: algebraically and graphically.

Algebraic Equations

Algebraic equations are numerical descriptions of natural processes. On the MCAT®, proportional relationships between variables as given in an equation can often be used to circumvent lengthy calculations. In some cases, the MCAT® question simply asks the test taker to identify the relationship directly. **When the MCAT® asks for the change in one variable due to the change in another, it is making the assumption that all other variables remain constant.**

In the equation $F = ma$, we see that if we double F while holding m constant, a doubles. If we triple F, a triples. The same relationship holds for m and F. This type of relationship is called a direct proportion.

$$\overset{\times 2}{\nearrow}\quad\overset{\times 2}{\nearrow}$$
$$F = ma$$

F and a are directly proportional.

If we change the equation to $F = ma + b$, the directly proportional relationships are destroyed. Now if we double F while holding all variables besides a constant, a increases, but does not double. **In order for variables to be directly proportional to one another, they must both be in the numerator or** denominator when they are on opposite sides of the equation, or one must be in the numerator while the other is in the denominator when they are on the same side of the equation. In addition, all sums or differences in the equation must be contained in parentheses and multiplied by the rest of the equation. No variables within the sums or differences will be directly proportional to any other variable.

If we examine the relationship between m and a, in $F = ma$, we see that when F is held constant and m is doubled, a is reduced by a factor of 2. This type of relationship is called an **inverse proportion**. Again the relationship is destroyed if we add b to one side of the equation. **In order for variables to be inversely proportional to each other, they must both be in the numerator or denominator when they are on the same side of the equation, or one must be in the numerator while the other is in the denominator when they are on opposite sides of the equation. In addition, all sums or differences in the equation must be contained in parentheses and multiplied by the rest of the equation. No variables within the sums or differences will be directly proportional to any other variable.**

$$F = ma$$

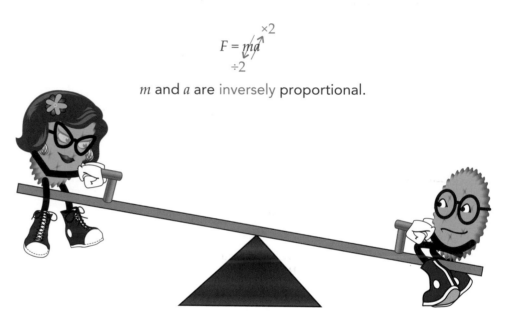

m and a are inversely proportional.

Equations can be used to better understand the scientific processes that they describe. On the flip side, considering the processes being described can make the equation easier to understand and recall. Suppose we are given the following equation:

$$Q = \frac{\Delta P \pi r^4}{8 \eta L}$$

This is Poiseuille's Law, which describes the flow rate of a real fluid through a horizontal pipe (Q). The volume flow rate Q of a real fluid through a horizontal pipe is equal to the product of the change in pressure ΔP, π, and the radius of the pipe to the fourth power r^4, divided by 8 times the viscosity and the length L of the pipe.

Poiseuille's Law will be covered in the context of the circulatory system. Despite the complicated appearance of the equation, it can be understood intuitively by considering the characteristics represented by each variable. Recall that the variables in the numerator of the right side of the equation must be directly proportional to Q. (π is a constant rather than a variable, so it does not have a proportional relationship with Q.) ΔP is the difference in pressure between the ends of the pipe; r is the radius of the pipe. Think about the effect that each of these has on water running through a hose. If you turn up the pressure, water comes out more quickly. What if you made the hose shorter? This also increases the rate of flow of the water. Simple intuition demonstrates the direct proportionality that is shown by the equation. If you were trying to remember Poiseuille's Law, this type of thinking would allow you to recall that ΔP and r belong in the numerator. Notice that the term in the equation is actually r^4. The exponent shows that even small changes in the radius of a pipe can have a dramatic effect on the velocity of the fluid flowing through it.

Now consider the variables in the denominator, which are there because they must be inversely proportional to Q. η is the viscosity of the fluid, meaning its thickness or resistance to flow; L is the length of the pipe. An increase in a fluid's resistance to flow will cause flow rate to decrease. (Which do you think will flow more quickly through a pipe—molasses or water? Water, which is less viscous than molasses.) Increasing the length will decrease flow rate because energy from the fluid is lost through friction against the walls of the pipe. (Imagine molasses running through an extremely long hose. You would expect the molasses to slow down or even stop before coming out the end of the hose.) As in the case of the variables in the numerator, reasoning about the variables in the denominator shows that their placement makes sense. An increase in these variables must lead to a decrease in flow rate; the variables are indirectly proportional to Q.

Narrating equations in this way makes both equations and the phenomena that they represent easier to understand and recall. Use this method to make sense of new equations and the relationships between variables.

> With rare exception, DON'T MEMORIZE. Instead, describe relationships and make connections. When you memorize there is a high risk that you do not understand what you are committing to memory. If you understand it, you won't need to memorize it. The MCAT® rewards understanding over memory.
>
> An equation is a shorthand for a story. If you tell the story and understand why it makes sense, you can use that understanding to rebuild the equation when you need it. Tell yourself the story: talk through the relationships between variables and notice why they are logical. "When pressure increases, it makes sense that flow rate would increase..." This approach is more reliable than your memory on MCAT® day!

MCAT® THINK

Water ($\eta = 1.80 \times 10^{-3}$ Pa s) flows through a pipe with a 14.0 cm radius at 2.00 L/s An engineer wishes to increase the length of the pipe from 10.0 m to 40.0 m without changing the flow rate or the pressure difference. What radius must the pipe have?

$$Q = \frac{\Delta P \pi r^4}{8 \eta L}$$

A.   12.1 cm
B.   14.0 cm
C.   19.8 cm
D.   28.0 cm

See answer on page 28

Practice Questions:

1. The coefficient of surface tension is given by the equation $\gamma = (F - mg)/(2L)$, where F is the net force necessary to pull a submerged wire of weight mg and length L through the surface of the fluid in question. The force required to remove a submerged wire from water was measured and recorded. If an equal force is required to remove a separate submerged wire with the same mass but twice the length from fluid x, what is the coefficient of surface tension for fluid x? ($\gamma_{water} = 0.073$ mN/m)

   A. 0.018 mN/m
   B. 0.037 mN/m
   C. 0.073 mN/m
   D. 0.146 mN/m

   $\gamma = \dfrac{(F - mg)}{(2)2L}$

   $0.07 \times 0.5 = 0.035$

2. A solid sphere rotating about a central axis has a moment of inertia

   $$I = \frac{2}{3}MR^2$$

   where R is the radius of the sphere and M is its mass. Although Callisto, a moon of Jupiter, is approximately the same size as the planet Mercury, Mercury is 3 times as dense. How do their moments of inertia compare?

   A. The moment of inertia for Mercury is 9 times greater than for Callisto.
   B. The moment of inertia for Mercury is 3 times greater than for Callisto.
   C. The moment of inertia for Mercury is equal to the moment of inertia for Callisto.
   D. The moment of inertia for Callisto is 3 times greater than for Mercury.

3. The force of gravity on an any object due to earth is given by the equation $F = G(m_o M/r^2)$ where G is the gravitational constant, M is the mass of the earth, m_o is the mass of the object and r is the distance between the center of mass of the earth and the center of mass of the object. If a rocket weighs 3.6×10^6 N at the surface of the earth what is the force on the rocket due to gravity when the rocket has reached an altitude of 1.2×10^4 km? ($G = 6.67 \times 10^{-11}$ Nm²/kg², radius of the earth = 6370 km, mass of the earth = 5.98×10^{24} kg)

   A. 1.2×10^5 N
   B. 4.3×10^5 N
   C. 4.8×10^6 N
   D. 9.6×10^6 N

   $(7 \times 10^{-11})(H \times 10^6)(6 \times 10^{24})$

   $(1 \times 10^4)^2$

   $= \dfrac{168 \times 10^{19}}{10^8}$

   $\approx 168 \times 10^3$

   $\approx 1.68 \times 10^5 N$

4. The kinetic energy E of an object is given by $E = \frac{1}{2}mv^2$ where m is the object's mass and v is the velocity of the object. If the velocity of an object decreases by a factor of 2 what will happen its kinetic energy?

   A. Kinetic energy will increase by a factor of 2.
   B. Kinetic energy will increase by a factor of 4.
   C. Kinetic energy will decrease by a factor of 2.
   D. Kinetic energy will decrease by a factor of 4.

5. Elastic potential energy in a spring is directly proportional to the square of the displacement of one end of the spring from its rest position while the other end remains fixed. If the elastic potential energy in the spring is 100 J when it is compressed to half its rest length, what is its energy when it is compressed to one fourth its rest length?

   A. 50 J
   B. 150 J
   C. 200 J
   D. 225 J

Answers

1. B is correct. γ and L are inversely proportional.

2. B is correct. Since the bodies are the same size and Mercury is 3 times denser, Mercury is 3 times more massive. Mass is directly proportional to moment of inertia.

3. B is correct. If you are good with scientific notation, it is easy to see that r is tripled. r is the distance from the center of the Earth to the earth's surface. The Satellite is two Earth radii from the surface, so it is three Earth radii from the center of the earth. Since the square of r is inversely proportional to F, F must be divided by 9.

4. D is correct. E is directly proportional to v^2.

5. D is correct. If we imagine a spring 100 cm long at rest (We can use any spring length but 100 is always a good choice.) then the initial displacement is 50 cm and the final displacement is 75 cm. The displacement is increased by a factor of 1.5, thus the energy is increased by a factor of 1.5^2. 1.5^2 is greater than 1.4^2 or greater than 2. Thus the energy is greater than 2×100.

Graphs

A graph visually demonstrates the change in one variable that occurs due to changes in another variable. The MCAT® requires that you recognize the graphical relationship between two variables in certain types of equations. The four graphs below are the most commonly used. Memorize them. The first is a directly proportional relationship, the second is an exponential relationship, the third is an inversely proportional relationship, and the fourth is a logarithmic relationship.

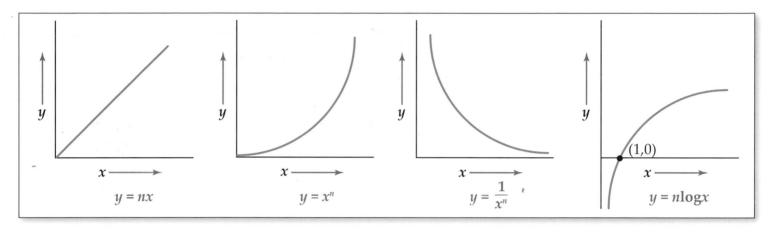

$$y = nx$$ $$y = x^n$$ $$y = \frac{1}{x^n}$$ $$y = n\log x$$

Let's look at the second graph and assume that $n = 2$.

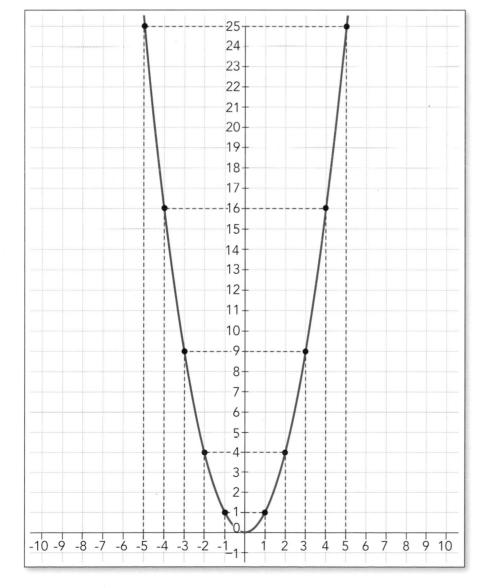

Note: n is greater than zero for the graph of $y = nx$. If n were equal to zero, the graph would simply be a straight line at $y = 0$. Also note that n is greater than one for the other three graphs. This is because x^1 is simply equal to x.

Don't worry if you don't remember the equation above. Just try and follow the math and how it corresponds to the graph.

When x is 2, y is $(2)^2$, which is 4. When x is 5, y is $(5)^2$, which is 25. As the graph shows, as n grows, y increases faster and faster. In other words, y experiences exponential growth. Consider the equation for an object moving with constant acceleration: $d = v_0t + \frac{1}{2}at^2$, where d is the distance travelled, v_0 is the initial speed of the object, a is the acceleration and t is the time elapsed. If we assume an object initially at rest ($v_0 = 0$) with constant acceleration of $2m/s^2$, the above relationship becomes, $d = t^2$. This relationship would be identical to the graph above with distance travelled as the y–axis and time as the x-axis.

As long as the value of n is within the given parameters, the general shape of the graph will not change.

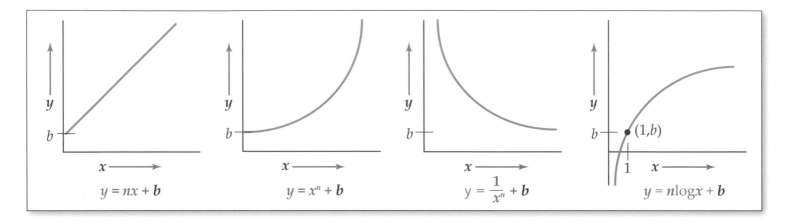

$$y = nx + b \qquad y = x^n + b \qquad y = \frac{1}{x^n} + b \qquad y = n\log x + b$$

When graphs are unitless, multiplying the right side of an equation by a positive constant will not change the shape of the graph. If one side of the equation is negative, or multiplied by a negative constant, the graph is reflected across the x axis.

Whenever the MCAT® asks you to identify the graphical relationship between two variables, assume that all other variables in the equation are constants unless told otherwise. Next, manipulate the equation into one of the above forms (with or without the added constant b) and choose the corresponding graph.

If you are unsure of a graphical relationship, plug in 1 for all variables except the variables in the question and then plug in 0, 1, and 2 for x and solve for y. Plot your results and look for the general corresponding shape.

Work through the following Practice Problems to see more examples of how equations can be represented graphically.

I must have been multiplied by a negative constant.

Practice Questions

$h = h_0 + t^2$ ~~(crossed out)~~
$h = h_0 - t^2$

1. The height of an object dropped from a building in the absence of air resistance is given by the equation $h = h_0 + v_0 t + \frac{1}{2}gt^2$, where h_0 and v_0 are the initial height and velocity respectively and g is -10 m/s^2. If v_0 is zero which graph best represents the relationship between h and t?

A.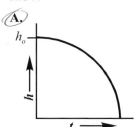

C.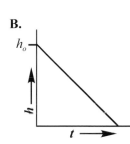

B.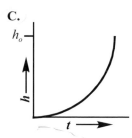

D.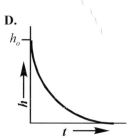

2. Which of the following graphs best describes the magnitude of the force (F) on a spring obeying Hooke's law ($F = -k\Delta x$) as it is compressed to Δx_{max}?

A.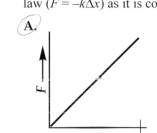

C.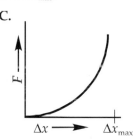

B.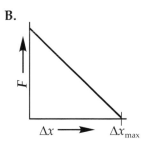

D.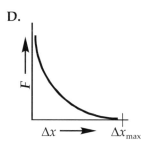

3. Which of the following graphs shows the relationship between frequency and wavelength of electromagnetic radiation through a vacuum? ($c = \nu\lambda$)

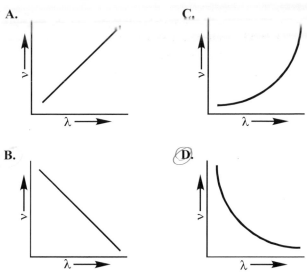

4. Which of the following graphs best describes the magnitude of the electrostatic force $F = k(qq)/r^2$ created by an object with negative charge on an object with a positive charge as the distance r between them changes?

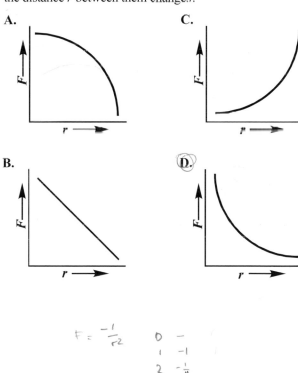

$F = \frac{-1}{r^2}$

0	$-$
1	-1
2	$-\frac{1}{4}$

5. Which of the following graphs demonstrates the relationship between power P and work W done by a machine? ($P = W/t$)

A.

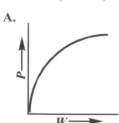

C.

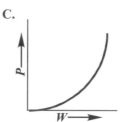

B.

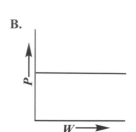

D.

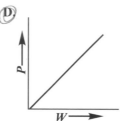

i.12 | Units

Often on the MCAT®, you must be able to quickly and confidently convert between one unit and another. Suppose we wanted to convert 34 centimeters to meters. First we must know the conversion rate between meters and centimeters, namely that 1 meter = 100 centimeters. We can rewrite this equality as:

$$\frac{1 \text{ meter}}{100 \text{ centimeters}} = \frac{100 \text{ centimeters}}{1 \text{ meter}} = 1$$

Of course, if we multiply any number by 1, the number is unchanged. 34 centimeters × 1 equals 34 centimeters. Likewise, $\frac{1 \text{ meter}}{100 \text{ centimeters}}$ is the same thing as 1 centimeter. If we cancel the centimeter units and divide by 100, we arrive at 0.34 meters:

$$34 \text{ centimeters} \times \frac{1 \text{ meter}}{100 \text{ centimeters}} = 0.34 \text{ meters}$$

If it helps, you can visualize this equation in two steps as follows:

$$34 \cancel{\text{ centimeters}} \times \frac{1 \text{ meters}}{100 \cancel{\text{ centimeters}}} = \frac{34 \cancel{\text{ centimeters}}}{100 \cancel{\text{ centimeters}}} \times 1 \text{ meter} = 0.34 \text{ meters}$$

But just as $4 \times \frac{6}{2}$ and $\frac{4}{2} \times 6$ both equal 12, it makes no difference how the equation is written in terms of the final answer.

Although converting from centimeters to meters is relatively straightforward, it is still helpful to know how to use the method above for two reasons. First, it is easy to mix up the direction of the conversion and arrive at 34 centimeters = 3400 meters (wrong) instead of 34 centimeters = 0.34 meters (correct). If you write out the equation, the numerator and denominator will only cancel if you have arranged the conversion factor correctly:

Problem: Convert 34 centimeters to meters. There are 100 centimeters per meter.

Wrong way: 34 × 100/1 = 3400 meters

Right way: 34 centimeters × (1 meter)/(100 centimeters) = 0.34 meters

---

Second, more complicated conversions can be carried out more easily using this method. For example, suppose we wanted to find out how many seconds are in 10 years. We would write the following equation:

$$10 \text{ years} \times \frac{365.25 \text{ days}}{1 \text{ year}} \times \frac{24 \text{ hours}}{1 \text{ day}} \times \frac{60 \text{ minutes}}{1 \text{ hour}} \times \frac{60 \text{ seconds}}{1 \text{ min}}$$
$$= 3.16 \times 10^8 \text{ seconds}$$

Another important aspect of unit manipulation is in understanding equations themselves. Knowing the units for a given physical property can be helpful in terms of understanding the equation, or even constructing a forgotten equation from scratch. For example, if you know that the SI units for speed are meters per second (m/s), it follows that since meters are a measurement of distance and seconds are a measurement of time, speed can be expressed as distance divided by time. More complex equations can also be constructed in a similar manner.

Let's turn to energy as an example. The SI unit for energy is the Joule, but let's suppose we wanted to express energy in terms of simpler units like meters, kilograms and seconds. In the example of gravitational potential energy, energy can be described as mass times acceleration due to gravity (g) times height, *Energy = Mass $\times$ g $\times$ Height*. The units for mass are kilograms (kg), the units for height are meters (m), and since g is an acceleration, its units are meters divided by seconds squared $\frac{m}{s^2}$. If we write out our equation in terms of units,

$$Energy = Mass \times Acceleration \text{ due to gravity} \times Height$$
$$Joules = (\text{kg}) \times \left(\frac{m}{s^2}\right) \times (m) \quad \frac{\text{kg } m^2}{s^2}$$

We've now arrived at a way of expressing energy in terms of the most fundamental units. The important thing to realize is that energy must have these same units in any equation. Let's consider another equation involving energy (as work), where energy is equal to force times distance, Energy = Force $\times$ Distance. The units for distance are meters (m), and the units for force are Newtons (N). If we write out the equation in terms of units,

$$Energy = Force \times Distance$$
$$Joules = N \times m = N \, m$$

But wait a minute. Didn't we just say that Joules had to equal $\frac{\text{kg } m^2}{s^2}$ in this equation as well? Whenever you come across a new equation, it is useful to break it down into its individual units. The more you do this, the faster you will be at spotting patterns. On the MCAT®, you may be able to eliminate wrong answers, or even arrive at the correct answers, simply by looking at the units. For instance, if an unfamiliar equation appears in a MCAT® passage and a question asks you to express energy with respect to new terms, it is possible that only one of the four answer choices will have a combination that leads to $Joules = \frac{\text{kg } m^2}{s^2}$. This answer is automatically correct.

SI units will be covered in more detail in the *Physics Manual*, so don't worry if the equations seem foreign to you at this point. Just focus on the units.

$$\sqrt[3]{27} = 3$$
$$4^{\frac{2}{3}} = \sqrt[3]{4^2} = \sqrt[3]{16} = ? \approx 2.5$$
$$\sqrt[3]{8} = 2$$
$$\sqrt{2} \approx 1.4 \; and \; \sqrt{3} \approx 1.7$$

TABLE I.1 > Sines and Cosines of Common Angles

θ	Sine	Cosine
0°	$\dfrac{\sqrt{0}}{2}$	$\dfrac{\sqrt{4}}{2}$
30°	$\dfrac{\sqrt{1}}{2}$	$\dfrac{\sqrt{3}}{2}$
45°	$\dfrac{\sqrt{2}}{2}$	$\dfrac{\sqrt{2}}{2}$
60°	$\dfrac{\sqrt{3}}{2}$	$\dfrac{\sqrt{1}}{2}$
90°	$\dfrac{\sqrt{4}}{2}$	$\dfrac{\sqrt{0}}{2}$

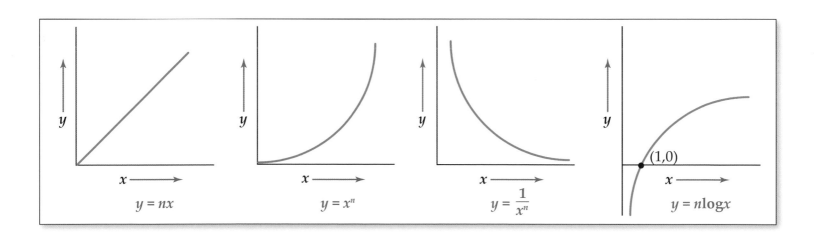

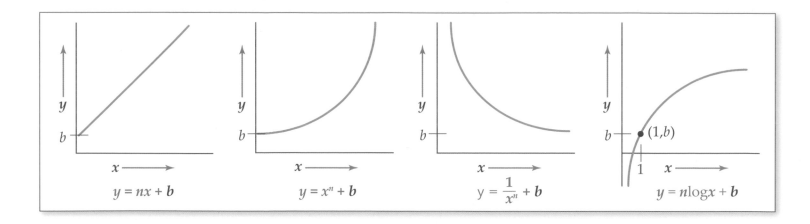

$$y = nx + b \qquad y = x^n + b \qquad y = \frac{1}{x^n} + b \qquad y = n\log x + b$$

MCAT® THINK ANSWER

The only way to answer this question is with proportions. Most of the information is given to distract you. Notice that the difference in pressure between the ends of the pipe is not even given and the flow rate would have to be converted to m³/s. To answer this question using proportions, multiply L by 4 and r by x. Now pull out the 4 and the x. We know by definition, $Q = \Delta P \pi r^4 / 8\eta L$; thus, $x^4/4$ must equal 1. Solve for x, and this is the change in the radius. The radius must be increased by a factor of about 1.4.

$14 \times 1.4 = 19.6$. The new radius is approximately 19.6 cm. The closest answer is C.

$$Q = \frac{\Delta P \pi r^4}{8\eta L}$$

$$Q = \frac{\Delta P \pi (xr)^4}{8\eta (4L)}$$

$$Q = \frac{\Delta P \pi r^4}{8\eta L} \times \frac{x^4}{4}$$

$$4 = x^4$$

$$x = \sqrt{2}$$

DON'T FORGET YOUR KEYS

1. The MCAT® rewards flexibility and connections. Study concepts in order to simplify, understand, and organize content.

2. Remove the disguise of complexity from MCAT® passages and questions to reveal the simple science tested.

3. Keep MCAT® math simple: use proportionality, rounding, units, and scientific notation.

Research and Reasoning
Skills for the MCAT®

ii.1 | Introduction

About fifty percent of questions in the Biological, Physical, and Psychosocial sections of the MCAT® will test research skills. These questions require analytical thinking and reasoning skills. Critical thinking about research is emphasized on the MCAT® because the ability to analyze research is crucial to practice as a physician. The field of medicine constantly adapts in response to new findings relevant to the causes, effects, and treatments of disease. Evidence-based medicine is centered on the principle that physicians should draw upon the results of current, high-quality studies when making clinical decisions about individual patients. In other words, although physicians' expertise and patients' wishes are still critical, physicians should also examine the latest research, or evidence, when determining a treatment plan.

The ability to interpret studies and their results is necessary to do well in all sections of the MCAT®. Passages that are explicitly based on particular studies are most common in the context of biology, biochemistry, sociology, and psychology. Passages about general chemistry, organic chemistry, and physics may simply describe reactions or other phenomena rather than presenting a hypothesis and study. However, each section will include questions that test research skills. This means that you must be comfortable with research questions in a variety of contexts.

This lecture will make it simple. Although various types of research methodology will appear on the MCAT®, the fundamental ideas are the same. You do NOT need years of lab experience or an advanced statistics class to gain the level of understanding of research required for the MCAT®. The research skills it will test are an extension of the critical and logical thinking that will help you gain success on the test as a whole. Many of the skills described in this lecture, particularly determining the key ideas of a passage and evaluating flaws, are closely related to the type of analytic thinking required to do well in the CARS section. For most passages on the MCAT®, it is crucial to be able to figure out what the author cares about (especially in CARS) and/or what an experiment is studying (in the other sections).

This lecture will first provide an overview of how the scientific method guides the practice of research, followed by research ethics. Next, it will cover issues of methodology and measurement. The lecture will then cover the basic skills of quantitative analysis that are required for the MCAT®, including common statistical analyses. The following section will discuss how researchers draw conclusions by analyzing and interpreting data, with an emphasis on the features of study design that are necessary for conclusions of causality. Finally, the lecture will conclude with an example of a passage that could be seen on the MCAT®, along with a demonstration of the analysis required to interpret research-based passages. The reading of the sample passage will also include the skill of interpreting graphical data, which is often key to understanding both the passage as a whole and any statistical analyses.

The major skills that you need to answer questions involving research methods are: identifying research questions and variables, considering strengths and weaknesses of measurements and methodologies, interpreting quantitative analysis of data, and evaluating the conclusions drawn from data analysis.

> **THE 3 KEYS**
>
> 1. In an experimental setup, the independent variable is manipulated and the dependent variable is measured and/or observed.
>
> 2. Correlated factors do not necessarily indicate a causal relationship.
>
> 3. Narrate as you read a research-based passage: identify the variables and hypothesis and interpret the data as it relates to the hypothesis.

Although you must understand how researchers think and how scientific research is conducted, you will obviously not carry out actual experiments as part of the MCAT®! Instead the emphasis will be on your ability to interpret the work carried out by others. Throughout the lecture there will be tips on how to translate your understanding of research to answering questions correctly on the MCAT®.

ii.2 | The Scientific Method

The scientific method represents the process by which researchers develop research questions, hypotheses, and studies. The standardized guidelines of the scientific method allow researchers to easily share their work and interpret the findings of others. The purpose of research is to create shared scientific knowledge. Therefore, the shared "language" of the scientific method is a crucial tool. Furthermore, the scientific method sets out the fundamental principles of research: the creation and evaluation of scientific questions.

Most students of the sciences have encountered the scientific method before. However, an abstract knowledge of the scientific method does not automatically translate to the ability to recognize and reason about each step in the context of an actual study. This section will review the scientific method in the context of the research-based skills required for the MCAT®.

The steps of the scientific method are presented in Figure ii.1 and are described further below. In broad terms, the scientific method involves asking a question; proposing a possible answer to that question; designing a study that will produce data that can support or undermine that possible answer; collecting the data; and then analyzing the data to determine the implications for the original question.

> You may have seen the steps of the scientific method split up in different ways in various textbooks. However, this version is the best way to think about the scientific method for the purposes of the MCAT®.

FIGURE ii.1 | The Scientific Method

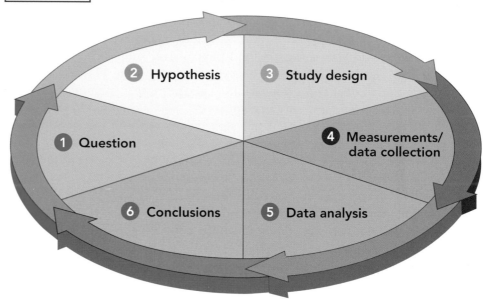

1. Question
2. Hypothesis
3. Study design
4. Measurements/data collection
5. Data analysis
6. Conclusions

> Sir Isaac Newton once said, "If I have seen further, it is by standing on the shoulders of giants." He meant that he was only able to discover so many scientific principles because he based his research questions on the results of other famous scientists before him.

1) Question: The purpose of a study is to find an answer to a specific question. A wide variety of possible questions can motivate the development of a study. However, a successful study is based on a testable research question. A testable research question is one that can be accurately modeled and evaluated through the methods used in scientific research.

Part of being a successful test-taker is reading actively rather than passively. As you read a research-based MCAT® passage, identify the research question and hypothesis. The results are impossible to understand and evaluate without a clear knowledge of the question that they are intended to answer!

A research question is often inspired by observation. In other words, the researcher observes some real-world phenomenon and develops a question about it. However, research is a collaborative enterprise; no one tries to reinvent the wheel. Instead, when researchers are developing their questions of interest, they are influenced by past findings. The process of background research, meaning the examination of the work of other researchers who have studied related questions, allows a researcher to learn from the mistakes and discoveries of other researchers. It also helps them to ask questions that have not been answered before and that will further the understanding of the field.

Theory also influences the development of research questions. A theory is a proposed explanation of the causes and mechanisms of a natural phenomenon. A theory is broader than a hypothesis, and is not testable in a single experiment. Instead, it is supported by the results of multiple studies that test smaller facets of the overall theory. Like the scientific method itself, the relationship between theory and research can be understood as a cycle. Theoretical claims inspire the development of research questions, and studies that answer those questions lead to modification of theory, which then leads to questions for future studies, and so on. Theory is discussed further in the first lecture of the *Psychology and Sociology Manual*.

Different types of research involve different types of research questions. One important distinction is the one between basic and applied research. **Applied research** attempts to find practical solutions to problems, while **basic research** tries to explain the fundamental principles of how the world works. Basic research can be thought of as the production of scientific knowledge for its own sake, rather than for application to a particular situation. This is not to say that basic research is somehow less useful than applied research. Basic research provides the necessary base for applied research.

Applied and basic research can be carried out in the context of many different fields, each of which ask questions about specific types of phenomena. Perhaps the most fundamental distinction is between natural and social science. **Natural science** is the study of processes in the natural world, such as the laws of physics or the life processes of biological organisms. In contrast, **social science**, as the name implies, examines phenomena in the social world, often focusing on behavior and interactions. The MCAT® will include studies from both the natural and social sciences. All research follows the principles laid out in the scientific method, but the goals of social and natural science research are often different. Natural science asks questions about laws of nature that will allow extremely reliable predictions. However, the issue of whether such laws even exist in the realm of the social world is debatable. Rather than attempting to find rigid laws such as those described by the natural sciences, social science research seeks to discover patterns of behavior and explain relationships between different social and psychological phenomena.

2) **Hypothesis:** The hypothesis is the researcher's prediction of the answer to the research question. Like the research question, a hypothesis is informed by past findings and scientific theories, so it is an educated prediction rather than a blind guess. Hypotheses must be testable, like research questions. In other words, a claim that cannot be tested scientifically cannot be used to develop a study and is not a scientific hypothesis. So what does it mean for a hypothesis to be testable? A testable hypothesis is a prediction that a study can either support or prove wrong. Usually this prediction concerns the relationship between two variables.

Variables are aspects of the study that can have different values and be measured or categorized. Suppose that the research question for a study was "Does daily consumption of aspirin reduce the incidence of myocardial infarction?" A research hypothesis associated with this question could be "Consumption of 81 mg of aspirin every day for twelve months leads to a decreased incidence of myocardial infarction during a two-year follow-up period." This hypothesis involves the components of a testable hypothesis: a prediction, a relationship, and variables.

The research hypothesis usually predicts that one variable causes a change in another variable. The variable that is predicted to have a causal effect is the **independent variable**. In an experimental setting, the independent variable is the one that researchers control and manipulate. The **dependent variable** is hypothesized to "depend" on the independent variable, and it is what the researchers measure.

Applied and basic research may cover similar topics, but have different goals. For example, basic research on the human genome could attempt to sequence a specific gene for a large sample of people to assess human variation and identify forms of the gene that may be linked with causing disease. Applied research might develop gene therapies that target and silence disease-causing forms of the gene.

The natural and social sciences often differ in their limitations on study design and, by consequence, conclusions that can be drawn from the results. This will be discussed later in the lecture.

Practice the skill of telling the difference between testable and untestable research hypotheses. One way is to consider whether a hypothesis can be proven wrong. A prediction that cannot be proven wrong is not testable and is not a scientific hypothesis. For example, consider the hypothesis that there are purple dogs in the world. This hypothesis cannot be proven wrong, because there could always be a purple dog hiding somewhere, waiting to be discovered. That means that this is NOT a testable hypothesis. On the other hand, the hypothesis that there are no purple dogs in the world is falsifiable, because finding just one purple dog would be enough to prove it wrong.

The hypothesis given above predicts that aspirin consumption (the independent variable) decreases the incidence of myocardial infarction (the dependent variable).

Although the two concepts are closely related, it is important to understand the difference between a research question and a hypothesis. Remember, a hypothesis is a proposed answer to the question that the study is designed to explore. For example, consider the following statements:

"The authors were interested in the relationship between aspirin consumption and incidence of myocardial infarction."

"The authors proposed that daily consumption of 81 mg of aspirin leads to decreased incidence of myocardial infarction."

The first describes a question, while the second refers to a hypothesis. Sometimes a passage will actually use the word "question" or "hypothesis." However, you must be able to identify the question and hypothesis when they are described but not explicitly named, as in the example above.

3) **Study design**: Once the question and hypothesis have been developed, a study is designed to produce results that have the potential to support or refute the hypothesis. In the example above, researchers might give aspirin to one study group but not the other, and then determine whether the group that receives aspirin has a lower incidence of myocardial infarction. Different types of research methods and how they affect the conclusions that can be drawn from the results will be discussed later in this lecture.

4) **Measurement/data collection**: To answer a hypothesis, it is necessary to come up with an appropriate method of measurement to collect data. This process includes *operationalization*, or approximating the true variables of interest with one that can be measured or tabulated. Consider a psychological study that is interested in the effect of stress on memory formation. The hypothesis might be that stress results in poorer memory formation. The independent variable is stress, and the dependent variable is quality of memory formation. But "stress" and "memory formation" are not items that can actually be measured in a lab. Operationalization of these variables is what makes the collection of data possible, and could occur in a variety of ways depending on the resources and preferences of the researchers. "Stress" could be operationalized as the presence of a particular event in the lab that is thought to cause stress, such as study participants witnessing a theft. "Memory formation" could be operationalized as a subject's score on a specific test of memory, such as recalling a list of items.

5) **Analysis**: Once data has been collected, statistical analyses provide methods of describing and interpreting the measured data. Statistical analysis can show whether the data support or undermine the hypothesis in mathematical terms. The goal of statistical analysis is to determine whether differences in the dependent variable can be attributed to changes in the independent variable, or whether they were due to chance. The basic knowledge of statistical analysis that is required for the MCAT® will be covered later in this lecture.

6) **Conclusions**: Statistical analysis generally returns numerical results that must be interpreted by the researcher. Statistics are a necessary step in evaluating whether the results support or undermine the hypothesis, but the researcher must take the final step of interpreting the statistical analysis and determining the implications of the study. Often the interpretation of the data will have to do with whether or not the independent variable caused a change in the dependent variable. The implications of the study involve the conclusions that can be drawn about the "real world" based on the group of subjects involved in the study. The features of study design that allow particular conclusions to be drawn will be examined later in this lecture.

Of course, for the MCAT®, you will not have to use the scientific method to design studies. Instead the scientific method is your key to understanding the passages that present the work of other researchers. You will notice that these passages are often roughly organized according to the steps of the scientific method. A typical research-based passage starts by considering past findings that influence the research question and then narrows in on the specific study by presenting the question and/or hypothesis, as well as the methods used (the study design). Then the passage presents the data graphically and/or verbally. The passage may then discuss data analysis and conclusions, or the test-taker may be asked to answer questions about these steps.

<table>
<tr><td>ii.3</td><td></td></tr>
</table>

ii.3 | Ethics of Research

The ultimate purpose of research is to create a model that can then be generalized to the real-world phenomena it is intended to represent. The elements of study design that allow scientists to draw conclusions about actual phenomena based on research will be discussed later in this lecture. In many cases, **ethical guidelines** necessarily place limitations on the models constructed for the purpose of research.

One of the most important components of research ethics is the protection of those who are involved as study participants, whether they are humans or other organisms. Any possible risks to participants must be necessary to the purpose of the study, outweighed by the expected benefits, and minimized as much as possible. For example, some psychological studies involve deception, meaning that the participants are not told the truth about some aspect of the study. In most studies, participants are fully informed of the purpose of the study. In deception studies, there is some risk that people will end up participating in an experiment to which they would not have knowingly consented. It is the responsibility of the researcher to minimize risk by telling the participants as much as possible before the experiment, revealing the true purpose afterwards, and providing an opportunity for the subjects to ask questions. In addition, deception can be used only if telling participants the whole truth prior to the experiment would make it impossible to test the hypothesis. Finally, the deception must be justified by the expectation that valuable scientific knowledge will be gained from the study.

MCAT® THINK

Stanley Milgram's studies of obedience to authority provide a prominent example of controversy over research ethics. Milgram recruited subjects to participate in a study about how punishment affects learning. The real purpose of his study, inspired by the Holocaust, was to examine people's willingness to break their moral code when ordered to do so by an authority figure. Milgram found that many people were willing to deliver extreme shocks to another participant (who was in fact an actor and did not actually experience shocks) when told to do so. Even though the participants experienced extreme psychological distress, they continued to obey the authority figure and deliver shocks. In this case, the study could not have taken place if the subjects had known its true purpose. However, some argued that the information gained about obedience to authority was not valuable enough to outweigh the stress experienced by the subjects during the experience and the possibility of lasting psychological effects. In other words, they argued that the study was not acceptable according to ethical standards.

In many cases, animal subjects are used in the place of human subjects when it is clear that the benefits of the study do not outweigh the risks to human participants. Any type of experiment that poses permanent damage to the organism will involve animals rather than humans. However, the same fundamental ethical consideration of whether the benefits of the study outweigh the risks applies to animal subjects. Researchers using laboratory animals in their research must follow standard guidelines for humane treatment and justify their research design by the expectation of gaining scientific knowledge with significant benefits.

In addition to protecting the rights of study participants, researchers must follow guidelines of **scientific integrity**, or intellectual honesty. Researchers are expected to act with integrity at every step of the research process, from formulating a research question to drawing conclusions and presenting the results to other researchers and the general public. This means that researchers cannot present the ideas and work of others as their own. They also cannot invent data, take measurements that are biased towards their desired result, or intentionally misrepresent the results of their study. In other words, researchers are required to present the actual data that they obtain, whether or not the results of the experiment are what they had hoped to find. This requirement of researchers extends to **protecting the interests of research consumers**. Researchers have a responsibility to report their results accurately to the public, without misrepresenting the data for monetary or any other type of gain.

ii.4 | Methods and Measurements

As discussed above, developing research questions and hypotheses are crucial to the scientific process. However, good research questions without appropriate research methods are useless for drawing conclusions. In order for research to be useful and successful, scientists must carefully choose measurement techniques and research methods that allow for the appropriate collection of data and interpretation of results that address the research questions.

Issues to Consider in Measurement

Recall that a variable is an aspect of the system under study that can vary, or have different values. This means that part of carrying out a study involves measuring or categorizing the variables of interest. The data collected fall into one of the following measurement scales: nominal, ordinal, interval, or ratio. The type of measurement scale employed in data collection is important because it is a factor in determining both the kind of statistical analysis that can be applied to the data and what conclusions can be drawn about the study.

In a *nominal scale,* data are classified into non-ordered categories. For example, eye color might be recorded as blue, grey, green, hazel, brown, or amber. Notice that there is no intrinsic ordering to these categories (i.e., there is no particular reason that blue should come before grey).

By contrast, an *ordinal scale* allows for classification into ordered categories. Pain, for instance, might be described as mild, moderate, or severe. However, it is difficult to compare values within an ordinal system. There is no way of knowing if the increase in pain from mild to moderate is equivalent to the increase from moderate to severe. In other words, ordinal scales do not convey relative degree of difference. Interval or ratio scales must be used to collect data that involve meaningful degrees of difference.

In an *interval scale*, the intervals between values on the scale are meaningful. For example, when measuring temperature in degrees Celsius, the difference in temperature between 40°C and 50°C is the same as the difference between 70°C and 80°C. However, a limitation of the interval scale is that the ratios between values in the scale are not meaningful. For example, water at 80°C is not twice as hot as water at 40°C. In order to make meaningful ratios between values, a ratio scale must be used. Unlike an interval scale, which has an arbitrary zero point, a *ratio scale* has an absolute zero. As a result, ratios between values are meaningful. For example, because the Kelvin scale of temperature measurement has a point of absolute zero, unlike the Celsius scale, it is accurate to say that 80 K is twice as hot as 40 K. Variables such as age, height, and weight are typically measured using ratio scales.

No matter what kind of measurement scale is used, variability is an inherent part of the data collection process. Any single measured value is unlikely to exactly represent the true value of the thing being measured. Deviation between observed measurements and the true value is referred to as *error*. Error can generally be broken down into two main categories: random error and systematic error.

Random error is present in all types of measurement and shifts measurements in unpredictable ways. Human error and lack of instrument sensitivity contribute to random error. Imagine a chemist is trying to determine the boiling point of an unknown liquid. He measures the boiling point ten times and records his results. When the mercury is between degree marks on the thermometer, the chemist may sometimes round up and sometimes round down, resulting in random error in his measurements. Random error decreases **precision**, which is a measure of how closely individual measurements of the same value agree with each other.

By contrast, **systematic error** shifts all measurements in a standardized way. Systematic error can arise from a variety of causes. For example, if the chemist's thermometer consistently reports temperatures at two degrees greater than what they really are, the chemist will incorrectly estimate the boiling point of his unknown liquid by two degrees. Systematic error decreases the accuracy of the measurements obtained, which is how well the measured values reflect the true value. In this way, systematic error can result in *bias*, a systematic difference between the results obtained and the true value. Biases in measurement are commonly introduced by the observer, instrument, or subject. *Observer bias* occurs when an observer intentionally or unintentionally records a distorted measurement, whereas *instrument bias* results from systematic malfunctioning of a mechanical instrument. Finally, *subject bias* is introduced when a study participant intentionally or unintentionally reports a distorted measurement. For example, suppose that researchers surveyed people to ask how many cigarettes they had smoked per day over the past twenty years. Respondents with cancer might, on average, overestimate their cigarette smoking compared to respondents without cancer because the experience of having cancer biases people to recall more smoking. This recall bias decreases the accuracy of the survey as an instrument to measure the true rate of smoking.

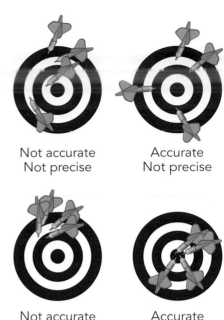

Not accurate
Not precise

Accurate
Not precise

Not accurate
Precise

Accurate
Precise

Accuracy and precision are often confused. Accuracy is how well measurements reflect the true value of something, while precision refers to how well multiple measured values agree with each other.

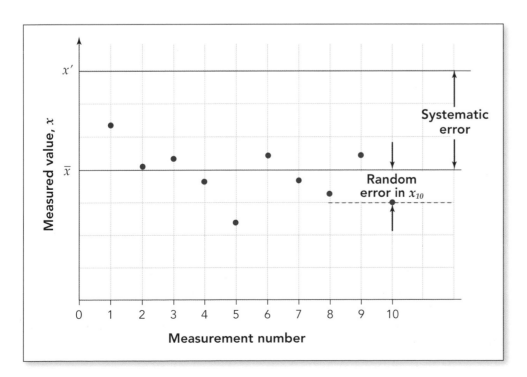

FIGURE ii.2 Random vs. Systematic Error

Any imprecision in the measurement process will cause a certain amount of random error for each measurement of a value. When several measurements of the same value are taken, their average is believed to represent the true value. However, if systematic error is present, all measurements may be shifted away from the actual true value (x') in a standardized way.

MCAT® THINK

The precision of a measurement is affected by the number of significant figures (also called significant digits) in that measurement. More significant figures are associated with a more precise measurement. Significant figures, and thus precision, are dependent on the measuring tools available. Take the example of a carpenter who wants to measure the length of a piece of wood. If he has a ruler with markings only every centimeter, he may record the length as 3.5 cm. However, with a ruler that has marks every millimeter, he may conclude that the length is actually closer to 3.45 cm. A measurement of 3.5 indicates that the true value is greater than 3 but less than 4, while the greater precision in the measurement of 3.45 indicates that the true value is between 3.4 and 3.5. Notice that measurements usually consist of those digits that are known exactly (in this case, the digits 3 and 4) and one additional digit that is estimated by the person taking the measurement (in this case, the digit 5). The number of significant digits therefore provides information about the precision of the measurement.

In determining whether a digit is significant, there are special rules when zero is a digit in the measurement. Zero digits that come at the end of a number are significant if followed by a decimal point (as in 400.) or preceded by a decimal point (as in the last zero of 0.040). However, zeros that come at the beginning of a number (as in the first two zeros of 0.040) are not significant. When multiplying or dividing measurements, the final answer has the same number of significant figures as the least precise measurement involved in the calculation. When adding or subtracting, the final answer has the same number of decimal places as whichever measurement in the calculation has the least number of decimal places.

You could see a question or two on the MCAT® about significant figures and their conventions. The most important thing is to understand that they reflect the precision of measurement by indicating the number of digits that can be reliably reproduced in multiple measurements of the same quantity.

Experimental Methods

As scientists develop a research question, they must choose a research method in order to refine their question into one that can be used to test a specific hypothesis. Research methods can be broadly classified as experimental or non-experimental. Each method allows researchers to refine the research question differently.

In **experimental studies**, scientists manipulate one or more variables in order to observe the outcome. To experimentally study the relationship between coffee and pancreatic cancer, scientists could manipulate the variable of coffee consumption by feeding different amounts of coffee to laboratory animals, such as mice. The research question, "Does drinking coffee cause pancreatic cancer?" would then be refined to something like, "Does consumption of four ounces of brewed coffee every day for six months by laboratory mice lead to an increased incidence of pancreatic cancer as determined by computed tomography scans during a one-year follow-up period?"

Sometimes, the proposed research question is difficult to approach with an experimental method for reasons related to feasibility, affordability, or ethics. For example, it would not be feasible to manipulate the amount of coffee consumed by a group of human research subjects for a long period of time. If our researchers wanted to study the relationship between coffee and pancreatic cancer in humans, they might choose a non-experimental research method. In non-experimental or observational studies, scientists merely observe variables without manipulating them. Researchers could choose to observe the amount of coffee consumed by a group of people and then measure the incidence of pancreatic cancer in the group. The research question would be refined to, "Do people with pancreatic cancer report having drunk more coffee during the past twenty years than do people without pancreatic cancer?" There are several different types of observational studies commonly used in medical research, described in the table below.

TABLE ii.1 > **Types of Observational Study Design**

Observational study design	Description	Example
Cross-sectional study	Studies a sample of the population at one point in time	A researcher measures current coffee intake and the current rate of pancreatic cancer.
Cohort study	Studies a sample of the population over time	A researcher measures baseline coffee intake and, later, the rate of pancreatic cancer.
Case-control study	Studies two sample populations, one with and one without an outcome	A researcher asks people with and without pancreatic cancer about past coffee intake.

When an experimental method is used, scientists often perform control experiments (see adjacent figure). These are particularly common in laboratory experiments in the biological sciences. Control experiments help scientists determine whether the whole experiment truly shows what it is intended to show. **Positive controls** are groups in which an effect is expected because scientists manipulate them in a way that is already known to produce the effect. By contrast, **negative controls** are groups in which no effect is expected.

In the study involving coffee and pancreatic cancer, scientists could perform a positive control experiment by manipulating a gene that is known to cause pancreatic cancer. Demonstrating the ability to detect cancer in the group with this gene helps validate the use of computed tomography (CT) scans as a measurement tool.

The scientists could perform a negative control experiment by keeping a group of mice in the exact same conditions as the experimental group, but giving them water instead of coffee. Any change in the incidence of pancreatic cancer in this group will be due to a factor other than coffee. Thus, in this example, the negative control experiment strengthens the argument that any change in prevalence of cancer in the coffee group is due to the coffee and not to other factors.

In summary, the choice of specific methods influences the conclusions that can be drawn from study results and allows scientists to refine their experimental question. Remember that the study design constrains the research question and that the results of the study will only answer a very specific question. The scientists in the given example will not get an answer to the general question, "Does drinking coffee cause pancreatic cancer?" from their experiment, and it would be a mistake to draw this conclusion from their study, no matter what the results are.

Negative control

Fed water

Results: negative

Experimental group

Fed coffee

Results: ?

Positive control

Genetic mutation

Results: Positive for pancreatic cancer

Even the best-crafted research methodology results in data that appear to be just a pile of numbers, and can be difficult to interpret without organization and analysis. The point of statistics is to take a set of numbers (however unwieldy) and turn it into an intelligible story. Statistics allow the researcher to answer research questions and draw conclusions that are supported by the research results.

For a quick check to know if a data set is continuous or discrete, think about how the data were obtained. If values were counted (as in the example of cancer relapses), the data are discrete. If the values were measured (as in the example of arm length), chances are the data are continuous..

Many of the most commonly used descriptive statistics may already be familiar to you. Use this section to refresh and solidify your knowledge so that these basic techniques are second nature. That way, when you encounter data interpretation on the MCAT®, you will have more time to spend on more difficult problems.

Research-based passages adapted from specific studies in both the natural and social sciences are likely to appear throughout the MCAT®. A basic understanding of statistics is necessary for understanding research methodology and interpreting data and results. This section will explain how statistics can be used to describe a data set, examine relationships between variables, and test specific hypotheses. It will cover some of the most commonly used statistical tools and will review how to draw conclusions about the meanings of data through statistical analysis. It's important to realize that the MCAT® does NOT require knowledge of advanced statistics! Questions about statistics on the MCAT® will likely appear in the context of specific information given in the passage, rather than requiring the selection of a specific test or complex reasoning about the features of different statistical tests.

Statistics are used to analyze data sets. A data set is a list of values for a certain variable or collection of variables. The values in a data set can be numerical or categorical. *Numerical data* (also called *quantitative data*) represent variables that can be measured and recorded as a number (either interval or ratio), such as height. *Categorical data* (also called *qualitative data*) represent variables that can be observed and recorded as a category. Categorical data can sometimes consist of numbers (such as a rating of 1 through 10 on a pain scale), but unlike quantitative data, the numbers are not a measurement of a value but rather represent a specific category (a little pain, moderate pain, etc.).

A closely related distinction is between *continuous* and discrete data. Data that are continuous are obtained through measurement and usually have values that fall somewhere on a continuous number line. For example, the length of your arm may be 22 inches, 22.4 inches, or 22.43 inches depending on the level of specificity in the measurement. In comparison, *discrete* data are counted, not measured, and are restricted to certain values or categories. Discrete data include both nominal and ordinal systems of measurement, but may also apply to data that are numerical, usually consisting of values restricted to whole numbers. For example, a researcher recording the number of relapses a patient experiences after treatment for cancer may record two relapses, but not 2.63 relapses.

Introduction to Statistics

Statistics are a way to increase the objectivity involved in analyzing data. Without mathematical guidelines, researchers might bring personal bias to data analysis and interpret results that are not actually supported by the data. Statistics also help organize and summarize data sets. Once data are collected, they can seem like a meaningless list of numbers. One way to make sense of the contents of the data set is through *descriptive statistics*, which are just what they sound like. Descriptive statistics describe the scope and content of the data set to show researchers the patterns present in their data. For the MCAT®, it is important to be familiar with commonly used descriptive statistics for both the central tendency (which estimates the center of a data set) and the dispersion (which shows how spread out the values are) of the data.

Consider the simple data set in Figure ii.4. A class of 15 students was given a pop quiz consisting of five multiple choice questions. Figure ii.4 contains the scores of each student on the quiz. As a mere collection of numbers, it is difficult to visualize the spread of the data even within this small data set. One technique that can be used to visualize the data is a *frequency distribution*, which displays the frequency of occurrence for each score and can be represented as either a table or a chart. Frequency distributions can be used with both quantitative and qualitative variables. They provide both a way to visualize the data at a glance and the ability to draw some quick inferences. Further insight into the nature of the data set can then be obtained through the use of descriptive statistics such as measures of central tendency and dispersion.

FIGURE ii.3 Examples of Normal and Skewed Distributions

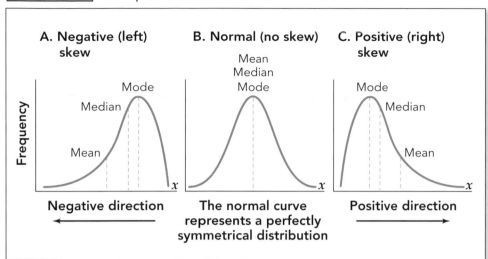

A. Negative (left) skew — Negative direction

B. Normal (no skew) — The normal curve represents a perfectly symmetrical distribution

C. Positive (right) skew — Positive direction

FIGURE ii.4 Construction of Frequency Distributions

A. Unorganized data

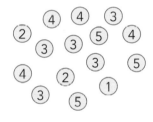

B. Data organized on a number line

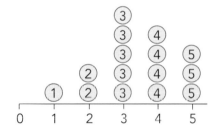

TABLE ii.2 > Data Frequency

4	4	3	5	3
3	2	5	1	2
3	3	4	5	4

C. The above organization is the foundation of a frequency chart

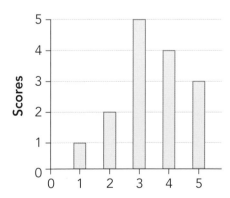

D. A frequency table serves the same purpose

Scores	Tally	Frequency
0		0
1	I	1
2	II	2
3	IIII	5
4	IIII	4
5	III	3

Measures of Central Tendency

Measures of **central tendency** include various methods of representing the "middle" of the data set. They provide a quick summary by identifying the central position of values within the data set. The most common measures of central tendency include mean, median, and mode. The mean, also called the *average*, generally refers to the arithmetic mean, which is calculated by dividing the sum of all values in the data set by the number of values within the data set. The advantage of the mean as a representation of central tendency is that it minimizes error in predicting any one value in the data set by taking all values into account. However, because of this, the mean is particularly sensitive to the influence of outliers. An *outlier* is a data point that is far away (either higher or lower) from the other values observed or measured. Even just one outlying data point can dramatically skew the mean, making it a less accurate representation of the central position of the majority of data points in the data set.

The mean cannot be used as a measure of central tendency in all data sets. In order for the mean to be a useful representation of central tendency, the difference between values for a variable must also be meaningful (i.e. data must be either interval or ratio).

The **median** of a data set is the middle value once all values have been placed in order of magnitude. For data sets with an odd number of values, the median is simply the middle value. When a data set contains an even number of values for a particular variable, the median is the average of the two middle values. The median divides the data set in half so that for a particular variable, there are as many values above the median as below it. Unlike the mean, the use of median as a measure of central tendency is appropriate for ordinal data.

The **mode** is the value that occurs most often for a variable in a data set. In other words, it is the most common outcome recorded for that variable. The mode is readily identifiable as the longest bar on a frequency chart or the highest incidence on a frequency table. Mode is the only measure of central tendency that is appropriate to use with nominal data.

To understand why the use of arithmetic mean is only useful for ratio or interval data, consider trying to calculate the mean for nominal data such as a comparison of type of pets owned. The arithmetic mean of cat, bird, and rabbit might be adorable, but would not be very statistically meaningful or relevant to the results of the study.

Do a self-test to check your understanding of mean, median and mode. Quickly calculate each of the three measures of central tendency for the data set given in Table ii.2. Check your answers on page 58..

Suppose you have a data set consisting of three numbers: 1, 101, and 102. 101 is the median because it is the middle value of the rank ordered data set, even though it is very far from the mean of the data. In this case, the mean would be a better measure of central tendency.

TABLE ii.3 > **Measurements of Central Tendency and Appropriate Applications**

Measurement Scale	Definition	Mode	Median	Mean
Nominal	Unordered categories	X	–	–
Ordinal	Ordered categories	X	X	–
Interval	Meaningful intervals between values	X	X	X
Ratio	Meaningful ratios between values	X	X	X

Although the central tendency of any data set resulting from interval or ratio measurement scales can be appropriately explored through mean, median, and mode, the preferred method for non-skewed data is the mean. For interval or ratio data that are skewed or contain outliers, the median is the best measurement. Only median and mode are appropriate for ordinal data, and the central tendency of nominal data can only be represented by mode.

Measures of Dispersion

Measures of dispersion describe how closely clumped together or widely spread apart the values are within a data set. Three of the most commonly used measures of dispersion are range, inter-quartile range, and standard deviation. The range of a data set is calculated by subtracting the value of smallest magnitude from the value of greatest magnitude. To use the example data set of the pop quiz scores, the highest score recorded was a 5 while the lowest score was a 1. The range of the data is therefore 5 − 1 = 4. If one or more students had scored a zero on the pop quiz, the range of the data would equal 5. A larger range indicates a greater amount of dispersion amongst the data points, while a small range suggests data that are clumped toward a central value.

The inter-quartile range also uses subtraction to gauge dispersion. To calculate inter-quartile range, the values in a data set must be organized by magnitude and quartiles must be determined. Just as the median divides a frequency distribution in half, quartiles divide a distribution into four equal parts. The distribution is divided into quartiles at the 25%, 50%, and 75% points. These are known as the first, second, and third quartiles, respectively. Note that the second quartile is the middle value, so it is equal to the median. The inter-quartile range is calculated by subtracting the value of the first quartile from that of the third quartile. Inter-quartile range provides a summary of the amount of dispersion present in the middle half of the data. Trimming the upper 25% and lower 25% of the data from analysis eliminates the influence of any outliers.

Calculating standard deviation is more mathematically rigorous than the calculations for range and inter-quartile range, but the underlying principles are the same. Like range and inter-quartile range, standard deviation is a measure of the dispersion of values in a data set, and is expressed in the same units as the values themselves. Unlike these statistics, the calculation for standard deviation takes each value into account and assesses how far, on average, values are from the mean value. The difference between each value in the data set and the mean is calculated and then squared. The standard deviation is then obtained by calculating the mean of these squared values and, finally, taking the square root of the result. A large standard deviation indicates widely dispersed data, while a small standard deviation indicates more tightly grouped values around a central point.

While measures of central tendency are a very useful in establishing approximately where the values of a data set exist along a number line, they provide no information about how tightly those values are grouped together. As is illustrated by these two frequency charts, two data sets may share identical means, medians, and modes, and yet vary significantly in terms of dispersion. In descriptive statistics, a measure of central tendency is most often used in conjunction with a measure of dispersion to provide a more complete picture of the nature of the data set. By summarizing how clumped or spread out the data are, the measure of dispersion indicates how well the measure of central tendency approximates individual values in the data set. A single, representative central value, such as a mean or a median, will more accurately reflect individual values in a data set that is crowded toward that middle value than it will if the data are widely dispersed over a large range.

FIGURE ii.6 | Range and Interquartile Range

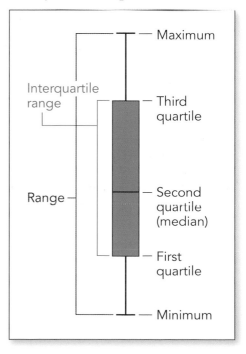

The MCAT® will NOT require you to calculate a standard deviation. You only need to be generally familiar with where this value comes from and what it represents. Remember, a greater standard deviation means data are more dispersed.

FIGURE ii.5 | Relative Dispersion

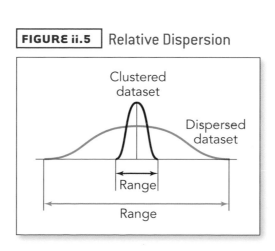

Examining Relationships between Variables

In scientific inquiry, statistics are used to determine whether the data collected support or refute the hypothesis of the experiment. Statistical tests generally address the question of how likely (or unlikely!) is it that any differences between the observed data and hypothesized outcomes have occurred by chance alone. When statistical tests indicate that any differences observed are very unlikely to have occurred by simple chance, the general assumption is that variables within the experiment must have some effect on each other. This section will briefly cover some of the most commonly used statistical tests and the conditions under which they can be applied.

Experimenters often set out to explore the relationship between an independent variable and one or more dependent variables in a study. Statistical tests can address the question of whether the values for one variable display a reliable pattern with corresponding values for the other variable. For instance, if the independent variable is increased, does the dependent variable reliably increase? Decrease? Or does it have no effect? The tests of this kind that are most likely to appear on the MCAT® are linear regression and correlation. Regression and correlation can be used when the all of the variables examined are continuous rather than categorical. Both of these tests are a way of getting a unbiased, mathematical view of the data. If researchers simply examined the data set on a scatter plot and attempted to spot a relationship between the variables, they might think that they observe the hypothesized relationship between variables, even if it is not truly present in the data set. Regression and correlation provide an accurate view of the existence and strength of a relationship between variables.

Simple *linear regression* describes the degree of dependence between one variable and another and is often used as a predictive tool. In linear regression, data are usually displayed in a scatter plot, such as the one in figure ii.8, with the independent (explanatory) variable on the x-axis and the dependent (responsive) variable on the y-axis. For an example of when linear regression might be used, consider that a researcher records observations of 100 lizards, measuring both ambient temperature and how many centimeters each lizard moved in a one hour period. Linear regression addresses the question of whether differences in ambient temperature will influence how far a lizard has moved in an hour by fitting a straight line (the line of best fit) to the data. Once an equation for the line of best fit is determined, the linear regression model can be used to estimate values for the dependent variable based on known values of the independent variable. Based on this model, a researcher might be able to predict that a lizard placed in a room at 40°C will move approximately 17 cm in an hour.

It is important to note that while linear regression makes an assumption about a one-way influence of one variable on another, it does not provide any information on causality. Even if a linear regression shows that lizards tend to move more in warmer temperatures, it doesn't say why that is the case. One researcher might argue that cold-blooded animals have more energy to move when they are warmer, while another might speculate that at high temperatures the floor becomes uncomfortable on the lizard's feet if it stays still too long. The point is that linear regression describes a mathematical relationship between two variables, but does not provide insight about why that relationship exists.

Correlation is similar to regression in that it also examines relationships between variables. However, unlike regression, correlation makes no assumptions about which variable is exerting influence on the other. Correlation estimates the degree of association between two variables with an outcome called a correlation coefficient. A correlation coefficient is a measure of linear association between two variables. The value of a correlation coefficient can vary between –1 and 1. If all values on a scatterplot fit perfectly on a line with positive slope, the correlation coefficient is equal to 1. Similarly, a correlation coefficient of –1 indicates a perfect linear relationship with negative slope between two variables. A correlation coefficient of 0 indicates no relationship between two variables whatsoever. Correlation only provides information on the degree of association between two variables without providing insight on causality.

Saying that two variables have a correlation coefficient of +1 is the same as saying that they are directly proportional. For example, in the equation $F = ma$, F and a are directly proportional, so they must have a correlation coefficient of +1.

FIGURE ii.7 | Correlation Coefficient

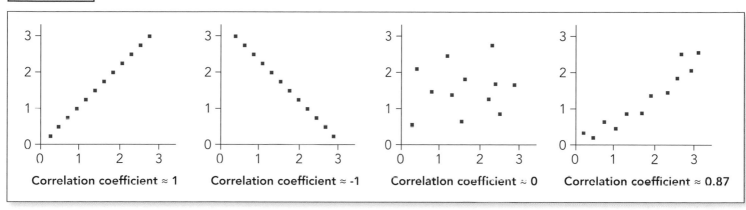

Correlation coefficient ≈ 1   Correlation coefficient ≈ -1   Correlation coefficient ≈ 0   Correlation coefficient ≈ 0.87

Regression and correlation are similar and sometimes confused with each other. Regression assumes that one variable influences another, while correlation simply describes the relationship between two variables without assuming the direction of influence or even the existence of influences at all. Let's consider two data sets to illustrate the difference between regression and correlation. One data set seems to indicate a relationship between leg length and arm length in adult men. However, it doesn't make sense to assume that longer arms cause legs to be longer. Nor does it make sense to assume that longer legs cause arms to be longer. We don't know which (if either) of these variables influences the other. It is possible that neither of these variables affects the other and both are controlled by outside influences. In this example, correlation would be an appropriate test to show that arm length and leg length tend to be correlated in men. For the second data set, consider the data recording inches of rainfall and maximum height of wheat grown during each of 50 consecutive years. We can make the assumption that rainfall may have some effect on wheat growth and test this hypothesis with a regression analysis. Correlation would not be appropriate in this case because no matter how high the wheat grows, it is not likely to make it rain more.

FIGURE ii.8 | Regression and Correlation

The variables leg length and arm length can be analyzed using correlation because neither causes the other. The lack of a clear independent and dependent variable means that a graph examining these two variables can assign either variable to either axis. By comparison, a change in rainfall may cause a change in wheat height, but a change in wheat height is not likely to cause a change in rainfall. By convention, the independent variable, rainfall, is placed on the x-axis while the dependent variable, wheat height, is on the y-axis. A regression should be used to explore a possible causal relationship between rainfall and wheat height.

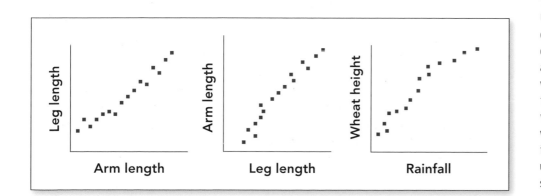

Hypothesis Testing

As discussed earlier in this section, statistical tests are often used to either support or refute specific hypotheses of the experiment. For these statistical tests, the default assumption or *null hypothesis* is that there is no difference between the observed results and those expected if the independent variable has no effect. Statistical tests are used to assess the likelihood that any differences found are attributable to chance. When the tests indicate that the observed results are likely to be the result of chance (within the realm of likely variation), the null hypothesis is accepted. When tests indicate that the results diverge from the expected in a way that is very unlikely to be due to chance alone, the null hypothesis is rejected and the *alternative hypothesis* is adopted. The following section examines the three most common statistical tools for hypothesis testing: the chi-square analysis, t-test, and analysis of variance.

The *chi-square test* (χ^2) can only be used when all variables in question are categorical. It shows whether two distributions of categorical data differ from each other. The chi-square test is often employed to determine whether the observed distribution of a categorical variable differs from the expected distribution for that variable. As an example, a researcher recreating Mendel's experiments with pea plants might expect that plants resulting from the self-pollination of heterozygotes would exhibit a 3:1 ratio of purple to white phenotypes. If the researcher produces 400 second generation offspring, the expected results would be 300 plants with purple flowers and 100 plants with white flowers. When the researcher tallies the actual incidence of purple vs. white flowers, she finds 228 with purple flowers and 172 with white flowers. The results are different than what was expected, but are they different enough to indicate that other forces are influencing flower color or could this variation from the expected have occurred by chance? This kind of question, because it deals with tallies of categorical responses, can be addressed with a chi-square test. In this case, the null hypothesis and alternative hypothesis would be as follows:

Null hypothesis (H_0): The tally of purple and white flowers do not differ significantly from the expected ratio of 3:1.

Alternative hypothesis: (H_1): The tally of purple and white flowers do differ significantly from the expected ratio of 3:1.

If the alternative hypothesis is accepted, it suggests to the researcher that outside variables were most likely involved in influencing the flower color results.

The *t-test* compares the mean values of a continuous variable (the dependent variable) between two categories or groups (where group membership is the independent variable). One group may be a population distribution or even a single mean value. Suppose that a researcher records the body temperatures of 100 people at rest. A t-test could be used to determine whether the average body temperature of those sampled differed significantly from the usual human body temperature of 98.6°F. The null hypothesis would be that the average temperature does not differ significantly from 98.6°F. The alternative hypothesis would state that the average temperature does differ significantly from 98.6°F.

In addition to comparing the mean of a group to a specific value, a t-test can also compare the means of two groups. For example, a t-test could be used to evaluate whether the average body temperature of males differed significantly from the average body temperature of females. In this case the categorical groups would be male and female, while the continuous variable would be body temperature.

A t-test is called one-tailed or two-tailed depending on the nature of the questions asked. A *two-tailed t-test* is used to explore the possibility of a relationship in both directions. Using the above example, if a researcher had no reason to believe that either women have a higher body temperature than men or that men have a higher body temperature than women, he would use a two-tailed test to allow for both options. However, suppose the researcher had seen previous research suggesting that men have a higher body temperature than women and wanted to see

FIGURE ii.9 | Flower Color in Mendel's Pea Plants

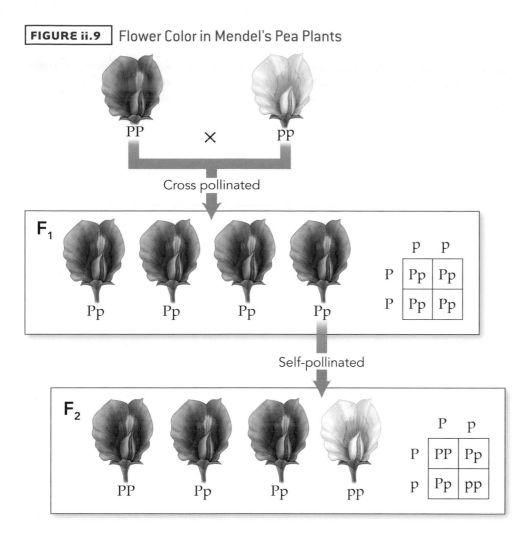

if his data support that claim. He would use a one-tailed t-test because he is only interested in whether the body temperature of men is higher than that of women, and is not interested in whether it might be lower. Compare the null and alternative hypotheses for such tests:

One tailed:

H_0: The body temperatures of men and women are equal.

H_1: The body temperatures of men are higher than the body temperatures of women.

Two tailed:

H_0: The body temperatures of men and women are equal.

H_1: The body temperatures of men and women are not equal.

The advantage of a two-tailed test is that it explores the possibility for difference in both directions. The advantage of a one-tailed test is that it has greater *statistical power* and is therefore more sensitive and able to recognize differences between groups.

The t-tests described above are more specifically known as *unpaired* or *independent sample* t-tests. In contrast, a *paired t-test* compares the distributions of two groups when each value within a group has a natural partner in the other group. Paired t-tests provide greater power to evaluate differences between groups and are useful when the variance within groups is large compared to the variation between groups. A paired t-test can be used in many experimental setups, but it is commonly used for before-and-after studies. For instance, if a study is trying to determine whether a new medication is effective at lowering blood pressure, the researchers may record "before" and "after" values of each participant's blood pressure. The blood pressures of the participants before medication will probably vary considerably. With so much variation within groups, it can be difficult to detect differences between the groups without a very large sample size. A paired t-test can be used to evaluate whether there is a significant difference in blood pressure between groups (before vs. after treatment) by taking into account that the individual values within the groups are paired, in that they come from the same participant.

As described above, t-tests are useful for a wide variety of experimental setups and can address many types of research questions by comparing the means of two groups. However, in some cases researchers need to compare data from more than two groups simultaneously. For instance, suppose a team of researchers designs a study to explore how diet effects cholesterol levels in rats. They randomly assign the rats into four groups, each of which is fed a different diet. At the end of six weeks, the researchers want to compare the mean cholesterol levels between the four groups of rats. This requires an *analysis of variance*, more commonly known as an *ANOVA*. An ANOVA is very similar to a t-test. It is used to compare the distributions of a continuous variable (cholesterol level) between the groups of a categorical variable (diet type). Like a t-test, ANOVAs begin with the null hypothesis that there is no difference between test groups. The distinction between an ANOVA and a t-test is that a t-test can only be used to analyze differences between two groups, while an ANOVA can be used when three or more groups are present.

> Remember that t-tests and ANO-VAs are used to answer the same kinds of questions, but when you are looking for differences between two groups or one group and a specific value, use a t-test. When you are looking for differences between three or more groups, use an ANOVA.

> Much of the information about statistical tests is background knowledge that will not be directly tested on the MCAT®. This table has everything you need to know if asked to choose a statistical test for a data set described in a passage.

TABLE ii.4 > **Common Statistical Tests**

Test	Test statistic	Variables	Used to...	Example research question
Regression	N/A	All continuous	Determine whether an independent variable influences a dependent variable	Do hot chocolate sales vary with temperature?
Correlation	N/A	All continuous	Determine whether change in one variable is reliably associated with change in another variable	Does the number of books read by a person correlate to his/her reading speed?
Chi-square	X^2	All categorical	Determine whether two distributions of categorical variables differ from each other (often comparing expected and actual results)	Does political affiliation differ by state?
t-test	t	1 continuous (DV); 1 categorical (IV, with 2 groups)	Determine whether two groups differ in their distributions of a single variable	Do men and women differ in IQ?
ANOVA	F	1 continuous (DV); 1 categorical (IV, with 3 or more groups)	Determine whether three or more groups differ in their distributions of a single variable	Do students learn best in low light, medium light, or bright light?

Results: Interpreting Data

Test Statistics

Hypothesis-testing statistics use mathematical calculations to compare the observed results to the expected results. The calculations involved in these statistical techniques are beyond the scope of the MCAT®. However, the numbers produced by the calculations indicate to researchers whether the null hypotheses of their experiments should be accepted or rejected. The end of these calculations produces a number known as a test statistic. The symbols representing the relevant test statistic for the chi-square, t-test, and ANOVA are χ^2, t, and F, respectively.

The calculated test statistic can be compared with a known likelihood distribution for that test statistic, such as the one shown of the student's t distribution in Figure ii.10. Each distribution represents the relative probability of all possible values for a given test statistic. The distributions follow a normal (bell) curve, where the center of the distribution represents the most likely outcome for the test statistic while the tails represent significantly less likely outcomes. Because all possible outcomes are represented, the area under the curve is equal to 1 (or 100 percent of outcomes). The area under the curve to the right of any specific value of t represents the likelihood of obtaining that value of t by chance and is represented by the symbol p.

Interpreting p Values

A *p value* is usually presented in any results summarizing statistical hypothesis testing. Interpreting the p value of a statistical test is how scientists decide if their data support or refute the hypotheses of their experiments. To see how p values are interpreted, examine the second part of Figure ii.10. In this graph, the likelihood of obtaining the given value of t is $p = 0.3$, or 30%. Whether any particular p value indicates a significant difference between the groups studied is open to interpretation. Most people would consider a 30% probability of any differences between groups occurring purely by chance to be a large probability, so they would likely not reject the null hypothesis. In other words, they would conclude that there were no differences between the groups studied. By contrast, Figure ii.10 also displays an example where $p = 0.04$. A 4% chance of differences between groups occurring by chance would be a low enough likelihood to convince many people that there are actual differences between the groups. Research studies generally set a "cut-off" point for p values they will consider statistically significant before beginning statistical analysis so the researchers' ideas about significance will not be biased by the results. The most common cut-off is $p < 0.05$, or a 5% probability of results occurring by chance, although many studies also use a value of $p < 0.01$ for a more conservative approach. When a test returns a p value below the established cut-off point, the test is said to have reached **statistical significance** and the null hypothesis is rejected.

When used in everyday language, the word significant simply means that something is important or meaningful. When used in the context of statistics, significance has a very specific meaning: the p value returned from a statistical test indicates that there are differences between groups tested that are unlikely to be due to chance.

The information in this section about how a p value is determined provides a useful background, but on the MCAT® you will likely just be asked to interpret a given p value. Remember, when a p value is SMALL, the difference between groups is SIGNIFICANT.

FIGURE ii.10 The Student's t Distribution and p Values

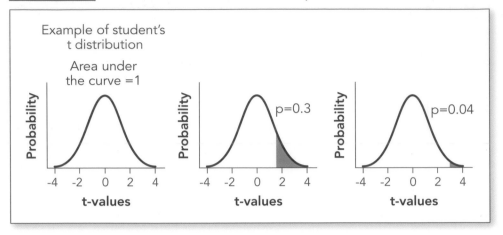

Uncertainty and Error in Statistics

Because all measurements are subject to error, error exists in any collection of data. One measure of error is standard deviation. Recall that standard deviation is a measure of how far values in a sample tend to fall from the mean of the sample. A small standard deviation indicates greater precision in data collection. Similar to standard deviation is *standard error.* The mean of one sample is unlikely to equal the population mean, but the distribution of means from many samples provide an estimate of the population mean. The standard deviation of a distribution of sample means is known as standard error and provides an estimate of the accuracy with which a sample represents a population.

Because of error, estimated values may not accurately reflect true values. There-fore, researchers often describe the **uncertainty** of their findings by including a range of values within which the true value is likely to fall. **Confidence intervals** use a normal distribution to provide an estimated range of values that is likely to include the true value. Similar to hypothesis testing, establishing the correct distributions for estimating uncertainty is dependent on sample size of the study. Most commonly, researchers employ a 95% confidence interval, meaning that there is a 95% chance that the true value lies between the upper and lower limits of the interval. However, other *confidence levels,* including 90% and 99%, are also common.

Results: Drawing Conclusions from Data

As described above, statistical methods are useful tools to organize data, recognize patterns, and identify relationships between variables. However, to obtain results from the data, the researcher must interpret the outcomes of the statistical tests. It is through this interpretation that scientists are able to answer research questions and draw conclusions from the results of their studies. Validity describes the degree to which conclusions based on the study's data are warranted. Studies have different levels of internal and external validity based on aspects of study design.

Internal validity is the degree to which a causal relationship between the independent and dependent variables is demonstrated. When asked to interpret data on the MCAT®, it is important to critically consider what elements of causality can reasonably be inferred as a result of the experimental setup and data analysis. A relationship between variables does not mean that some form of causality can automatically be assumed. This idea is often described by saying that "correlation is not causation." A correlation between variables must be present for the possibility of causality to even be considered, but correlation does not automatically mean that there is a causal relationship.

Confounding variables are a common threat to internal validity. A *confounding variable* (or "confounder") is a variable that is correlated with the independent variable and has a causal effect on the dependent variable. Suppose that a researcher wanted to see if exposure to sunlight effects running speed in white rats. If she placed all of the largest rats into one grouping for level of sun exposure, and size is correlated with running speed, size would be a confounding variable.

The best way to minimize the effects of both known and unknown confounders is to use **random assignment** to divide participants into different treatment groups. This means that differences between the research subjects that are not being measured or manipulated by the researchers, and thus could act as confounding variables, are evened out across the groups. In practice, the requirement of random assignment means that experimental methods can lead to inferences of causality but non-experimental methods cannot. In other words, if the researchers observe the effect of the independent variable after the fact rather than actually controlling the independent variable, correlation is the most that can be concluded.

MCAT® THINK

The issue of inferring causality often arises in social science research, which tends to be interested in variables that cannot be controlled by researchers for ethical or practical reasons. For example, suppose a social science researcher is interested in the effect of the quality of environmental stimulation on neurological development in youth. An experimental study design would take young children and randomly assign them to enriched or deprived environments and then measure neurological development. Obviously, such a study cannot actually be carried out, and the researcher will choose an observational method that can at least establish a correlation between the variables of research. (In fact, in the actual study on which this example is based, the researchers chose to use an animal model so that random assignment could be used. As a result, inferences of causality were possible.)

Random assignment makes it unlikely that an unknown third variable is responsible for any relationship that is found between the dependent and independent variable. However, the question of which variable has a causal influence on the other still needs to be resolved. To conclude that the independent variable has a causal influence on the dependent variable, the condition of temporality must be met. **Temporality** means that the cause comes before the effect. In other words, variable A can only cause a change in variable B if it happens before the observed change.

Temporality is a very simple concept, but understanding how the need for temporality to establish causation influences the progress of research is not as intuitive. Consider the following hypothetical example: a researcher in the lab observes that at the end of embryological development, chick embryos producing high levels of protein X also have particularly large beaks. In other words, a correlation has been observed. The researcher can use statistical analysis to describe the data and confirm that there is a correlation, but there is no way to know whether a rise in the level of protein X during development actually caused an increase in beak size. Another possible explanation is that a larger amount of beak tissue causes an increase in the production of protein X. To address the question of which change might cause the other, the researcher must determine which came first: an increase in the level of the protein or the development of unusually large beaks. The researcher might observe a new batch of chicks, recording both protein X level and beak volume every day throughout development. The researcher finds that when embryos experience a rise in protein X, beak size dramatically increases a few days later. Because beak size increases AFTER protein X increases, increased beak size cannot cause increased protein levels. According to the condition of temporality, it is still possible that higher protein levels can cause greater beak size. Simply observing that something happens first is insufficient to establish that it causes what happens later, though. In order to explore causality, the researcher would need to design an experiment in which he would randomly divide a new set of developing embryos into two groups. After taking initial measurements of beak size, the chicks in one group would receive an injection of the protein. If the chicks in this group then developed significantly larger beaks than those of the other group while all other variables were held constant, the researcher could then conclude that protein X causes an increase in beak size.

In summary, prior to inferring that an association represents a causal relationship, a researcher must consider four rival explanations: chance, bias, effect-cause and confounding variables. The first and second explanations suggest that the association was false. False associations due to chance follow from random error resulting in poor precision, whereas those due to bias follow from systematic error resulting in poor accuracy.

The third and fourth explanations, by contrast, maintain that a real association exists but is not a cause-effect relationship. Instead, the relationship may be effect-cause. In other words, the causal relationship may be opposite of the one that was hypothesized. For example, if the hypothesis was that increased coffee consumption leads to hypothyroidism, it may in fact be the case that hypothyroidism leads to increased coffee consumption. Appropriate temporality, where the cause comes before the effect, is required to eliminate the possibility of an effect-cause relationship. Alternatively, the relationship may be confounding, meaning that some third variable associated with coffee consumption leads to hypothyroidism. Random assignment protects against confounding. See the Table ii.5 for a summary of the potential explanations for an observed association between variables.

TABLE ii.5 > **Explanations for an Observed Association Between Variables X and Y**

Explanation	Type of association	Conclusion
Chance (random error)	False	X is not associated with Y
Bias (systematic error)	False	X is not associated with Y
Effect-cause	Real	Y is a cause of X
Confounding	Real	Z is associated with X and is a cause of Y
Cause-effect	Real	X is a cause of Y

The issues with inferring causality all have to do with the internal validity of a study. **External validity**, or generalizability, is the degree to which the results of a study can be generalized to other situations. Remember that scientists select a sample of subjects to study from a larger population. If the sample differs from the larger population in a way that affects the variables of the study, the external validity of the study is reduced. For example, many studies use college students as test subjects, but the results of research performed on a group composed entirely of young, healthy participants may not accurately extrapolate to the population at large. Additionally, external validity diminishes if the conditions of the study cause the subjects to behave differently from the larger population in a way that affects the variables of interest.

Appropriately analyzing data is essential to identifying pertinent results and drawing relevant conclusions. As discussed in the previous section, data analysis can reveal relationships between variables. An ANOVA may indicate that diet affects blood cholesterol level; a correlation analysis could demonstrate that when there is more rain, wheat tends to grow taller. Data analysis can even be used to make predictions that are beyond the scope of the data. For example, through extrapolations of their regression analysis, scientists could speculate that lizards in the hottest climates in the world would tend to be the most active. A well-constructed experimental method combined with careful and appropriate data analysis allows scientists to answer a variety of research questions and to draw conclusions from their data. However, it is also important to recognize that there are limits to the conclusions that can reasonably be drawn from data. These limits are affected by the methods and analysis techniques the researcher chooses, as well as factors beyond their control. Critical thinking about these limits is likely to be tested on the MCAT®.

ii.9 | Reading Research–Based MCAT® Passages and Interpreting Graphs

As you practice reading research-based passages in all of the sciences, you will gain a better understanding of how the knowledge and logic described throughout this lecture will be tested in the context of an actual passage. This section presents a sample passage to demonstrate the process of understanding a research-based passage, including the interpretation of complex graphs. As you read the passage, try to identify the research question, hypothesis, and independent and dependent variables.

Sample Passage I

Insulin resistance is a condition in which cells exhibit a diminished response to insulin, a hormone that promotes glycogen synthesis. In order to overcome this resistance and maintain glucose homeostasis, pancreatic β-cells must produce additional insulin. If β-cells cannot produce a sufficient quantity of insulin, type 2 diabetes, a condition characterized by a failure of insulin to properly maintain glucose homeostasis, results.

Insulin resistance can lead to β-cell failure, and reduction in β-cell mass is relentless in patients with insulin resistance and type 2 diabetes. Why β-cells fail in some individuals is a central issue in diabetes research today.

Glycogen synthase kinase-3β (Gsk-3β) is a serine/threonine kinase that inactivates glycogen synthase (GS), thereby inhibiting glycogen synthesis. Insulin inhibits Gsk-3β, and inactivation of Gsk-3β appears to be the major route by which insulin activates glycogen synthesis. Gsk-3β has been shown to affect many cellular processes, including cell proliferation and apoptosis. When elevated, it can impair replication and increase cell death.

Researchers found that mice missing two alleles of the insulin receptor substrate 2 (Irs2$^{-/-}$) had a 4-fold elevation of Gsk-3β activity, a decrease in β-cell proliferation, and an increase in β-cell apoptosis. Irs2$^{-/-}$ mice are insulin resistant and develop profound β-cell loss, resulting in diabetes.

Researchers hypothesized that decreasing Gsk-3β activity would reduce insulin resistance and increase β-cell mass in Irs2$^{-/-}$ mice. To test this hypothesis they crossed insulin resistant Irs2$^{-/-}$ Gsk-3β$^{+/+}$ mice with mice haploinsufficient for Gsk-3β (Irs2$^{+/+}$ Gsk-3β$^{+/-}$).

Experiment 1

Insulin resistant mice missing two alleles of the insulin receptor substrate 2 (Irs2$^{-/-}$ Gsk-3β$^{+/+}$) were crossed with mice haploinsufficient for Gsk-3β (Irs2$^{+/+}$ Gsk-3β$^{+/-}$). Fed blood glucose concentration in wild-type (Irs2$^{+/+}$ Gsk-3β$^{+/+}$) mice was compared with that in mice deficient in Irs2 and/or haploinsufficient in Gsk-3β.

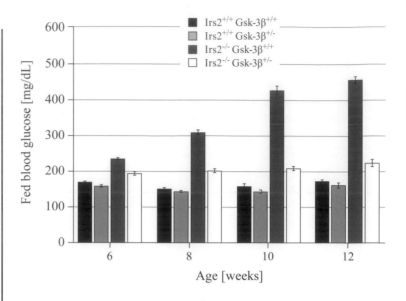

Figure 1 Effects of glycogen synthase kinase-3β genotype and insulin receptor 2 genotype on fed blood glucose concentration at 6, 8, 10 and 12 weeks of age

Experiment 2

β-cell mass in wild-type (Irs2$^{+/+}$ Gsk-3β$^{+/+}$) mice was compared with that in mice deficient in Irs2 and/or haploinsufficient in Gsk-3β.

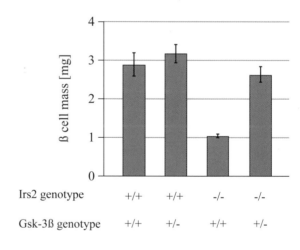

Figure 2 Effects of glycogen synthase kinase-3β genotype and insulin receptor 2 genotype on β-cell mass

STOP.

This is the type of complex passage that will be found on the MCAT®, but don't panic! With time and practice, it will become easier to interpret a passage in the context of your prior knowledge and gain the new information needed to answer the questions. Similarly to reading CARS passages, as described later in this manual, there are strategies that a reader can use to identify the most important aspects of a passage. As in the given example, it is likely that complex words that you have never seen before will appear in passages. Many students get so hung up on new vocabulary that they forget to apply what they already know. Be confident in your ability to interpret complicated new words and phrases using simpler background knowledge.

An example of the type of narration that a successful test taker uses to understand a research-based passage is given in yellow highlighting on the next page.

Sample Passage I: Successful Narration

Insulin resistance is a condition in which cells exhibit a diminished response to insulin, a hormone that promotes glycogen synthesis. In order to overcome this resistance and maintain glucose homeostasis, pancreatic β-cells must produce additional insulin. If β-cells cannot produce a sufficient quantity of insulin, type 2 diabetes, a condition characterized by a failure of insulin to properly maintain glucose homeostasis, results.

Insulin resistance can lead to β-cell failure, and reduction in β-cell mass is relentless in patients with insulin resistance and type 2 diabetes. Why β-cells fail in some individuals is a central issue in diabetes research today. So far there isn't enough information to determine the hypothesis and variables of the actual study. This is all background information that the researchers used to develop their question. But I can expect that the dependent variable will have something to do with β-cells.

Glycogen synthase kinase-3β (Gsk-3β) is a serine/threonine kinase that inactivates glycogen synthase (GS), thereby inhibiting glycogen synthesis. The unfamiliar name can be interpreted in terms of background knowledge. The suffix "-ase" is used in the names of enzymes, so glycogen synthase kinase-3β is an enzyme (and thus probably a protein). As the passage suggests, because it is an enzyme, it will influence activation or inhibition of reactions. Insulin inhibits Gsk-3β, and inactivation of Gsk-3β appears to be the major route by which insulin activates glycogen synthesis. The information can be organized into a mental chain of events: Gsk-3β inactivates GS and thus inhibits the reaction catalyzed by GS (glycogen synthesis). In other words, Gsk-3β decreases glycogen synthesis. Insulin inhibits this whole chain of events by inhibiting Gsk-3β. In other words, insulin increases glycogen synthesis. This is consistent with background knowledge about the role of insulin in metabolism. Gsk-3β has been shown to affect many cellular processes, including cell proliferation and apoptosis. When elevated, it can impair replication and increase cell death.

Researchers found that mice missing two alleles of the insulin receptor substrate 2 (Irs2$^{-/-}$) had a 4-fold elevation of Gsk-3β activity, a decrease in β-cell proliferation, and an increase in β-cell apoptosis. Given what the information in the passage says about Gsk-3β so far, the cellular processes that go along with the Irs2$^{-/-}$ genotype are probably due to the elevated Gsk-3β activity. Irs2$^{-/-}$ mice are insulin resistant and develop profound β-cell loss, resulting in diabetes. Irs2$^{-/-}$ is simply a symbolic description of the genotype. Whenever you see it, think of the associated phenotype: high Gsk-3β activity and insulin resistance. These two aspects of the phenotype are related, since insulin normally functions to inhibit Gsk-3β activity. The overall result of insulin resistance and high Gsk-3β activity will be very low rates of glycogen synthesis.

Researchers hypothesized that decreasing Gsk-3β activity would reduce insulin resistance and increase β-cell mass in Irs2$^{-/-}$ mice. The hypothesis is easy to find and is clearly related to the background research presented by the passage. The independent variable is level of Gsk-3β activity, and the dependent variables are β-cell mass and insulin resistance in Irs2$^{-/-}$ mice. To test this hypothesis they crossed insulin resistant Irs2$^{-/-}$ Gsk-3β$^{+/+}$ mice with mice haploinsufficient for Gsk-3β (Irs2$^{+/+}$ Gsk-3β$^{+/-}$). The unfamiliar term "haploinsufficient" can be interpreted using background information and the symbol for the genotype. "Haplo" means half (as in haploid cells). The genotype shows a +/− which, like the "half," implies one dominant and one recessive allele. Also, notice that the same name (Gsk-3β) is used for both the enzyme and its related genotype. You can tell them apart based on context and the fact that the genotype is italicized.

Experiment 1

Insulin resistant mice missing two alleles of the insulin receptor substrate 2 (Irs2$^{-/-}$ Gsk-3β$^{+/+}$) were crossed with mice haploinsufficient for Gsk-3β (Irs2$^{+/+}$ Gsk-3β$^{+/-}$). Fed blood glucose concentration in wild-type (Irs2$^{+/+}$ Gsk-3β$^{+/+}$) mice was compared with that in mice deficient in Irs2 and/or haploinsufficient in Gsk-3β. The variables in the hypothesis have been operationalized for the purposes of the experiment. Level of Gsk-3β activity has been operationalized as different genotypes that will be associated with different levels of Gsk-3β. Presumably haploinsufficiency for Gsk-3β will be associated with a lower level of Gsk-3β activity. We also know from the passage that the Irs2$^{-/-}$ genotype is associated with high levels of Gsk-3β activity. Insulin resistance has been operationalized as fed blood glucose concentration, since insulin resistance is associated with higher blood glucose.

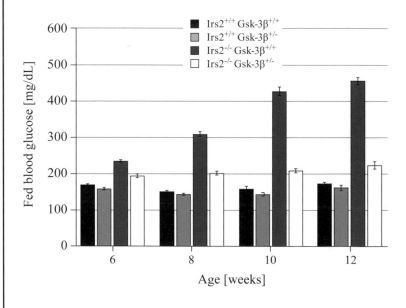

Figure 1 Effects of glycogen synthase kinase-3β genotype and insulin receptor 2 genotype on fed blood glucose concentration at 6, 8, 10 and 12 weeks of age

GO ON TO THE NEXT PAGE.

The interpretation of graphical data will be talked about in more detail for Figure 2, but we can get a general sense of the results by considering each category of the independent variable. In an experiment involving genotype, wild type is almost always a control group. In this case, it provides a baseline for fed blood glucose in mice that are not insulin resistant and have normal levels of Gsk-3β. The next group is haploinsufficient for Gsk-3β, meaning that it has lower levels of Gsk-3β, but is wild type for insulin receptor substrate. The graph indicates that this genotype is no different from wild type. The third group is wild type for Gsk-3β and is missing the two alleles for insulin receptor substrate—that is, it has normal levels of Gsk-3β and is insulin resistant. As expected based on the background research, fed blood glucose levels are much higher than in the previous two groups. Finally, the fourth group allows the researchers to observe blood glucose level in mice who are both insulin resistant and have lowered levels of Gsk-3β. As hypothesized, the result of this genotype is lowered fed blood glucose compared to the group that is insulin resistant and has normal levels of Gsk-3β. However, blood glucose is still elevated compared to the groups that are wild type for insulin receptor substrate.

Experiment 2

β-cell mass in wild-type (Irs2$^{+/+}$ Gsk-3β$^{+/+}$) mice was compared with that in mice deficient in Irs2 and/or haploinsufficient in Gsk-3β. The independent variable in this experiment is the same as in the previous one, but now the other dependent variable of interest, β-cell mass, is being examined.

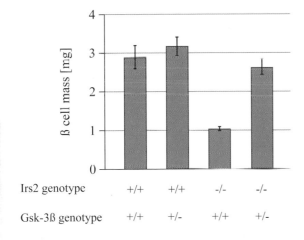

Figure 2 Effects of glycogen synthase kinase-3β genotype and insulin receptor 2 genotype on β-cell mass

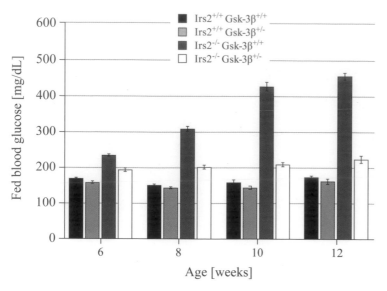

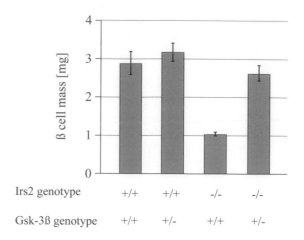

Figure 1 Effects of glycogen synthase kinase-3β genotype and insulin receptor 2 genotype on fed blood glucose concentration at 6, 8, 10 and 12 weeks of age

Figure 2 Effects of glycogen synthase kinase-3β genotype and insulin receptor 2 genotype on β-cell mass

As you can see in Figure 2, research-based passages often use graphs to present the data. This means interpeting these graphs to determine the important findings of the study. Like the passages themselves, the graphs appear intimidating but will get easier to interpret with practice. Use the following method to systematically interpret and extract information from figures:

1) Read the figure and axis titles.

2) Determine what the data suggest.

3) Look at the range of error.

To illustrate, consider Figure 2, taken from the sample passage.

Read the figure and axis titles

At first, ignore the data and look only at the figure and axis titles, using them to determine the overall purpose of the figure.

In this case, the figure title suggests that the independent variable is genotype, since the effects of genotype are being demonstrated. Because two different genes are being considered, there are four categories of the independent variable: 1) wild type for both, 2) altered for both (+/- for Gsk-3β and -/- for Irs2), 3) wild type for Gsk-3β and altered for Irs2, and 4) altered for Gsk-3β and wild type for Irs2. β-cell mass must be the dependent variable, since the graph shows the effects of genotype on β-cell mass. The independent variable should appear on the x-axis, and the dependent variable should appear on the y-axis. This is the case here, indicating that the figure is intended to show how β-cell mass changes according to changes in Irs2 and Gsk-3β genotype. Notice that the four genotype combinations are each represented on the x-axis.

Determine what the data suggest

Only after determining the overall purpose of the passage should you attempt to interpret the data. Keeping in mind the background research and hypothesis of the study, examine the graph to see what differences between groups it indicates. This passage suggested that, relative to wild-type mice, those deficient for Irs2 exhibit reduced β-cell mass. Therefore, you might expect β-cell mass to be lower in Irs2$^{-/-}$ mice. The researchers hypothesized that increased Gsk-3β activity contributes to reduced β-cell mass in Irs2 deficient mice. In other words, if the hypothesis is correct, β-cell mass will be lower in Irs2$^{-/-}$ Gsk-3β$^{+/+}$ mice than in Irs2$^{-/-}$ Gsk-3β$^{+/-}$ mice.

The first column indicates that mice wild-type for both *Irs* 2 and Gsk-3β ($Irs2^{+/+}$ Gsk-3β$^{+/+}$) have a β-cell mass of approximately 3 mg. By contrast, as indicated by the third column, mice wild-type for Gsk-3β but missing two alleles of Irs2 ($Irs2^{-/-}$ Gsk-3β$^{+/+}$) have a β-cell mass of just 1 mg. Together, the third and fourth columns indicate that, as expected, β-cell mass is lower in Irs2 deficient mice wild-type for Gsk-3β ($Irs2^{-/-}$ Gsk-3β$^{+/+}$) than in those haploinsufficient for Gsk-3β ($Irs2^{-/-}$ Gsk-3β$^{+/-}$).

Look at the Range of Error

Looking at Figure 2, you may have been tempted to conclude that β-cell mass is higher in $Irs2^{+/+}$ Gsk-3β$^{+/-}$ mice than in $Irs2^{+/+}$ Gsk-3β$^{+/+}$ mice. However, the error bars indicate that this conclusion is not warranted. When interpreting a figure, always look at the range of error if it is given.

The T-shaped bars at the top of each column, called error bars, indicate the uncertainty, or possible error, present in each reported measurement. To determine the full range of error, extend the error bar an equal distance below the reported measurement. Eyeballing the range of error can be useful in making quick assumptions about statistical significance. If the ranges of error for two measurements do not overlap, the difference between them is statistically significant. If there is considerable overlap, then the difference between the two measurements is not significant. A moderate amount of overlap may indicate statistically significant differences or not, and further statistical testing is needed. Furthermore, the size of the error bars indicates the amount of uncertainty. The larger the error bar, the less precise the data are. In summary, be cautious about concluding that there is a statistically significant difference between groups if the error bars are both large and overlapping.

The MCAT® is unlikely to ask questions about ambiguous error bars. In this figure, the ranges of error for columns one and two overlap considerably. For this reason, it would be inappropriate to conclude that β-cell mass is higher in Irs $2^{+/+}$ Gsk-3β$^{+/-}$ mice than in Irs $2^{+/+}$ Gsk-3β$^{+/+}$ mice. However, the range of error for column three clearly does not overlap with any of the other columns. This supports the conclusion that, as expected, this group is significantly different from the others.

This lecture contains everything that you need to know to interpret research-based passages and answer questions involving research skills. With every passage that you read, practice finding the hypothesis and the independent and dependent variables. Eventually it will become second nature.

The rest of this manual discusses the skills needed for success on the CARS section. As you will see, the interpretation of CARS passages draws upon the same skills of critical and logical thinking that are required for tackling research-based passages.

Answers to sidebar on page 40:

Mean: 3.4

Median: 3

Mode: 3

DON'T FORGET YOUR KEYS

1. In an experimental setup, the independent variable is manipulated and the dependent variable is measured and/or observed.

2. Correlated factors do not necessarily indicate a causal relationship.

3. Narrate as you read a research-based passage: identify the variables and hypothesis and interpret the data as it relates to the hypothesis.

Introduction to CARS: Strategy and Tactics

1.1 Introduction

The *Critical Analysis and Reasoning Skills* (CARS) Section of the MCAT® (formerly known as Verbal Reasoning) is composed of nine passages, averaging 500-600 words per passage. Five to seven multiple-choice questions follow each passage for a total of 53 questions. Answers to these questions do not require information beyond the text of the passage. The test taker has 90 minutes to complete the entire section.

Topic Areas Covered by CARS passages

CARS passages are excerpted from books, magazines, journals, and other sources, and they cover a wide variety of disciplines from the humanities and social sciences. These disciplines are laid out in Tables 1.1 and 1.2. All the information that you need to know to answer test questions is contained in the passages and question stems; no outside knowledge is necessary. However, familiarity with the subject areas will enhance your understanding. Use the table as a guide to acquaint yourself with the subject areas. Some students taking the MCAT® may have a broad liberal arts background and feel comfortable with all of these topics; others may need to gain familiarity with several of these areas. A good way to gauge your understanding is to imagine yourself in a conversation with someone who is wholly unfamiliar with the topic area. Practice giving a brief definition of that field. In addition, imagine several potential MCAT® topics beyond what is listed in the table. If you can do these two things, you are ready for whatever the MCAT® throws at you.

THE 3 KEYS

1. Review the Strategies before each practice test, evaluate after: energy, focus, confidence, timing.

2. Use the Tactics every step of the way from passage to questions to answer choices.

3. Leave your outside knowledge and bias at the door for the CARS section.

This table is meant to familiarize, but is by no means exhaustive. Be ready for anything!

TABLE 1.1 > **Humanities Disciplines Tested on the MCAT®**

Topic
Architecture
Art
Dance
Ethics
Literature
Music
Philosophy
Popular Culture
Religion
Theater
Studies of Diverse Cultures

TABLE 1.2 > **Social Science Disciplines Tested on the MCAT®**

Topic
Anthropology
Archaeology
Economics
Education
Geography
History
Linguistics
Political Science
Population Health
Psychology
Sociology
Studies of Diverse Cultures

*These lists are not exhaustive; other humanities and social science disciplines may be tested.

Other CARS Strategies

Dogma about the CARS section is abundant and free, and that's an accurate reflection of its value. There are many cockamamie CARS strategies touted by various prep companies, academics, and well-wishers. **We strongly suggest that you ignore them.** Some test prep companies design their CARS strategy to be marketable (to make money) as opposed to being efficient ("raising your score"); the idea being that unique and strange will be easier to sell than commonplace and practical.

Some colleges offer classes designed specifically to improve reading comprehension in the MCAT® CARS section. Typically, such classes resemble English 101 and are all but useless at improving your score. They are often taught by well-meaning humanities professors who have never even seen a real MCAT® CARS section. Being a humanities professor does not qualify you as an expert on the MCAT® CARS section. The emphasis in such classes is usually on detailed analysis of what you read, rather than how to eliminate wrong answers and find correct answers. Improvements are predictably miserable.

There are those who will tell you that a strong performance on the CARS section requires speed-reading techniques. This is not true. Most speed-reading techniques actually prove to be an impediment to score improvements by shifting focus from comprehension to reading technique. It is unlikely that you will improve both your speed and comprehension in a matter of weeks. As you will soon see, speed is not the key to a good score on the CARS section. Finishing the CARS section is within the grasp of everyone who follows the advice given in this manual.

If your college professor hasn't taken the MCAT®, why would you take his advice on it?

A favorite myth among MCAT® students is that copious amounts of reading will improve scores on the CARS section (formerly on the Verbal Section). This myth originated years ago when prep companies having insufficient practice materials suggested that their students "read a lot" rather than use the other companies' materials. The myth has perpetuated itself ever since. "Reading a lot" is probably the least efficient method of improving your CARS score. If you intend to take the MCAT® four or five years from now, you should begin "reading a lot." If you want to do well on the CARS section this year, follow the guidelines given in this manual.

Take Our Advice

Most smart students listen to advice, then pick and choose the suggestions that they find reasonable while disregarding the rest. This is not the most efficient approach for preparing to take the MCAT® CARS section. In fact, it is quite counter-productive. Please abandon all your old ideas about CARS and follow our advice to the letter. Don't listen to your friends and family. They are not experts at teaching students how to score well on the CARS section. We are.

Expected Improvement

Taking the CARS section is an art. Like any art form, improvement comes gradually with lots of practice. Imagine attending a class in portraiture taught by a great artist. You wouldn't expect to become a Raphael after your first lesson, but you would expect to improve after weeks of coaching. The CARS section is the same way. With the tools you will learn here and with regular practice, you will see dramatic improvements over time.

How to Study for the CARS section

Of course, you'll want to practice in the most efficient way that will give you the best results. Once you have learned the effective Examkrackers method, covered in the next three CARS lectures, use the algorithm below to guide your studying. We believe that this is the most effective way to improve your CARS score.

1. Take a CARS test under strict timed conditions and score yourself.

2. Take a break from CARS for at least one day.

3. Take the set of questions for the first passage in the CARS exam that you recently finished and examine the questions and answer choices as if you had never read the passage, as demonstrated in Lecture 3 of this manual. If this step takes you less than 30 minutes per passage, do it again because you missed quite a bit.

4. Repeat step 3 for each passage.

5. Take a break from CARS for at least one day.

6. Carefully read the first passage in the same CARS test, and write out a precisely worded main idea in one or two complete sentences being certain that your main idea expresses the author's opinion or stance on the issues.

7. Match your main idea to each question and all the answer choices and see what insights you gain into answering MCAT® questions.

8. Repeat steps 6 and 7 for each passage.

If you learn our method and use this algorithm for studying, you will see marked improvement in your CARS score.

"Reading a lot" isn't going to get you a better score on the CARS section. Using the Examkrackers method will. Book clubs, reading, and study groups are a good way to increase your reading comprehension, but are not effective tools for raising your CARS score in a short amount of time.

1.3 | The Examkrackers Approach: Strategies for Success

The rest of this lecture will examine the CARS section on two levels: strategic and tactical. The strategic point of view, presented in this section, will encompass the general approach to the CARS section as a whole. The tactical point of view is the subject of the following section and will explain exactly what to do, passage by passage, and question by question.

It is extremely important to have a good strategy before you begin the CARS section. The Examkrackers strategy has four components:

1. Maintain energy

2. Stay focused

3. Be confident

4. Mind timing

Maintain Energy

Sit up straight, young man!

Pull your chair close to the table. Sit up straight. Place your feet flat on the floor, and be alert. This may seem to be obvious advice to some, but it is rarely followed. Test-takers often look for the most comfortable position in which to read the passage. Do you really believe that you do your best thinking when you're relaxed? Webster's Dictionary gives the definition of relaxed as "freed from or lacking in precision or stringency." Is this how you want to be when you take the MCAT®? Your cerebral cortex is most active when your sympathetic nervous system is in high gear, so don't deactivate it by relaxing. Your posture makes a difference to your score.

One strategy used by the test writers is to wear you down with the CARS section before you begin the Biological section. You must mentally prepare yourself for the tremendous amount of energy necessary for a strong performance on the CARS section. Like an intellectual athlete, train yourself to concentrate for long periods of time. It is crucial to improve your reading comprehension stamina. **Practice! Practice! Practice!** always under timed conditions. **And always give 100% effort when you practice.** If you give less than 100% when you practice, you will be teaching yourself to relax when you take the CARS section, and you will be lowering your score. It is more productive to watch TV than to practice with less than complete effort. If you are not mentally worn after finishing three or more CARS passages, you have not tried hard enough, and you have trained yourself to approach the section incorrectly; you have lowered your score. Even when you are only practicing, sit up straight in your chair and attack each passage.

Stay Focused

The CARS section is made up of nine passages with both interesting and boring topics. It is sometimes difficult to switch gears from "the migration patterns of the Alaskan tit-mouse" to "economic theories of post-Soviet Russia." In other words, sometimes you may be reading one passage while thinking about the prior passage. Learn to **focus your attention on the task at hand.** Methods to increase your focus will be discussed in the section on tactics.

During the real MCAT®, it is not uncommon for unexpected interruptions to occur. People get physically ill, nervous students breathe heavily, air conditioners break down, and lights go out. Your score will not be adjusted for unwelcome interruptions, and excuses will not get you into medical school, so learn to focus and **ignore distractions.**

Be Confident

There are two aspects to confidence on the CARS section: 1) **be confident of your score** and 2) **be confident when you read.**

1) CONFIDENCE IN YOUR SCORE Imagine taking a multiple choice exam and narrowing 50% of the questions down to just two answer choices, and then guessing. On a physics exam, this would almost certainly result in a very low grade. Yet this exact situation describes a stellar performance on the CARS section of the MCAT®. Even those who have earned a perfect score (including many of our own students) guessed on a large portion of the answers. The test writers are aware that most students can predict their grades on science exams based on their performance, and that guessing makes science majors extremely uncomfortable. The CARS section is the most dissatisfying in terms of perceived performance. Realize that even the best test takers finish the CARS section with some frustration and insecurity concerning their performance. A perceived dissatisfactory performance early in the testing day is likely to reflect poorly in scores on the Biological and Psychosocial sections if you let your confidence waver. Instead, assume that you have answered every question of the CARS section correctly and get psyched to ace the Biological section.

2) CONFIDENCE WHEN YOU READ The second aspect of confidence concerns how you read CARS passages. Read the passages as if you were a Harvard professor grading high school essays. Read critically. If you are confused while reading the passage, assume that it is the passage writer, not you, who is at fault. If you find a contradiction in the reasoning of the argument, trust in your reasoning ability and that you are correct. The questions will focus on the author's argument, and you must be confident in your understanding of the strong and weak points. In order to identify the strong and weak points, you must read with confidence, even arrogance.

Mind the Timing

Generally speaking, timing can be broken down into three smaller components:

1) **start with a five second break;**

2) **read and attempt every passage and every question, in order; and**

3) **check time only once and finish with 5 minutes left.**

1) THE FIVE SECOND BREAK If we observed a room full of MCAT® test takers just after beginning a section, we would see many students read for 20 to 30 seconds, pause, and then begin rereading from the beginning. Why? Because as they race through the first passage, they are thinking about what is happening to them ("I'm taking the real MCAT®! Oh my God!"), and not thinking about what they are reading. They need a moment to become accustomed to the idea that this MCAT® section has actually begun. They need a moment to focus. However, they don't need 20 to 30 seconds! They take so much time because they are trying to do two things at once: calm themselves down and understand the passage. They end up accomplishing neither. This loss of concentration may also occur at the beginning of each new passage, when the test-taker may still be struggling with thoughts of the previous passage while reading the new passage.

...Three One Thousand
..Four One Thousand
...Five One Thousand

If we continued to observe the test-takers, we would see them in the midst of a passage suddenly stop everything, lift up their head, stretch, yawn, or crack their knuckles. Their beleaguered minds are forcing them to take a break. No one has an attention span 90 minutes long. If you don't allow yourself a break, your mind will take one. How many times have you been reading a passage when suddenly you realize that you weren't concentrating? You're forced to start the passage over. More time is wasted.

There is a simple method to prevent all this lost time. Instead of taking breaks at random, inconvenient moments, plan your breaks. **Before each passage, including the first passage, take five seconds to focus your thoughts.** Remind yourself to forget the last passage and all other thoughts not related to the task at hand. Remind yourself to sit up straight, concentrate, and focus. For these five seconds, look away from the page, stretch your muscles and prepare to give your full attention to the next passage. Then begin and don't break your concentration until you have finished answering all the questions to that passage. The five second break is like a little pep-talk before each passage.

Unfortunately, most students will not take the five second break. Understand one thing. All students will take breaks during the CARS section. Most will take them without realizing it, and most will take them at inopportune moments. If your goal is to get the highest CARS score of which you are capable, you should take the five second break at planned intervals.

Note that you can apply these strategies regarding focus, confidence, and taking a 5 second break to every section, not just CARS!

2) READ AND ATTEMPT EVERY PASSAGE AND EVERY QUESTION, IN ORDER

If you want a 127 or better on the CARS section, you must read every passage and attempt to answer every question. If you want to go to medical school, you should attempt to score 127 on the CARS section. Therefore, read every passage in the order given, and attempt every question.

You don't get penalized for missed questions anyway, so why would you leave a question blank?

Skipping around in the CARS section to find the easiest passages is a marketable strategy for a prep company but an obvious waste of time for you. It is a bad idea that makes a lot of money for some prep companies because it's an easy trick to sell. 'Cherry picking' is an unfortunate carryover from SAT strategy where it works because the questions are prearranged in order of difficulty. On the MCAT®, some passages are difficult to read, but have easy questions; some passages are easy to read, but have difficult questions. Some passages start out difficult and finish easy. You have no way of knowing if a passage is easy or difficult until you have read the entire passage and attempted all of the questions, so 'cherry picking' is a waste of precious time and lowers your score.

If you begin reading a passage and are asking yourself "Should I continue, or should I move on to the next passage? Is this passage easy or difficult?", you are not reading with confidence; you are not concentrating on what the author is saying; and you are wasting valuable time. Your energy and focus should be on doing well on each passage, not on trying to decide which passage to do first.

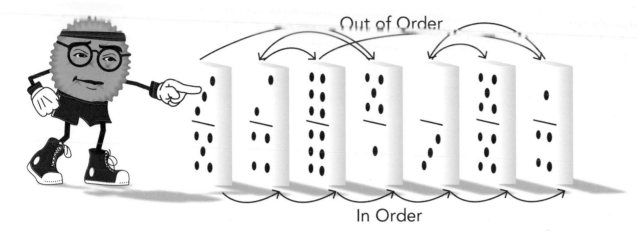

Out of Order

In Order

Hmmm. Let's see. I must knock down all seven dominos. Is it faster and more efficient to knock them down in order, or is it faster to decide which one is heaviest and then run back and forth and knock them down out of order?

3) CHECK TIME ONLY ONCE AND FINISH WITH 5 MINUTES LEFT Check your time only once during the CARS section. Constantly checking your time is distracting and not very useful since some passages take longer to finish than others. Instead, **check your time only once, and after you have finished the 5th passage.** You should have about 40 minutes left. A well-practiced test taker will develop an acute sense of timing and will not need to look at the time at all.

Don't spend too much time with the difficult questions. **Guess at them and move on.** Guessing is very difficult for science students, who are accustomed to either being certain of the answer on an exam or getting the answer wrong. Test writers are aware of this, and use it to their advantage. Learn to give up on difficult questions so that you have more time to spend on easier questions. Accurate guessing on difficult questions is one of the keys to finishing the exam and getting a high score. To accurately guess, practice learning to use all of your tools for answering the questions. We will discuss this when we discuss tactics.

Finish the entire section with five minutes to spare, no more, no less. If you have more than five minutes to spare, you missed questions on which you could have spent more time. The stress of exam taking makes you more perspicacious while you take the exam. When you finish an exam, even if you intend to go back and check your work, you typically breathe a sigh of relief. Upon doing so, you lose your perspicacity. The best strategy is to use your time efficiently during your first and only pass through the exam.

Some people have difficulty finishing the exam. These people often think that they can't finish because they read too slowly. This is not the case. In the next section, we will discuss how finishing the exam does not depend on reading speed; in fact, anyone can finish the exam.

> Many test-takers are able to guess on difficult questions during a practice exam, but when it comes to the real MCAT®, they want to be certain of the answers. This meticulous approach has cost such students dearly on their scaled score. Learn to guess on difficult questions so you have time to answer the easy questions.

Finish the entire section with five minutes to spare.

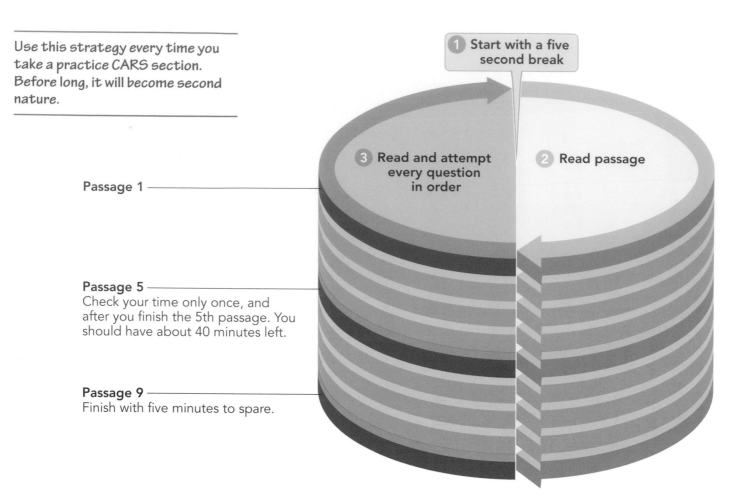

Use this strategy every time you take a practice CARS section. Before long, it will become second nature.

1 Start with a five second break

3 Read and attempt every question in order

2 Read passage

Passage 1

Passage 5
Check your time only once, and after you finish the 5th passage. You should have about 40 minutes left.

Passage 9
Finish with five minutes to spare.

1.4 | The Examkrackers Method: Test Taking Tactics

The following techniques are designed to increase your pace and efficiency. Practicing them may initially take longer – that is true of learning any skill. Over time these tactics will increase your pace, efficiency, and score. Many students begin to pick and choose CARS methods that they think best suits their own personalities. Please don't do this. Follow our strategies and tactics exactly for each passage and with practice your CARS score will increase.

Reading the Passage

Most test takers have difficulty finishing the CARS section in the 90 minutes allowed. Strangely enough, the vast majority of premeds are capable of reading 5000 words in around 25 minutes. A very slow reader can easily read every word of a 600 word passage in 3 minutes. Try it! It's true! This leaves about 65 minutes to answer the questions, or around 70 seconds per question. In other words, over two thirds of your time is spent answering questions on the MCAT® CARS section, and less than one third is spent reading. If you read TWICE as fast as you

It's not your reading speed that you need to improve; it's your efficiency at answering the questions.

Improving your efficiency at answering questions will be more profitable than increasing your reading speed. Improving your efficiency at answering the questions will also give you more time to read the passages. If you increase your reading speed by 10%, a strong improvement, you will only gain 2 and a half minutes on the entire exam. Spread over 53 questions, this allows you less than 3 extra seconds per question. Not too fruitful. If you increase your efficiency at answering questions by 10%, a rather simple task as you will soon see, you gain 6 and a half minutes. This is easily enough time to read one or more entire additional passages!

Work on your efficiency at answering the questions, NOT your reading speed.

do now, you would have about 85 seconds, instead of 70 seconds, to answer each question. So increasing your reading speed has very little effect on your CARS score. If you're not finishing now, you won't be able to finish by reading faster.

So why do so many test-takers fail to finish the CARS section? The answer is that they spend too much time hunting for the answer in the passage, and end up reading the passage many times over. We'll talk more about "looking back" in Lecture 3. For now, just believe us that **you can read every word in the CARS section and easily finish the exam,** so you should.

Have you ever tried skimming through a novel, not reading every word? Try it and see how much you understand. If you don't usually understand much when you skim, why would you skim on the most important test of your life, especially when it won't give you much more time to answer the questions? **Don't skim.**

Have you ever mapped out a novel by writing a brief synopsis alongside each paragraph as you read? Try it. We think you will fall asleep from boredom. You will understand less of what you read, not more. Passages are intended to be read in their entirety as a single work presenting one overriding theme. The MCAT® expects you to understand this theme. The details within the theme are far less important. **Don't distract yourself by taking notes.**

The people that write the MCAT® know that most of us are scientists who like to find the exact answers to questions. Give us a mysterious powder and let us analyze it, and we will tell you exactly what it is. Show us the exact words in a passage as an answer choice and we will probably choose it. Don't fall for this trap. The CARS section tests your ability to detect and understand ambiguities and gray areas, not details. Rely heavily on your main idea and give little weight to details. If you are highly certain of all your answers on the CARS section, you have probably fallen for all of its traps. **Mastering this section is as much an art as a science.** With practice, you will develop a 'feel' for a good MCAT® answer, which will help you move faster through the CARS section. If you teach yourself not to expect the concrete certainty that you get with science questions, you will become more comfortable with the CARS section and your score will increase.

The biggest mistake you can make on the CARS section is to consciously attempt to remember what you are reading. The vast majority of the questions will not concern the details of the passage and will not be answerable by searching the passage for facts. Most questions are about the main idea of the passage. The main idea will not be found in a list of details. In order to learn the main idea, the passage as a whole must be understood. Read the passage the way you would read an interesting novel; **concentrate on the main idea, not the details.**

An often posited tactic is to read the questions first; don't do it! You will not remember even one question while you read the passage, much less the 5 to 7 questions that accompany every passage. Not only that, reading the questions first will force you to read for detail, and you will never find the main idea. You will probably end up rereading the passage many times but never straight through. This results in a tremendous waste of time.

Some of the CARS topics will fascinate you and some will bore you. The challenge will be to forget the ones that fascinate you as soon as you move to the next passage, and to pay close attention to the ones that bore you. **Train yourself to become excited and interested in any and every passage topic.** This will increase your comprehension. However, don't become so engrossed in a passage that you slow your pace.

Likewise, **free yourself from outside bias.** We all have outside knowledge and bias that we want to bring into our reading. Although this is natural in real life, don't do it on the MCAT®! CARS passages and questions are designed to be read and answered based solely on the information provided in the passage. If you like or dislike a topic or point of view, your opinion may color your reading. If a topic hits close to home, or if you dislike a subject, it is easy to get distracted, allow your reading to be disrupted, and misunderstand the main idea or author's point of view. Strive to be an open-minded, mentally objective reader for each and every CARS passage.

Don't use fancy speed reading techniques where you search for meaningful words or try to read entire phrases in one thought. This will only distract you from your goal. Read the way you normally read. Your reading speed is unlikely to change significantly in 10 weeks, and your reading speed is not the problem anyway. Finishing the entire section depends on how long you spend answering the questions, not how long it takes you to read the passages. You also cannot assume that the passages are written well enough that you could read just the first and last sentence of each paragraph. They are sometimes barely intelligible even when you read every word.

Read each passage like you are listening to a friend tell you a very interesting story. Allow the details (names, dates, times) to slip in one ear and out the other, while you wait with bated breath for the main point. The funny thing about this type of reading is that, when you practice it, you can't help but remember most of the details. Even if you were to forget some of the details, it only takes about 5 seconds to find a name, number, or key word in a 600 word passage. Thus, when you run into a rare question about a detail that you've forgotten, it is easy to find the answer. Another convenient aspect of this tactic is that you are trying to accomplish exactly what the CARS section will be testing: your ability to pick out the main idea. The best thing about this type of reading is that you have practiced it every day of your life. This is the way that you read novels, newspapers, and magazines. Read the passages the way that you read best; read for the main idea.

When I create a great soup, you do not taste the salt, and each spice separately. You must experience the whole soup as a single, wonderful consommé.

Aim to clear your cache after every passage, and be a blank slate!

When you read, ask yourself, "What is the author trying to say? What is his point? Is he in favor of idea A or against it? If this author were sitting right in front of me, would he want to discuss idea A or is his real interest in idea B?" **Creating an image of the author in your mind will help you understand him.** Use your life experiences to stereotype the author. This will help you make quick, intuitive decisions about how the author might answer each MCAT® question about the passage. Make careful mental note of anything the author says that may not fit your stereotype. Use the stereotype to help guide your intuition on the questions.

FOLLOW OUR PASSAGE READING TACTICS:

• Don't skim.

• Don't distract yourself by taking notes.

• Concentrate on the main idea, not the detail.

• Don't read the questions first.

• Train yourself to become excited and interested in every passage topic.

• Free yourself from outside bias.

• Don't use fancy speed reading techniques.

• Read each passage like you are listening to a friend tell you a very interesting story. Allow the details (names, dates, times) to slip in one ear and out the other.

• Create an image of the author in your mind.

The Main Idea

As you read the passage, you will construct the main idea that the author is trying to communicate. Then, when you have finished reading a passage, take twenty seconds to state the main idea in the form of one or two complete sentences. Lecture 2 of this manual contains detailed techniques for constructing a main idea. On a timed MCAT®, writing the main idea requires too much time, so spend 20 seconds mentally contemplating the main idea before you begin the questions. After you have completed an entire timed practice exam, scored yourself, and taken a break, go back to each passage and write out the main idea for practice.

Answering the Questions

Use the following four tools as you answer the questions:

1. going back;

2. the main idea;

3. the question stems; and

4. the answer choices.

Answering the questions utilizing the four tools will be covered thoroughly in Lecture 3. For now, attempt to answer the questions based upon the main idea and not the details.

DON'T FORGET YOUR KEYS

1. Review the Strategies before each practice test, evaluate after: energy, focus, confidence, timing.

2. Use the Tactics every step of the way from passage to questions to answer choices.

3. Leave your outside knowledge and bias at the door for the CARS section.

The Main Idea

2.1 Introduction

The main idea is a thematic summary of the passage in one or two sentences. It should reflect the author's opinion (if presented or implied), and it should emphasize minor topics to the same extent that they are emphasized in the passage. It is not a list of topics discussed in the passage, nor is it an outline of those topics. It is a statement about the passage topics, and includes the author's opinion. The main idea does not get bogged down by detail. Instead, it presents the author's overarching point of view, which ties together the most important ideas presented in the passage. A good main idea represents the middle ground that the author eventually reaches after presenting alternative points of view. A good main idea usually does not present an extreme viewpoint. Instead, the main idea, like the passage itself, will settle on a middle ground between opposing perspectives. This idea is explored further in the last lecture of this manual.

In one form or another, 90% of the CARS Section questions will concern the main idea. Notice that the main idea cannot be found by going back to the passage and searching for details. You must concentrate on the main idea while you read the entire passage. If you read for detail and try to remember what you have read rather than processing what you are reading, you will have to guess at 90% of the questions.

It is important to have a clear concept of the main idea before reading any questions. MCAT® CARS Section questions are designed to take your inchoate thoughts concerning the passage and subtly redirect them away from the true main idea. Each successive question embellishes on insidious pseudo-themes steering unwary followers into an abyss from which there is no return. Like a faithful paladin, your clearly stated main idea unmasks these impostors and leads you toward the holy grail of CARS Section perfection.

Writing the main idea on paper is an important step toward improving your ability to find the main idea; however, it requires too much time while taking the exam. Instead, a few days after taking a practice exam, go back to each passage and write out the main idea. While taking the exam, pause for 20 seconds after reading a passage and construct the main idea in your head. Say the main idea "out loud" in your head before moving on to the questions.

Most students resist writing out their main idea until they are halfway through the course and the materials. At this point they begin to realize how important the main idea is. Unfortunately, they must start from scratch and begin writing out the main idea with only four weeks until the MCAT®. Don't do this. Start now by going back to used passages and writing out the main idea. **It is very painful at first, but it will get easier, and it will dramatically improve your score.**

2.2 | Constructing the Main Idea

A good main idea can be formed as follows:

1. After finishing the passage, write down a list of main topics. Each item should be one to four words long.

2. Choose the most important topics, two or three at a time, and write a short phrase relating them to each other and the passage.

3. Now connect the phrases into one or two sentences which still concern the most important topics but incorporate the other topics as well. Be sure to include the author's opinion if it was given or implied. Try to emphasize each topic to the same extent to which it was emphasized in the passage. This is your main idea. Over time, you will be able to construct the main idea in your head.

The last lecture of this manual will revisit the main idea from the particular perspective of placing ideas in the passage along a continuum between extreme viewpoints.

Confidence

Often on the MCAT®, passages seem incomprehensible. Don't get bent! Remember, most questions are answered correctly by 60% or more of test takers, and only two or three are answered incorrectly by fewer than 40%, so no group of questions will be that difficult. Have the confidence to keep reading. **Don't reread a line or paragraph over and over until you master it.** If a line or paragraph is incomprehensible to you, then it is probably incomprehensible to everyone else, and understanding it will not help your score. Instead, continue reading until you get to something that you do understand. Just get the general sense of what the author is trying to say. Chances are good that this will be enough to answer all the questions. As discussed further in the next lecture, after you read the passage you will have four additional tools to help you answer the questions.

Because I'm good enough, I'm smart enough and doggone it, people like me!

Know Your Author

Become familiar with the author. Who is he or she? Is the author young or old; rich or poor; male or female; conservative or liberal? Do you love or hate this author? Take a guess. Create a picture of the author in your mind. Use your prejudices to stereotype the author. Your harsh judgment of the author is everything to understanding what he is trying to say. The better you understand the author, the easier the questions will be. Read with a critical eye and judge harshly.

Statements presented in the passage will often reflect the author's unique "voice," but they can also represent a counterpoint or a specific example. Knowing your author will allow you to recognize the author's voice. This idea will be explored further later in the lecture.

Once you know the author intimately, when you get to a question, ask yourself "If this author were right here in front of me, how would he answer this question?" The way that the author would answer the question is the correct answer.

Details and the Big Picture

There is no reason to remember the details of a passage. They can be found in seconds and are rarely important to answering a question. Instead, focus on the big picture. Ask yourself "What is the author trying to say to me? What's his beef?" The author's 'beef' will be the main idea, and the key to answering 90% of the questions.

STOP!

DO NOT LOOK AT THE FOLLOWING PASSAGE AND
QUESTIONS UNTIL CLASS.

IF YOU WILL NOT BE ATTENDING CLASS, READ THE PASSAGE IN
THREE MINUTES AND ANSWER THE QUESTIONS WHICH FOLLOW.

Passage I

It is roughly a century since European art began to experience its first significant defections from the standards of painting and sculpture that we inherit from the early Renaissance. Looking back now across a long succession of innovative movements and stylistic revolutions, most of us have little trouble recognizing that such aesthetic orthodoxies of the past as the representative convention, exact anatomy and optical perspective, the casement-window canvas, along with the repertory of materials and subject matters we associate with the Old Masters—that all this makes up not "art" itself in any absolute sense, but something like a school of art, one great tradition among many. We acknowledge the excellence which a Raphael or Rembrandt could achieve within the canons of that school; but we have grown accustomed to the idea that there are other aesthetic visions of equal validity. Indeed, innovation in the arts has become a convention in its own right with us, a "tradition of the new," to such a degree that there are critics to whom it seems to be intolerable that any two painters should paint alike. We demand radical originality, and often confuse it with quality.

Yet what a jolt it was to our great-grandparents to see the certainties of the academic tradition melt away before their eyes. How distressing, especially for the academicians, who were the guardians of a classic heritage embodying time-honored techniques and standards whose perfection had been the labor of genius. Suddenly they found art as they understood it being rejected by upstarts who were unwilling to let a single premise of the inherited wisdom stand unchallenged, or so it seemed. Now, with a little hindsight, it is not difficult to discern continuities where our predecessors saw only ruthless disjunctions. To see, as well, that the artistic revolutionaries of the past were, at their best, only opening our minds to a more global conception of art which demanded a deeper experience of light, color, and form. Through their work, too, the art of our time has done much to salvage the values of the primitive and childlike, the dream, the immediate emotional response, the life of fantasy, and the transcendent symbol.

In our own day, much the same sort of turning point has been reached in the history of science. It is as if the aesthetic ground pioneered by the artists now unfolds before us as a new ontological awareness. We are at a moment when the reality to which scientists address themselves comes more and more to be recognized as but one segment of a far broader spectrum. Science, for so long regarded as our single valid picture of the world, now emerges as, also, a school: a *school of consciousness*, beside which alternative realities take their place.

There are, so far, only fragile and scattered beginnings of this perception. They are still the subterranean history of our time. How far they will carry toward liberating us from the orthodox world view of the technocratic establishment is still doubtful. These days, many gestures of rebellion are subtly denatured, adjusted, and converted into oaths of allegiance. In our society at large, little beyond submerged unease challenges the lingering authority of science and technique, that dull ache at the bottom of the soul we refer to when we speak (usually too glibly) of an "age of anxiety," an "age of longing."

Source: Adapted from T. Roszak, The Making of a Counter Culture. 1969 Doubleday.

Answer the following questions without going back to the passage. If you don't know the answer, guess.

YOU MAY NOT LOOK AT THE PASSAGE!

- Is the author male or female?
- Does the author have long or short hair?
- How old is the author?
- What political party is the author a member of?
- Would the author prefer a wild party or a night at the opera?
- Do you think you would like the author?
- What does the author do for a living?

These are the types of questions that you should be able to answer with prejudice if you have read the passage correctly. If you can answer these questions, you have compared the author to people of your past and categorized the author accordingly. This means that you have a better understanding of who the author is, and how he would answer the MCAT® questions about his own passage.

The previous questions were asked to make you realize how you should be trying to understand the author. Do not ask yourself these questions on a real MCAT®. Here are some questions to ask yourself on a real MCAT®:

YOU MAY NOT LOOK AT THE PASSAGE!

- If the author were sitting in front of you, would he or she want to discuss science or art?
- What emotion, if any, is the author feeling?
- Is the author a scientist?
- Is the author conservative, liberal, or somewhere in the middle?

The answers to these questions are unequivocal. This author is discussing science, not art. Art is used as a lengthy, nearly incomprehensible introduction to make a point about science. The author doesn't even begin discussing the main idea until the beginning of the third paragraph. "In our own day, much the same sort of turning point has been reached in the history of science." When you read this, you should have been startled. You should have been thinking "Where did science come from? I thought we were talking about some esoteric art history stuff that I really wasn't understanding." This one sentence should have said to you "Aha! That other stuff was just an appetizer; now the author is going to discuss his real interest." Notice that it is at the beginning of the third paragraph that the writing actually becomes intelligible. In other words, the second two paragraphs are much easier to read. This is because the author is interested in this topic and knows what he wants to say. If you spent lots of time rereading the first two paragraphs, trying to master them, you wasted your time. However, as discussed later in this lecture, these paragraphs are still useful in that they provide a window into the author's opinions about his true interest.

The author is frustrated and possibly even bitter. He is so angry that he is name-calling. For instance, he calls the scientific community "the technocratic establishment." The tone of the passage is like that of a whining child. He blames scientists for being too conservative and thus creating "an age of anxiety," as if the anxiety of most people would be relieved if scientists were less practical. In the last sentence, he even blames us, his reader, for not taking *his* issue more seriously. The author is positively paranoid. Notice that his adversaries move against him "subtly" as if trying to hide their evil intentions. They take "oaths of allegiance" like some kind of cult. This is way overdone when you consider that the author's only complaint is that science isn't liberal enough in its approach.

> Know your author and find your author's opinion. When answering questions, the author will help you choose the best answer.

The author is certainly not a scientist. First of all, he writes like a poet, not a scientist: "orthodox world view of the technocratic establishment," "subterranean history of our time," "gestures of rebellion subtly denatured." Secondly, his whole point is that he is upset with scientists. (A separate argument can be made that his point results from a misunderstanding of how science progresses.) And finally, he talks like a member of some pyramid cult, not a scientist: "alternative realities" and "ontological awareness." This author probably flunked high school physics and just can't get over it.

The author is certainly liberal, or anti-establishment. He talks about "liberating us" and "rebellion" among other things.

Now, with this understanding of the author, answer the questions on the next page.

YOU MAY NOT LOOK AT THE PASSAGE!

Passage I (Questions 1–9)

Item 1

The author believes that in "the subterranean history of our time" (paragraph 4) we find the beginnings of a:

- ○ A) renewal of allegiance to traditional values.
- ○ B) redefinition of art.
- ○ C) redefinition of science.
- ○ D) single valid picture of the world.

Item 2

The author compares art and science mainly in support of the idea that:

- ○ A) the conventions of science, like those of art, are now beginning to be recognized as but one segment of a far broader spectrum.
- ○ B) aesthetic orthodoxies of the past, unlike scientific orthodoxies of the present, make up only one tradition among many.
- ○ C) artistic as well as scientific revolutionaries open our minds to a more global conception of art.
- ○ D) artists of the past have provided inspiration to the scientists of the present.

Item 3

The two kinds of art discussed in the passage are the:

- ○ A) aesthetic and the innovative.
- ○ B) dull and the shocking.
- ○ C) traditional and the innovative.
- ○ D) representative and the traditional.

Item 4

The author's statement "How far [new perceptions of science] will carry toward liberating us from the orthodox world view of the technocratic establishment is still doubtful" (paragraph 4) assumes that the:

- ○ A) technocratic establishment is opposed to scientific inquiry.
- ○ B) traditional perception of science is identical to the world view of the technocratic establishment.
- ○ C) current perceptions of science are identical to those of art.
- ○ D) technocratic establishment has the same world view as the artistic revolutionaries of the past.

Item 5

Which of the following concepts does the author illustrate with specific examples?

- ○ A) Scientific innovations of the present
- ○ B) Scientific innovations of the past
- ○ C) Aesthetic innovations of the present
- ○ D) Aesthetic orthodoxies of the past

Item 6

The claim that the unease mentioned in the fourth paragraph is "submerged" most directly illustrates the idea that:

- ○ A) our great-grandparents were jolted by the collapse of academic certainty.
- ○ B) we have grown accustomed to the notion that there is more than one valid aesthetic vision.
- ○ C) so far, new perceptions of science are only fragile and scattered.
- ○ D) the authority of science is rapidly being eroded.

Item 7

Based on the information in the passage, the author would most likely claim that someone who did NOT agree with his view of science was:

- ○ A) dishonest.
- ○ B) conformist.
- ○ C) rebellious.
- ○ D) imaginative.

Item 8

Based on information in the passage, which of the following opinions could most reasonably be ascribed to the author?

- ○ A) It is misguided to rebel against scientific authority.
- ○ B) The world views of other disciplines may have something valuable to teach the scientific community.
- ○ C) Art that rebels against established traditions cannot be taken seriously.
- ○ D) The main cause of modern anxiety and longing is our rash embrace of new scientific and artistic theories.

Item 9

Adopting the author's views as presented in the passage would most likely mean acknowledging that:

- ○ A) it is not a good idea to accept traditional beliefs simply because they are traditional.
- ○ B) we must return to established artistic and scientific values.
- ○ C) the future is bleak for today's artists and scientists.
- ○ D) the scientific community has given us little of benefit.

STOP

Don't worry about the correct answers yet.

YOU MAY NOT LOOK AT THE PASSAGE YET!

The first thing to notice is that only question 5 requires any information from the first two paragraphs, and question 5 was a question about detail, not concept. This is because the first two paragraphs are not about the main idea.

The second thing to notice is that none of the questions require us to go back to the passage, even though some refer us to specific paragraphs. All but question 5 are answerable directly from the main idea. Question 5 is a detail question, but before you run back to the passage to find the answer, look at the possibilities. Chances are that you remembered Raphael and Rembrandt from the first paragraph. These are specific examples of "aesthetic orthodoxies of the past," answer choice D.

Notice that many of the questions can be rephrased to say "The author thinks _____." In fact, the word "author" is mentioned in 7 of them. This is typical of an MCAT® passage, and that's why you must "know your author."

Question 1: Forget about the quote for a moment. Simplify the question to say "The author thinks that we find the beginnings of a:." Answer C is the main idea. Certainly the author would disagree with A, B, and D.

Question 2: "The author thinks:" that science is like art, and that conventions of both are but part of a larger spectrum. Choice B says science is not like art; the opposite of what the author thinks. Choice C says that scientific revolutionaries are changing science; the author is frustrated because this is not really happening. Choice D says scientists of the present are opening their minds to new ideas; the author complains that they are not.

Question 3: The main idea of the passage contains the theme of traditional vs. innovative.

Question 4: Ignore the quotes until you need them. Without the quotes, the question says "The author's statement assumes that the:." In other words, "The author thinks _____." Choices C and D are exactly the opposite of what the author thinks. Choice A plays a common game on the MCAT®. They take the author's view too far. They want you to think "the author doesn't like the scientists; therefore, he thinks the scientists can't even do science." Even this author wouldn't go that far; A is incorrect. Choice B requires you to realize that the "technocratic establishment" is conservative.

Question 6: Choice D is out because it disagrees with the main idea, and Choice C is the only answer that supports the main idea. This question is best answered by comparing the answer choices with the question. The question asks for an example of "submerged unease." "Jolted" in choice A certainly doesn't describe submerged unease. "Grown accustomed" in choice B certainly does not describe submerged unease. Choice C could describe submerged unease, and it does describe the main idea. It is the best answer.

Question 7: The author is rebellious and imaginative. If you disagree with him, he thinks you are a conformist, which, by the way, is worse than dishonest as far as he's concerned.

Question 8: "The author thinks _____." The whole point of the introduction is that the scientific community should learn from the discipline of art. The other answer choices directly contradict the author's main point.

Question 9: "The author thinks ___ _____." The author is a rebel. He thinks you should always question authority. Notice that choice D is another example of taking things too far. No sane individual could argue that science has provided little benefit. Choice C would be incorrect even if it had not included 'artists.' It would have been too extreme.

Hopefully, we have demonstrated the power of knowing the author and understanding the main idea. In the next lecture, you will see that answering CARS questions requires the test taker to repeatedly apply the main idea.

Remember to read and answer questions with confidence. If you are having problems with energy, focus, confidence, or timing, go back to the basics of this manual. Figure out what part of our strategy you aren't using, and use it.

2.3 | A Close Reading: Narrating toward the Main Idea

You have a good idea of what the main idea looks like and how important it is to know your author. A close reading of the passage will allow you to find the components of the main idea in order to construct it. Success on the CARS section requires reading every word; a close reading is a way of gaining as much information as possible from the passage. Narrating in your own voice as you read will allow you to construct the main idea.

Close reading is a way of reading interactively, rather than passively. Close reading allows you to notice every clue to the author's opinions. It uses an analysis of language to find meaning and to find the author. A close reading looks at not just what the author says but also how he says it. This technique originates with the study of literature and is highly relevant to medicine. Reading a passage closely is like listening closely to a patient. Just as you attend to the nuance of a passage, physicians attend to their patients—to their histories and thereby their physical states and needs. The ability to construct a narrative is essential for success as a physician, not only to understand the patient's experience, but also to make an accurate diagnosis. A good physician is able to listen to patients; a successful test taker is able to read CARS passages closely.

Reading closely means engaging with the text, asking questions, and considering the author's writing decisions. Construct the main idea by narrating the passage in your own voice: restate information, examine word choice, and parse phrases and sentences -- i.e., read in small chunks. The specific skills that you can use to build a narration will be described further at the end of this lecture. Success on the CARS section will come as you develop your own voice. You will learn to trust that your own voice is a reliable guide to interpreting the passage.

Use a close reading to align yourself with the author's opinion. This process is similar to trying on the author's opinion like a set of clothes. For the time that it takes to read the passage and answer the questions, be the author. This process allows you to select the answer that the author would choose. Recall from Lecture 1 how important it is to fully concentrate on each passage. A close reading will help you achieve complete immersion in the passage. Read as though you are deeply interested in the topic. The passage becomes your whole world. Between passages you take that five-second break before moving to the next passage—so that one can become your world!

Let's now subject the passage you just read to a close reading and narration. The original passage is in black type. This section will give you a better idea of the strategies that a successful test taker uses to tackle a CARS passage and form the main idea.

The MCAT® student's narration is highlighted in yellow. Connecting words and phrases, which indicate transitions in the author's idea, are highlighted in green.

Begin your narration by reading the citation at the end of the passage to gain any information you can. The title often gives a clue to the main idea. The journal may suggest your author's profession or bias.

By doing a close reading of the passage, I get to try on the author's opinion!

Lecture 4 will help you construct the main idea by building a spectrum. A spectrum lays out opposite ideas that appear in a passage, such as change and tradition in this passage.

The Making of a Counter Culture, 1969.

The author wrote a whole book with "Counter Culture" in the title. He is interested in social movements that are opposite of the mainstream.

It is roughly a century since European art

The author cares about art and history. He references a time 100 years ago.

began to experience its first significant defections from the standards of painting and sculpture that we inherit from the early Renaissance.

"Defection" is dramatic. A defector leaves for a good reason. Defector is a positive word. Author, do you like or dislike change? I think you like change.

Notice how much you can determine about your author and his opinion from a close reading of the first sentence alone!

Looking back now across a long succession of innovative movements and stylistic revolutions

"Innovative" and "revolutions" are positive words that mean new or change. "Revolutions" is similar to "defections." When I see the author repeating himself, I'm on the right track to the main idea.

most of us have little trouble recognizing

This phrasing is casual and confident, indicating that this is the author's opinion.

that such aesthetic orthodoxies of the past

The author offers the opposites of old and new: orthodoxy and revolution versus tradition and change. I predict that he prefers what is new. He likes change.

as the representative convention, exact anatomy and optical perspective, the casement-window canvas,

This is a list of *examples* of traditional art. The author may be an art historian.

along with the repertory of materials and subject matters we associate with the Old Masters—

Old Masters represent tradition-the author is respectful, but not complimentary.

that all this makes up not "art" itself in any absolute sense,

The use of "not art" to refer to traditional art is not positive. The author still prefers the new to the old.

but something like a school of art, one great tradition among many.

The use of "but" indicates that the part of the sentence that will follow will be opposite the first part. Often the author's opinion follows the use of "but." After the "but," the author takes all of art history and shrinks it in significance.

We acknowledge the excellence which a Raphael or Rembrandt could achieve within the canons of that school;

The author is respectful of these classics but not enthusiastic.

but we have grown accustomed to the idea that there are other aesthetic visions of equal validity.

"We" indicates that the author includes himself - this is his opinion and not a counterpoint. The author says that "other" visions are equally valid to the classics.

Indeed, innovation in the arts has become a convention in its own right with us, a "tradition of the new,"

"Indeed" is casual and the sentence will be in the author's "voice."

Innovation equals convention - the new equals the old? What's going on? Until now, the author treated change and tradition as opposites, and he preferred change; but now he says that change has turned into a convention or tradition.

to such a degree that there are critics to whom it seems to be intolerable that any two painters should paint alike. We demand radical originality, and often confuse it with quality.

The author is using strong opinion words like "intolerable" and "radical," which are negative and indicate that he does not like something here. We know that he likes change. He explains that a constant demand for change can itself become a restrictive tradition.

Yet what a jolt it was to our great-grandparents to see the certainties of the academic tradition melt away before their eyes.

How distressing, especially for the academicians, who were the guardians of a classic heritage embodying time-honored techniques and standards whose perfection had been the labor of genius.

This is different from everything so far. This is a counterpoint. The author is presenting the other side by offering sympathy to those who do not like change.

Suddenly, they found art as they understood it being rejected by upstarts who were unwilling to let a single premise of the inherited wisdom stand unchallenged,

This language is dramatic. The author likes change, but not when it is too extreme.

Now, with a little hindsight, it is not difficult to discern continuities where our predecessors saw only ruthless disjunctions.

The author is pointing out how change can include continuity. The author's main idea is closer to the middle than to the extremes of change or tradition.

To see, as well, that the artistic revolutionaries of the past were, at their best, only opening our minds to a more global conception of art which demanded a deeper experience of light, color, and form.

The author puts down the art of the past, even that of revolutionaries, by using the word "only." The author likes the new.

Through their work, too, the art of our time.

Now the author is referencing the present.

has done much to salvage the values of the primitive and childlike, the dream, the immediate emotional response, the life of fantasy, and the transcendent symbol.

This is a list of *examples* to support the previous sentence. It lists the ways that new art is the same, "salvaging" or keeping the best of the old. This paragraph can be given the simple reference – "moderate change."

In our own day, much the same sort of turning point has been reached in the history of science.

What is happening? I thought the author worked in the field of art. Now he is talking about science. Is he an artist or a scientist? Maybe neither; he may be a historian or philosopher.

It is as if the aesthetic ground pioneered by the artists now unfolds before us as a new ontological awareness.

"Pioneered" is a positive word. The author is still the author – he likes the new. This sentence extends the *same* idea from the previous paragraph into the realm of science. I don't know what "ontological" means, but no single word ever matters much because the author will repeat himself to make his point.

when the reality to which scientists address themselves comes more and more to be recognized as but one segment of a far broader spectrum. Science, for so long regarded as our single valid picture of the world, now emerges as, also a school: a *school of consciousness*, beside which alternative realities take their place.

The author is making the *same* point about science that he made about art. The author shrinks the significance of traditional science and prefers "alternative realities" because he likes change. What does the author care more about: science or art? Did the author set up the first half of the passage as an analogy to explain his position on science?

There are, so far,

The passage started with the past, moved to the present, and is now hinting at possibilities for the future.

only fragile and scattered beginnings of this perception. They are still the subterranean history of our time.

The language here is emotional. "This perception" is fragile and scattered. What perception? This likely refers back to a perception of "alternative realities." Is the author happy or sad about the fact that the beginnings are fragile and scattered? These are negative words. The author likes change and is unhappy that "alternative realities" are not yet accepted.

How far they will carry toward liberating us from the orthodox world view
"Liberating us" indicates that the author includes himself and feels restricted by tradition. This is the *same* idea made earlier in the art section.
of the technocratic establishment is still doubtful.
I don't know what technocratic means here, but I recognize "establishment". "Technocratic" is associated with the "orthodox world view" from which the author wants us to be "liberated." He does not like "technocratic". Looking back a sentence, technocratic is the mainstream of science, not the "alternative realities".
These days, many gestures of rebellion are subtly denatured, adjusted,
I know that the author likes rebellion and he writes that it is being "denatured". I recognize that word--it is when a molecule comes apart. The rebellion falls apart.
and converted into oaths of allegiance.
The author likes change, so he would not like rebellion turning into allegiance. The author's emotions come through here - frustration, bitterness. This sentence has a tone of disgust. The author is sad that change is not successful.
In our society at large, little beyond submerged unease
This is a similar word to "subterranean." "Little beyond" is negative.
challenges the lingering authority of science and technique,
"Challenges" is like rebellion. This is the type of change that the author likes. Authority reminds me of tradition or convention from the beginning of the passage. The author equates science with tradition which he did not like. He has moved past art and now he does not like science either. He has been consistent through the passage in his love of change.
that dull ache at the bottom of the soul we refer to when we speak (usually too glibly) of an "age of anxiety," an *age of longing*."
The author is extremely emotional here, showing his tendency for drama and poetic language. We can complete the main idea. The author longs for change in modern times: the acceptance of alternative realities beyond the mainstream of science.

2.4 | Tools for Close Reading on the MCAT®

Narrating the passage can be done using concrete tools that you can apply to any passage to find the author and construct the main idea: 1. animated voice; 2. reading for the author; 3. asking questions; 4. naming; 5. title for each paragraph; 6. word choice; and 7. same or different.

These skills are suggestions to help you build the skill of close reading. They are not intended as a list to be memorized! You already have an intuitive feel for how to narrate a passage as narration is thinking along as you read. These techniques will allow you to take that ability further. After reading the following descriptions, go back to the passage narration demonstrated above and find examples of how the skills were used.

Using an *animated voice* as you read is a crucial instrument in your close reading toolbox. When you read a CARS passage, the voice in your head should be excited and engaged, as though you are reading a story to a young child. You will not remember or understand anything that you read in a boring, dull monotone. When you read with animation, you notice each word the author chose and its positive or negative valence. You will have an easier time staying interested which will allow you to listen more closely for the author.

Parsing sentences allows you to consider parts of a sentence separately. Some CARS sentences are so lengthy and convoluted that by the end of the sentence it is impossible to remember the beginning. Pausing part of the way through is the best way to make sense of your author's point. Once you determine the meaning and significance of a clause, move on to the next until you have read the whole sentence.

Reading for the author from the very first word is the best way to stay oriented and find the author's main idea. Frame your narration in terms of what the author likes and does not like. New information should be evaluated with simple statement like "the author says…" or "the author thinks…" Repeating these phrases will remind you that the CARS section is testing how well you find the author's opinion, not your comprehension of facts. No matter how disorganized the passage may seem, you will stay in touch with the author.

Asking questions is a tool for building an idea of what the author cares about. The strategy of asking yourself questions about what the author thinks was presented earlier in this lecture. You can also imagine speaking directly to the author. Do you like this? What did you mean by ___? Is this your opinion?

Identifying and *naming* the purpose of a sentence will help you follow the author's argument. Most statements in a CARS passage can be named as one of the following: author's voice, counterpoint, or example. Any statement that feels as though the author is speaking directly to the reader is the author's voice. A counterpoint will oppose the author's opinion, and is there to show the opposite perspective. Often the author will move in the direction of the counterpoint. The main idea usually includes a nuance gained from the counterpoint. Noticing lists of examples or evidence is useful when answering questions about whether the passage provided support for a particular idea.

At the end of each paragraph, *title the paragraph*. The title should be short and simple - a few words at most. The title will not capture every nuance of the paragraph, as you know, taking lengthy notes is a waste of precious time. Use a simple word or phrase to remember the point of that paragraph. Almost all CARS questions depend on your knowledge of the passage as a whole, and the titles you create will help you construct the author's argument as it develops from the beginning of the passage to its end. A mental paragraph title allows you to "carry forward" the ideas of each paragraph to the next so that new arguments or topics can be connected to previous ones.

Examining *word choice* allows you to find the author's beliefs. The words that appear in a passage were chosen deliberately by the author to convey a certain message. Ask yourself if a word is positive or negative. You do not need to look for adjectives and adverbs to find connotations. All word types, not only adjectives and adverbs but also nouns and verbs, have positive or negative connotations. Ask yourself why the author decided to use one particular word instead. Considering word choice is valuable for evaluating the author's tone. The use of casual or extreme language reveals what the author likes or dislikes. When you don't know a word, don't worry. The author will give you many different opportunities to hear her opinion.

Word choice can also provide information about the author's profession and position. The use of technical jargon in a passage about a scientific discovery might indicate that the author is a specialist within the field discussed.

Noticing transition words such as "but", however", or "yet" will help you find the author's voice and follow the argument, even when the passage is disjointed. Connecting words leaves a trail of bread crumbs that allow you to follow the author's train of thought. Putting emphasis on connecting words also helps you read in an animated way.

As you read, classify each statements as *same or different*. As you read, compare and connect each new sentence and paragraph with what you've read so far. If it is the same, the author is using repetition for emphasis of the main idea. Carrying

The repetition of a word or idea is like the author holding up a big sign saying, "Look here! This is what I care about!"

forward what you've read and comparing it to each new statement will help you navigate a disjointed passage and translate it into an argument you can follow.

When a statement presents an idea that is different from what you have read so far, ask yourself "how different is it?" Is it a slight adjustment to or does it oppose what has been stated so far. If opposite, it is a counterpoint and likely not the author's opinion. If it is similar to something you have read, but makes a new point, it is an important adjustment to the author's opinion. Pay attention to the way it adds critical nuance to the main idea. Certain words indicate that the author is spending extra time on a certain idea ("furthermore", "in addition") while others mark the shift to a new idea or perspective ("but", "however", or "yet"). Comparing what you have read to each new statement as "same or different" is key to the spectrum, an advanced CARS concept discussed in the last lecture of this manual.

Narrating as you read a passage closely makes it easy to identify the main idea. The main idea is your most powerful tool to finding the correct answers to CARS questions. Now that you have practiced narrating a close reading of the passage, the next lecture focuses on the questions and answers.

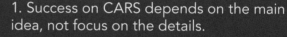
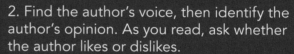

DON'T FORGET YOUR KEYS

1. Success on CARS depends on the main idea, not focus on the details.

2. Find the author's voice, then identify the author's opinion. As you read, ask whether the author likes or dislikes.

3. Read closely and narrate each CARS passage. Use the connotations of words-- nouns, verbs, adjectives, and adverbs -- to reveal the author's opinion.

Answering the Questions

3.1 Introduction

For most students, the CARS Section is literally a test of their ability to comprehend what they have read. Such students read a question and choose the correct answer based on what was said in the passage. If they do not arrive at an answer, they eliminate answer choices based on what was said in the passage. If they still don't arrive at an answer, they search the passage for relevant information that they may have missed or don't recall. If they still don't arrive at a single correct answer choice, which is likely to be about 50% of the time with this method, they repeat the process until they give up and make a random guess in frustration. This method uses only about 50% of the information provided by the test. When you can't identify an answer, 'thinking harder' (whatever that means) is not an effective strategy. Nor is it effective to search the passage until the answer jumps out at you. Both of these methods simply consume your precious time.

A successful test taker does more than just look for the answer in the passage.

In addition to your understanding of the passage, there are four tools that you can use to answer the questions. These four tools go beyond simply understanding the passage. They force you to consider additional information presented in the question stems and answer choices that is often overlooked or noticed only on a subconscious level.

The four tools are:

1. Looking Back;

2. The Main Idea;

3. The Question Stems; and

4. The Answer Choices.

Just thinking harder won't work.

Use your four tools.

THE 3 KEYS

1. Rephrase complex wording in the question stem to find the simple question being asked.

2. Through the question set, stay in touch with the passage and the author: after reading each question stem, restate the main idea and predict an answer.

3. The best answer matches the passage and the question stem.

Looking Back

'Looking back' refers to rereading parts of the passage to search for an answer. Only use 'looking back' when:

1. you are regularly finishing an exam on time;

2. you know what you're looking for; and

3. you know where you can find the answer.

'Looking back' is the most time consuming and least useful of the four tools. Unfortunately, it is the tool most often relied upon by inexperienced test takers. It is true that forgotten details can be found by rereading the passage. However, most questions require an understanding of the main idea, not your memory of details. **The main idea cannot be found by rereading parts of the passage.**

'Word-for-word' and other traps have been set for the unwary test taker looking for the 'feel-good' answer. The 'feel-good' answer is an answer where a section of the passage seems to unequivocally answer the question so that the test taker *feels good* when choosing it. The 'feel-good' answer choice may even use a phrase from the passage word-for-word. This is often a trap. Remember, the CARS Section is ambiguous and a simple clear answer is rarely correct.

Learn to use 'looking back' as seldom as possible. Force yourself to choose the best answer without looking back at the passage. This is a difficult lesson to accept, but it is extremely important to achieving your top score. Looking back at the passage for anything but a detail will take large amounts of your testing time and will allow the test writers to skew your concept of the main idea by directing you toward specific parts of the passage. **If you are unable to finish the test in the time given, it is because you are overusing the 'looking back' tool.** If you are not finishing, do not look back at all until you can regularly finish an entire CARS section with time left over.

If you're not finishing in time, it is probably because you are using the 'looking back' tool too often and for too long.

If you usually *don't* have time to finish the CARS section, try taking a practice exam where you read each passage once through and then don't allow yourself to look back at the passage no matter what. You will finish with time left to spare, and your score will probably go up.

As discussed in the Strategy and Tactics Lecture, you can read quickly enough to finish the exam. On the next practice exam, you can use the extra time that you know you will have at the end to take an occasional look back at the passage. But don't look too often or for too long. Looking back is why you weren't finishing the exam in the first place.

It's not bad to use your 'looking back' tool. Just don't overuse it.

Your number one goal is to finish the CARS Section. Difficult questions are worth no more than easy questions. **Don't sacrifice five easy questions by spending a long time answering a single difficult question.** If you usually finish the CARS section with time to spare, you can 'look back' to the passage more often; if you don't usually finish the CARS section, you should stop looking back to the passage until you begin finishing within the allotted time on a regular basis.

'Looking back' is a useful tool. Just use it wisely.

Main Idea

The main idea, discussed in the previous lecture, is the most powerful tool for answering MCAT® CARS questions.

3.2 | Question Stems

The question stems hold as much information as the passage. Read these question stems and see how much you can learn about the passage without even reading it.

1. The author of the passage believes that the fiction written by the current generation of authors:

2. The overall point made by the passage's comparison of movies to fiction is that:

3. According to the passage, John Gardner concedes that preliminary good advice to a beginning writer might be, "Write as if you were a movie camera." The word concedes here suggests that:

4. The fact that the author rereads Under the Volcano because it has been made into a movie is ironic because it:

5. The passage suggests that a reader who is not bored by a line-by-line description of a room most likely:

6. The passage suggests that if a contemporary writer were to write a novel of great forcefulness, this novel would most likely:

7. The passage places the blame for contemporary writers' loss of readers on the:

Ask yourself some questions about the author. What does the author do for a living? How does the author dress? How does the author vote? How old is the author? Is the author male or female? Look closely at each question stem and see what kind of information you get from it. Why are certain adjectives used? Who is John Gardner? What can I learn about the passage from these question stems?

Now, in the space below, write down everything that you can think of that is revealed about the passage from each stem. Write an answer for each of the seven question stems. (Warning: If you read on without writing the answers, you will miss an important opportunity to improve your CARS skills. Once you read on, the effect of the exercise will be ruined.)

1. _different generation, change, male, older, critic, books +_
   movies, not like both (irony), blame = critic

2. _similar_

3. _"gives in"_

4. _____

5. _____

6. _____

7. _____

Information that can be gained from the seven previous question stems:

1. The author of the passage believes that the fiction written by the current generation of authors:

From the first question stem, we immediately know that the passage was about the writing of fiction. The word 'current' suggests a comparison between authors of fiction from the past and the present.

2. The overall point made by the passage's comparison of movies to fiction is that:

From the second question stem we learn that there is a comparison between movies and fiction. We also know that this was central to the author's point. The movies are a 'current' medium, while 'written fiction' might be considered older or in the past. Hmmm. What is the significance of this?

3. According to the passage, John Gardner concedes that preliminary good advice to a beginning writer might be, "Write as if you were a movie camera." The word concedes here suggests that:

In question stem three, you need to wonder, "Who is John Gardner?" A named person will likely be someone whom the author used either to support his point or as an example of someone who has a bad idea. You should decide which. Now, even if the question hadn't asked this, you should have asked yourself about the word 'concedes,' because it provides valuable information about the context of the quote. When you concede, you give in. So 'concedes' here indicates that Mr. Gardner is giving in to a point when he says "Write as if you were a movie camera." Mr. Gardner's argument must be that written fiction is not good when it's like the movies, but it is okay to write like a movie camera when you are a beginning writer. Notice how hesitant the wording is. 'Beginning' is emphasized by the use of both 'preliminary' and 'beginning,' and the word 'might' is also used. At this point, you should be getting a feeling of what this passage was about: movies versus fiction, current fiction versus past fiction, and someone implying that movies don't make good fiction. The author believes something about current fiction and makes a point about fiction and movies. Given three question stems with no passage and not even answer choices to the questions, we can already get a sense of the passage. The remaining question stems will confirm what the passage is about.

4. The fact that the author rereads Under the Volcano because it has been made into a movie is ironic because it:

The fourth question stem indicates that a movie makes the author read a book. The question states that this is ironic. That means that the actual result is incongruous with the expected result. Apparently, according to the author's argument, watching a movie should not make him read the book. Thus, part of the author's argument in the passage must be that movies make people less interested in reading. Based on this question stem, it is also reasonable to assume that the author used John Gardner in question stem #3 to support his argument, so the author probably believes that fiction written like a movie is not good fiction. Extrapolating further from the comparison of movies to fiction and the stated dichotomy between current and past fiction, the author is probably arguing that current fiction is not as good as old fiction.

5. The passage suggests that a reader who is not bored by a line-by-line description of a room most likely:

The fifth passage compares the phrase 'line-by-line description' with the idea of boredom. It is a simple logical jump to equate 'line-by-line description' with past fiction as opposed to current fiction or movies. From our conclusions thus far about the author's argument, it is logical to conclude that someone who is NOT bored by 'line-by-line descriptions' would NOT be bored by past fiction, but would, in fact, appreciate it as the author obviously does.

6. The passage suggests that if a contemporary writer were to write a novel of great forcefulness, this novel would most likely:

Question stem #6 reinforces our conclusion about the author's argument. The 'if' indicates that 'contemporary writers' do not 'write novels of great forcefulness.' Instead, they must be writing novels that resemble movies. The only question is "What would a novel of great forcefulness do?" Answering this question is as simple as seating the author in front of you and asking him. The amazing thing is that we already have a stereotypical idea of this author just by reading six question stems! This guy is a college English professor fed up with the quick fix satisfaction offered by movies. He would love a novel of great forcefulness. Does he think that we would appreciate it? Be careful here. He appreciates the novel because he truly believes that the novel itself is great, not because he thinks he is great or better than everyone else. The answer is yes, he thinks that we would appreciate a novel of great forcefulness as well.

7. The passage places the blame for contemporary writers' loss of readers on the:

This last question stem answers the previous question. The seventh question stem says that current fiction is losing readers. It asks for the explanation. Of course, the author's whole point is to explain why current fiction is losing readership. It is because it is like movies and not forceful like past fiction. What should be revealing and even shocking to you is that we can accurately answer every question without reading the passage. In fact, on this particular passage, we can accurately answer every question without reading the passage OR the answer choices. Most MCAT® passages are like this. Did you realize that there was this much information in the question stems alone? Have you been using this information to answer the questions on the MCAT®? If you haven't, you are capable of scoring many points higher on the CARS Section. You can't expect to always be able to answer questions without the passage or the answer choices (and you shouldn't try to on the actual test), but you can expect to gain a lot of information about the passage from the question stems.

Compare your answers with the actual answer choices below and choose a best answer.

Item 1

The author of the passage believes that the fiction written by the current generation of authors:

○ A) lacks the significance of fiction written by previous generations.
○ B) is, as a whole, no better and no worse than fiction written by previous generations.
○ C) brilliantly meets the particular needs of contemporary readers.
○ D) is written by authors who show great confidence in their roles as writers.

Item 2

The overall point made by the passage's comparison of movies to fiction is that:

○ A) contemporary authors have strengthened their fiction by the application of cinematic techniques.
○ B) the film of Under the Volcano is bound to be more popular than the novel.
○ C) great fiction provides a richness of language and feeling that is difficult to re-create in film.
○ D) contemporary authors would be well advised to become screenwriters.

Item 3

According to the passage, John Gardner concedes that preliminary good advice to a beginning writer might be, "Write as if you were a movie camera." The word "concedes" here suggests that:

I. Gardner's approach to writing has been influenced by the competing medium of film.
II. Gardner must have written screenplays at one point in his life.
III. Gardner dislikes the medium of film.

○ A) I only
○ B) II only
○ C) I and II only
○ D) II and III only

Item 4

The fact that the author rereads Under the Volcano because it has been made into a movie is ironic because it:

I. seems to go against the overall point of the passage concerning fiction and film.
II. implies that the film version was a box-office failure.
III. hints that the author was dissatisfied with the novel.

○ A) I only
○ B) II only
○ C) III only
○ D) II and III only

Item 5

The passage suggests that a reader who is not bored by a line-by-line description of a room most likely:

○ A) prefers the quick fix of the movies.
○ B) would be bored by a single shot of a room in a film.
○ C) has no tolerance for movies.
○ D) displays the attitude demanded by good fiction.

Item 6

The passage suggests that if a contemporary writer were to write a novel of great forcefulness, this novel would most likely:

I. confuse and anger lovers of great literature.
II. exist in stark contrast to the typical contemporary novel.
III. win back some of the readers contemporary writers have lost.

○ A) I only
○ B) II only
○ C) I and II only
○ D) II and III only

Item 7

The passage places the blame for contemporary writers' loss of readers on the:

I. competition presented by movies.
II. writers themselves.
III. ignorance of the public.

○ A) I only
○ B) II only
○ C) I and II only
○ D) I, II, and III

STOP

Answers to the Questions

Question 1

Choice A, the answer to question #1, is exactly what we expected: past fiction is better than current fiction. Notice that we can simplify the choices to:

- ○ A) Current fiction is not as good as past fiction.
- ○ B) Current fiction is equal to past fiction.
- ○ C) Current fiction is good.
- ○ D) Current fiction is good.

Simplifying the question and the answer choices can make the correct answer easier to find. We'll discuss simplification later in this lecture. The main idea is all you need to answer this question.

Question 2

Choice C, the answer to question #2, is also exactly what we expected. The choices can be rephrased to:

- ○ A) Movies have been good for fiction.
- ○ B) Movies are more likeable than fiction.
- ○ C) Movies aren't as good as good fiction.
- ○ D) Authors of fiction should make movies.

When we put these questions to our author, the choice is obvious.

Question 3

The answers to question #3 are not what we expected. We expected a more sophisticated question pertaining to the use of the word "concedes." Although the question told us a lot about the passage, the answer choices match a much simpler question than we anticipated: "Who is John Gardner?" The choices can be rephrased as:

- I. John Gardner has been influenced by movies.
- II. John Gardner wrote movies.
- III. John Gardner dislikes movies.

Clearly John Gardner has been influenced by movies if he is suggesting that writing like a movie might be good advice for a beginning writer. From the answer choices, we can see that if option I is correct, option III is likely to be incorrect. If Gardner dislikes movies, it is unlikely that he would be influenced by them. Option II is incorrect because Gardner can be influenced by movies without having actually written them. Even if option III could be correct, and even assuming that Gardner is like the author, liking good fiction more than movies isn't the same as disliking movies. Choice A is correct.

Question 4

The answer to question #4 is exactly what we expected. The choices can be rephrased to:

- I. Seeing the movie shouldn't have made the author read the book.
- II. The movie flopped.
- III. The author didn't like the book.

Only option I addresses the 'irony' suggested in the question. and pertains to the main idea. The answer is choice A.

Question 5

Choice D, the answer to question #5, is exactly what we expected. The choices can be rephrased to:

- ○ A) If you're patient, you'll prefer the fast pace of movies.
- ○ B) If you're patient, you won't like waiting for action.
- ○ C) If you're patient, you won't have the patience for the fast pace of movies.
- ○ D) If you're patient, you'll like the careful pace of good fiction.

Choices A, B, and C seem to be self contradictory.

Question 6

Choice D, the answer to question #6, is exactly what we expected. Remember that "a novel of great forcefulness" describes past fiction according to our author, and that our author would expect us to like past fiction. This is consistent with options II and III.

Question 7

Choice C, the answer to question #7, is exactly what we expected. Option I restates the main idea that movies have hurt fiction. Certainly, our author is criticizing current authors, so option II is also true. Option III is not true, based upon our belief that the author would expect us to like a forceful novel. The answer here is C.

For practice, try this exercise again for another passage. Read these question stems and write answers in the blank lines given.

1. The passage suggests that most medieval thinkers of the 13th century were:

2. In the late 15th century, Christopher Columbus proposed an alternate passage to the Indies which would take him around the Earth. According to the passage, most of his educated contemporaries probably believed:

3. Based upon the information in the passage, which of the following events most likely occurred before 1300 A.D.?

4. The author probably believes that science in the 13th century:

5. Based upon the information in the passage, an educated person of the 13th century might explain the perpetual motion of the planets as:

6. The 13th century friar Roger Bacon argued that the progress of human knowledge was being impeded by excessive regard for ancient authorities. This information:

7. "Aristotle taught that natural science should be based on extensive observations, followed by reflection leading to scientific generalizations" (paragraph 1). The author would most likely agree with which of the following statements concerning this scientific method proffered by Aristotle?

1. _____

   _____

2. _____

   _____

3. _____

   _____

4. _____

   _____

5. _____

   _____

6. _____

   _____

7. _____

   _____

Information that can be gained from the seven previous question stems:

1. The passage suggests that most medieval thinkers of the 13th century were:

From the first question stem, we immediately know that the author has some opinion about "thinkers of the 13th century." Do not ignore the adverb "most." It doesn't tell us much, but it does hint of some moderation in the tone of the passage. Compare the tone if we were to replace the word "most" with "all": "The passage suggests that all medieval thinkers of the 13th century were:"

Of course, we cannot yet answer the question with any accuracy, but let's just consider some possibilities. Does the author suggest that 13th century thinkers were naïve, well informed, foolish, clever, careful, brash, guided by religion, guided by reason, or what? Keep this in mind.

2. In the late 15th century, Christopher Columbus proposed an alternate passage to the Indies which would take him around the Earth. According to the passage, most of his educated contemporaries probably believed:

The second question stem tells us that we are not dealing with just the 13th century, but with a broader era of history that spans at least until the 15th century.

Again, we cannot answer the question yet, but we can make a reasonable guess. What beliefs might contemporaries have had about Columbus' journey? The words "proposed" and "alternate" show that he was taking a new path. Columbus was sailing into the unknown, so the questions are likely to be about what he might find.

The question stem repeats the theme of "thinkers" with the words "educated contemporaries." We now know not only that the author is discussing educated thinkers from medieval times, but also that he is giving his opinion as to how they thought. He is making some kind of suggestion about what these educated contemporaries probably believed about Columbus sailing around the Earth.

"Educated" is a key word here. Imagine the question stem without the word "educated." "According to the passage, most of his contemporaries probably believed:" How does it change the answer? What is the difference between a "contemporary" and an "educated contemporary"? The question specifically mentions "around the Earth," drawing attention to the question of whether or not the world was thought to be round. Does the author suggest that educated contemporaries believed Columbus would fall off the edge of the world, or does he suggest that they believed that Columbus would find the new world? The word "educated" implies that the author is making the point that the 15th century thinker's thoughts may have been more accurate than we would expect.

We can expect an answer that says "educated contemporaries probably had reasonable expectations about Columbus' journey."

3. Based upon the information in the passage, which of the following events most likely occurred before 1300 A.D.?

Since we are asked to predict the chronology of certain events, the author must be discussing not just educated thought, but the progression of educated thought.

We can begin to narrow in on the time period beginning before the 13th century and ending around 1500 A.D. (Remember that the 13th century is during the 1200s.) We can infer that educated thought was progressing during this time period.

Because the question asks about the early part of the progression of educated thought (before the 13th century) and not the later part (the 15th century), the answer choice should be an event that reflects less highly developed educated thought. Keep in mind that this is the MCAT® and not a high school exam. The answer isn't likely to be as simple as "Thinkers were naïve in the 13th century and brilliant by the 15th century."

4. The author probably believes that science in the 13th century:

From this question stem, we see that the author is discussing scientific thought, not just educated thought in general.

Like question #3, this question asks about the early part of the progress discussed in the passage. Again, we will choose an answer choice with this in mind.

We can assume that science in the 13th century was less like modern science than science in the 15th century, but we still don't have enough information from the question stems alone to know how science changed.

5. Based upon the information in the passage, an educated person of the 13th century might explain the perpetual motion of the planets as:

This is almost the same question three times in a row. We might rephrase them as "Which of the following reflects a way of thinking prior to or toward the beginning of the progress in thinking discussed in the passage?" We are still waiting to learn more about the nature and extent of the change. One thing we do know is that the explanation will be different from a modern scientific explanation because there must be a progression to modern science.

6. The 13th century friar Roger Bacon argued that the progress of human knowledge was being impeded by excessive regard for ancient authorities. This information:

Finally we are given a clue about the aspect of change. The stem tells us that Bacon thought thinkers of the 13th century relied too heavily upon ancient thinkers. You should ask yourself, "13th century thinkers relied on ancient thinkers as opposed to relying on what?" In other words, instead of just believing whatever ancient thinkers say, they should have done what? The answer should be obvious to any modern science student: investigate and think for yourself!

Based on our analysis thus far, it appears that Bacon was used to support the author's argument.

The answer to this question will probably be something like "This information supports the author's argument because it is evidence that 13th century thinkers were relying too much on ancient thinkers rather than thinking for themselves."

7. "Aristotle taught that natural science should be based on extensive observations, followed by reflection leading to scientific generalizations" (paragraph 1). The author would most likely agree with which of the following statements concerning this scientific method proffered by Aristotle?

As an MCAT® student with a strong science background, you can see that the method proposed is not only practical, but is the method currently in use by today's scientists. Using the reasoning from question #6, we might be tempted to say that the author would disagree with an ancient source, but we cannot override common sense. We must assume that the author would agree with this common sense and modern-seeming statement by Aristotle and that there is some kind of twist to this question that we are unable to predict from the question stem alone. We know the author thought early thinkers relied too heavily on ancient sources, but, in this case, it must have been a good thing. The MCAT® is tricky like this.

We now have enough information to revisit and answer the earlier questions.

1. REVISITED: Based on information from question #6, the passage suggests that most medieval thinkers of the 13th century were too trusting of the work of the ancient thinkers, which impeded progress.

2. REVISITED: We already answered this to some extent, but the new information confirms: In the late 15th century, Christopher Columbus proposed an alternate passage to the Indies which would take him around the Earth. According to the passage, most of his educated contemporaries probably believed his trip was at least possible.

3. REVISITED: We still have no clue as to what events the answer choices will include, so we can only give a general answer. Based upon the information in the passage, the event that most likely occurred before 1300 A.D. was one that, though perhaps more impressive than many modern students would expect, did not require too much advanced science.

4. REVISITED: The author probably believes that science in the 13th century was not completely primitive but not advanced either; or (based on question #6) that it relied upon ancient knowledge with few innovations.

5. REVISITED: Based upon the information in the passage, an educated person of the 13th century might explain the perpetual motion of the planets as similar to the way ancient thinkers would have explained it, which is also somehow less scientific than Renaissance science or modern science.

6. REVISITED: As previously stated, the answer to this question is likely something like: This information supports the author's argument because it is evidence that 13th century thinkers were relying too much on ancient thinkers rather than thinking for themselves.

7. REVISITED: As previously stated, we must assume that the author would most likely agree that natural science should be based on extensive observations, followed by reflection leading to scientific generalizations; and that there is some kind of twist to this question that we are unable to predict from the question stem alone.

Compare your answers with the actual answer choices below and choose a best answer.

Item 1

The passage suggests that most medieval thinkers of the 13th century were:

- A) impractical mystics.
- B) good empirical scientists.
- C) somewhat superstitious.
- D) confident of the veracity of Aristotelian physics.

Item 2

In the late 15th century, Christopher Columbus proposed an alternate passage to the Indies which would take him around the Earth. According to the passage, most of his educated contemporaries probably believed:

- A) Columbus would fall off the edge of the earth.
- B) the trip was possible in theory.
- C) the sun was the center of the universe.
- D) in Aristotelian physics.

Item 3

Based upon the information in the passage, which of the following events most likely occurred before 1300 A.D.?

- A) Spectacles for reading were invented.
- B) Nicholas of Cusa conceived the idea of an infinite universe.
- C) Scientists abandoned Aristotelian physics.
- D) Raw sugar was refined.

Item 4

The author probably believes that science in the 13th century:

- A) laid the groundwork for modern science.
- B) was the beginning of a scientific revolution.
- C) is underestimated by modern historians.
- D) was more practical than theoretical.

Item 5

Based upon the information in the passage, an educated person of the 13th century might explain the perpetual motion of the planets as:

- A) propelled by a mysterious prime mover.
- B) *impetus* resulting from an initial, tremendous push.
- C) movement due to lack of any opposing force.
- D) a violation of Aristotelian physics.

Item 6

The 13th century friar Roger Bacon argued that the progress of human knowledge was being impeded by excessive regard for ancient authorities. This information:

- A) weakens the claims made by the author because it is an example of a direct criticism of Aristotle's scientific presuppositions.
- B) weakens the claims made by the author because it demonstrates that religion still dominated science in the 13th century.
- C) strengthens the claims made by the author because it is evidence that 13th century thinkers were not questioning the scientific suppositions of Aristotle.
- D) strengthens the claims made by the author because Aristotle was Greek, not Roman.

Item 7

"Aristotle taught that natural science should be based on extensive observations, followed by reflection leading to scientific generalizations." (lines 3-5) The author would most likely agree with which of the following statements concerning this scientific method proffered by Aristotle?

- A) This method had a stultifying effect on medieval science.
- B) This method was faithfully practiced by most thirteenth century thinkers.
- C) Practice of this method led to the *first major break with Aristotelian physics* (paragraph 2) in the fourteenth century.
- D) Extensive scientific observations of the thirteenth century resulted in gross inaccuracies in the interpretation of Aristotelian physics.

Answers to Questions

Notice that, although there was less information in the question stems for this passage than in the previous exercise, the lack of information was made up for by information in the answer choices. In other words, for this passage, much of the information was in the answer choices. Still, the point is that you need to use all of the information to answer a question, not just the words in the passage. In the next section we will discuss extraction of information from the answer choices. For now, let's consider the answers to this passage.

Question 1: Choice D is just what we thought: too much trust in ancient sources.

Question 2: Choice B is, again, exactly what we might predict. Notice that choices C and D are what we expect from early thinkers, not later thinkers. Choices C and D also do not answer the question as precisely, since they do not refer to Columbus' trip. Choice A does not represent the theme that 15th century thinkers were advancing in educated thought.

Question 3: Choice A is correct. Our limited knowledge from only the question stem allows us to narrow the answer to A or D, but it may not be enough to choose between the two. Choice B is a theoretical advance. Recall from question #6 that early thinkers were relying on ancient thinkers rather than innovative thought. Choice C is wrong since the question refers to early thinkers. Again, question #6 tells us that early thinkers were embracing ancient thinkers, not abandoning them.

Question 4: This one is very tough. Choice D is correct, and makes sense given our idea that there was little innovative thinking going on. However, choices A and B seem to be possibilities. "Modern" science cannot have arrived by the 15th century, so perhaps we can eliminate choice A. The weakness of choice B is the word "revolution," but it is still not a bad answer based on only the information in the question stems. Based on our analysis of the question stems, choice C seems unlikely.

There is no need to be concerned if we can't answer a question with absolute certainty based on only the question stems. We still have the passage and the analysis of answer choices (discussed in the next section) to consider. A close reading of all answer choices of all questions in this passage will reveal an underlying theme that is simply not in the question stems. The underlying theme is that science at the beginning of this period of scientific progression was more practical than theoretical. Of course, reading the passage would make this theme even more apparent.

Question 5: Choice A is correct. Choices B and C are close to how we would explain planetary motion today, so they are wrong answers for how an early thinker would explain it. It turns out that choice B is specifically described in the passage as an example of 14th century thought and thus must be a wrong answer. Choice D contradicts the idea that 13th century thinkers were relying on ancient thinkers without thinking for themselves.

Question 6: Choice C is correct and fits well with what we predicted.

Question 7: Choice C is correct. It makes the most sense given our conclusion that the method was sound and used today and that there is some kind of twist. The twist is that Aristotle's advice to base knowledge on observation led to the evidence that his own theory of physics was wrong. Thus, by following Aristotle's advice, the late thinkers were breaking with Aristotle. An irony that makes for a tricky MCAT® question.

Each MCAT® question has four possible answer choices. One of these will be the correct answer and the other three we will call *distractors*. Typically, when a CARS question is written, the correct answer choice is written first and then distractors are created. Because the correct answer is written to answer a specific question and a distractor is written to confuse, the two can often be distinguished without even referencing the question. In other words, with practice, a good test taker can sometimes distinguish the correct answer among the distractors without even reading the question or the passage. This is a difficult skill to acquire and is gained only through extensive practice.

Begin by learning to recognize typical distractor types. Among other things, an effective distractor may be: a statement that displays a subtle misunderstanding of the main idea, a statement that uses the same or similar words as in the passage but is taken out of context, a true statement that does not answer the question, a statement that answers more than the question asks, or a statement that relies upon information commonly considered true but not given in the passage.

In order to help you recognize distractors, we have artificially created five categories of **suspected distractors**. It is unlikely, but not impossible, that the correct answer choice might also fall into one of these categories. Thus, you must use this tool as a guide to assist you in finding the correct answer, rather than as an absolute test.

- Round-About: a distractor that moves around the question but does not directly answer it
- Beyond: a distractor whose validity relies upon information not supplied by (i.e., information *beyond*) the passage
- Contrary: a distractor that is contrary to the main idea
- Simpleton: a distractor that is very simple and/or easily verifiable from the passage
- Unintelligible: a distractor that you don't understand

The Round-About

Round-about distractors simply don't answer the question as asked. They may be true statements. They may even concur with the passage, but they just don't offer a direct answer to the question. A *round-about* is the answer you expect from a politician on a Sunday morning political talk show; a lot of convincing words are spoken but nothing is really said.

Beyonds

A distractor will often supply information beyond that given in the question and passage without substantiating its veracity. These distractors are called beyonds. While reading a beyond, you will typically find yourself thinking something like "This answer sounds good, but the passage was about the economics of the post Soviet Union. I don't remember anything about the Russian revolution."

Beyonds can also play upon current events. A passage on AIDS may have a question with an answer choice about cloning. Cloning may be a hot topic in the news, but if it wasn't mentioned in the passage or in the question, be very suspicious of it in an answer choice.

Don't confuse a *beyond* with an answer choice that directly asks you to assume information as true.

As you answer each question, align yourself with the author. BE the author! The best answer is usually the one the author would choose, unless asked for the opposite, i.e. what would weaken the argument.

Think of round-abouts as the kind of answer a politician would give. It sounds really good but it doesn't answer the question.

Contraries

A *contrary* distractor contradicts the main idea. If the question is not an EXCEPT, NOT, or LEAST, the answer choice is extremely unlikely to contradict the main idea. **Most answer choices support the main idea in one form or another.**

Simpletons

If the correct answers on the CARS Section were simple, direct, and straightforward, everyone would do well. Instead, the correct answers are vague, ambiguous, and sometimes debatable. An answer choice that is easily verifiable from a reading of the passage is highly suspect and often incorrect. These answer choices are called *simpletons*. Simpletons are not always the wrong answer choice, but you should be highly suspicious when you see one.

Typical of simpletons is extreme wording like *always* and *never*.

Here's a manufactured example of a simpleton:

> **13.** In mid-afternoon in December in Montana, the author believes that the color of the sky most closely resembles:
>
> **B.** cotton balls floating on a blue sea.

If this were the answer, everyone would choose it. This is unlikely to be the correct answer.

Unintelligibles

Unintelligibles are answer choices that you don't understand. Whether it's a vocabulary word or a concept, avoid answer choices that you don't understand. These are likely to be traps. Strangely enough, many test takers are likely to choose an answer that confuses them. This is apparently because the MCAT® is a difficult test and students expect to be confused. Test writers sometimes purposely use distractors with obscure vocabulary or incomprehensible diction in order to appeal to the test taker who finds comfort in being confused. As a general rule, don't choose an answer that you don't understand unless you can positively eliminate all other choices. Be confident, not confused.

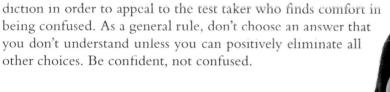

3.4 | Identifying the Correct Answer

Besides identifying distractors, familiarize yourself with the look and feel of a typical correct answer choice.

Typical correct answer choices contain *softeners*. Softeners are words that make the answer true under more circumstances, such as *most likely, seemed, had a tendency to*, etc. An answer choice with a softener is not necessarily correct; it is just more likely to be correct than an answer choice with more extreme language.

3.5 | Simplification of the Question and Answer Choices

It is often helpful to simplify the question and answer choices in terms of the main idea. For instance, reexamining the questions and answer choices from our original seven AAMC question stems in section 3.2, we have a passage with the following main idea:

"Great fiction provides a richness of language and feeling that is difficult to recreate in film. Contemporary authors emulating film have lost this richness and their audience with it."

This is a nice, complete main idea, but it can be difficult to understand all at once. It is helpful to simplify it as follows: past fiction, current fiction, and movies.

• Past fiction is good;

• Current fiction is bad; and

• Current fiction is like movies.

When analyzing the question stems and answer choices, restate them in terms of these ideas, keeping in mind that this is a simplification. For instance, any reference to "a great, forceful novel" or "a line-by-line description" can be replaced by "past fiction." "The passage suggests" can be replaced by "the author thinks." This technique is much like using the concept of an ideal gas to approximate the behavior of a real gas and then accounting for the characteristics of a real gas when more details are needed.

Compare the following restatements with the original seven AAMC questions (if you want to practice, fold the page so you can't see the restatements):

Original Question	Restatement

Original Question

Item 1

The author of the passage believes that the fiction written by the current generation of authors:

- ○ A) lacks the significance of fiction written by previous generations.
- ○ B) is, as a whole, no better and no worse than fiction written by previous generations.
- ○ C) brilliantly meets the particular needs of contemporary readers.
- ○ D) is written by authors who show great confidence in their roles as writers.

Item 2

The overall point made by the passage's comparison of movies to fiction is that:

- ○ A) contemporary authors have strengthened their fiction by the application of cinematic techniques.
- ○ B) the film of Under the Volcano is bound to be more popular than the novel.
- ○ C) great fiction provides a richness of language and feeling that is difficult to re-create in film.
- ○ D) contemporary authors would be well advised to become screenwriters.

Item 3

According to the passage, John Gardner concedes that preliminary good advice to a beginning writer might be, "Write as if you were a movie camera." The word concedes here suggests that:

- I. Gardner's approach to writing has been influenced by the competing medium of film.
- II. Gardner must have written screenplays at one point in his life.
- III. Gardner dislikes the medium of film.

Item 4

The fact that the author rereads Under the Volcano because it has been made into a movie is ironic because it:

- I. seems to go against the overall point of the passage concerning fiction and film.
- II. implies that the film version was a box-office failure.
- III. hints that the author was dissatisfied with the novel.

Restatement

Item 1

The author believes that current fiction is:

- ○ A) not as good as past fiction.
- ○ B) equal to past fiction.
- ○ C) good.
- ○ D) good.

Item 2

The author compares movies to fiction in order to show that:

- ○ A) movies have been good for fiction.
- ○ B) movies are more likable than fiction.
- ○ C) movies aren't as good as good fiction.
- ○ D) authors of fiction should make movies.

Item 3

John Gardner says, "Write like the movies," therefore:

- I. he has been influenced by movies.
- II. he wrote movies.
- III. he dislikes movies.

Item 4

The author sees a movie that causes him to read a book. This:

- I. weakens his argument.
- II. means the movie was bad.
- III. means the author didn't like the book.

Original Question	Restatement

Item 5

The passage suggests that a reader who is not bored by a line-by-line description of a room most likely:

○ A) prefers the quick fix of the movies.
○ B) would be bored by a single shot of a room in a film.
○ C) has no tolerance for movies.
○ D) displays the attitude demanded by good fiction.

Item 5

The author says that if you like past fiction:

○ A) you'll like movies.
○ B) you'll be bored by past fiction.
○ C) you won't like movies.
○ D) you'll like past fiction.

Item 6

The passage suggests that if a contemporary writer were to write a novel of great forcefulness, this novel would most likely:

I. confuse and anger lovers of great literature.
II. exist in stark contrast to the typical contemporary novel.
III. win back some of the readers contemporary writers have lost.

Item 6

If a new novel were like old fiction:

I. people who like old fiction wouldn't like the new novel.
II. the new novel would not be like current fiction.
III. people would like to read it.

Item 7

The passage places the blame for contemporary writers' loss of readers on the:

I. competition presented by movies.
II. writers themselves.
III. ignorance of the public.

Item 7

No one reads current fiction because:

I. movies are just as good.
II. current fiction writers write bad fiction.
III. people are ignorant.

You have four tools for finding the correct answer: looking back, the main idea, the question stems, and the answer choices. Use all of them in order to get your best MCAT® score. The fourth tool is the most difficult to master. When evaluating the answer choices for distractors, keep in mind that there are no absolutes, just suspects. When necessary, restate complicated questions using simplified concepts from the main idea.

Use the following questions and answer choices to practice using your four tools.

Passage I (Questions 1–7)

Item 1

According to the passage, an image is a versatile tool that:

- ○ A) is always visual, never abstract.
- ○ B) can be either abstract or visual.
- ○ C) is always abstract, never visual.
- ○ D) is neither visual nor abstract.

Item 2

An experiment found that dogs can remember a new signal for only five minutes, whereas six-year-old children can remember the same signal for much longer. Based on the information in the passage, this finding is probably explained by the fact that:

- ○ A) a human being possesses a larger store of symbolic images than a dog possesses.
- ○ B) the human brain evolved more quickly than the brain of a dog.
- ○ C) the children were probably much older than the dogs.
- ○ D) most dogs are color-blind.

Item 3

In order to defend poets from the charge that they were liars, Sidney noted that "a maker must imagine things that are not" (paragraph 2). Sidney's point is that:

- ○ A) a true poet must possess a powerful imagination.
- ○ B) in order to create something, one must first imagine.
- ○ C) poets are the most creative people in our society.
- ○ D) imagination is not a gift unique to poets, but is possessed by all creative people.

Item 4

In the context of the passage, the statement "if thereby we die a thousand deaths, that is the price we pay for living a thousand lives" (paragraph 3) is most likely meant to suggest that:

- ○ A) we must guard against using our imaginations toward destructive ends.
- ○ B) although imagination sometimes causes pain, its positive aspects outweigh its negative ones.
- ○ C) it is possible to be too imaginative for one's own good.
- ○ D) without imagination, the uniquely human awareness of death would not exist.

Item 5

Which of the following findings, if true, would most weaken the claim that the use of symbolic imagery is unique to humans?

- ○ A) Chimpanzees are capable of learning at least some sign language.
- ○ B) Certain species of birds are able to migrate great distances by instinct alone.
- ○ C) Human beings have larger frontal lobes than do other animals.
- ○ D) Some animals have brains that are larger than human brains.

Item 6

It has been said that language does not merely describe reality but actually helps bring reality into existence. Which point made in the passage provides the strongest support for this claim?

- ○ A) To imagine means to make images and move them about in one's mind.
- ○ B) The tool that puts the human mind ahead of the animal's is imagery.
- ○ C) There is no specific center for language in the brain of any animal except the human being.
- ○ D) Images play out events that are not present, thereby guarding the past and creating the future.

Item 7

According to the author, the most important images are:

- ○ A) words.
- ○ B) poetic images.
- ○ C) images of the past.
- ○ D) images of the future.

Answers to Questions
Before you look at the answers, let's discuss them.

Question 1: Common sense tells us that an image can be both abstract and visual. The word "versatile" in the question also helps us find the answer. Choices A, C, and D are incompatible with versatility.

Question 2 : Ask yourself, "Why might a child remember a signal longer than a dog?" Choices B, C, and D don't seem reasonable. For choice B, what does it mean for a human's brain to evolve more quickly? This answer is somewhat unintelligible. Choice C compares the age of a human child to that of a dog in terms of memory as if they were equivalent. This doesn't seem to be reasonable. At best, it calls for specific information about a dog's ability to remember based upon its age. For answer choice D, the question doesn't say anything about vision. Why would color-blindness be relevant? Choice D is a beyond.

Question 3: Notice that the question asks what is meant by the quote. For this type of question, just match the answer to the quote. Choice B is a paraphrase of the quote. Sidney himself is superfluous information.

Question 4: This is the same type of question as the last. Match the answer to the quote. Answer choice D is provided to tempt those who want to see things in black and white and take the quote very literally. It also does not match the quote.

Question 5: What would weaken the claim that the use of symbolic imagery is unique to humans? Answer: An example of a non-human using symbolic imagery. Choice A is correct.

Question 6: Here we are asked to interpret a paraphrase. Just match the paraphrase to the answer choice. "Bringing reality into existence" is the same as "creating the future."

Question 7: This is difficult to answer without the passage. However, look at the other questions. Ask yourself, "What is the main idea of this passage?" It is certainly about images, symbols, and language. Which answer fits most closely? Notice that the word "image" is in all of the answers except for the correct one. This makes choices B, C, and D simpletons. Notice also that language and poets were mentioned in other question stems and answer choices; the author cares about words. Choice A is correct.

The correct answers are: 1. B, 2. A, 3. B, 4. B, 5. A, 6. D, 7. A.

_____

STOP HERE UNTIL CLASS!

(DO NOT LOOK AT THE FOLLOWING QUESTIONS UNTIL CLASS.

IF YOU WILL NOT BE ATTENDING CLASS, GIVE YOURSELF 30
MINUTES TO COMPLETE THE FOLLOWING SET OF QUESTIONS.)

Passage I (Questions 1-7)

Item 1

When a beaver senses danger, it will instinctively slap its tail on the water, warning other beavers. According to the passage, this is not "a true form of communication" because it:

- ○ A) is instinctive.
- ○ B) is not language.
- ○ C) is unidirectional.
- ○ D) lacks emotion.

Item 2

According to the passage, which of the following are reasons that apes are better communicators than monkeys?

    I. Apes are capable of a greater variety of facial expressions.
   II. Apes are capable of a greater variety of sounds.
  III. Apes have a greater intelligence with which to interpret signals.

- ○ A) I and II only
- ○ B) I and III only
- ○ C) II and III only
- ○ D) I, II, and III

Item 3

Suppose researchers selected three adult chimpanzees from a wild troop and taught them sign language. Based on information in the passage, if the researchers returned to the same troop four years later, which chimpanzees in the troop might they expect to be using sign language?

- ○ A) Only the chimpanzees that were originally taught sign language
- ○ B) Only the chimpanzees that were originally taught sign language and their offspring
- ○ C) All chimpanzees in the troop
- ○ D) No chimpanzees in the troop

Item 4

According to the passage, which of the following is the most important difference between humans and chimpanzees that explains why humans developed language and chimpanzees did not?

- ○ A) Genetic makeup
- ○ B) Personal relationships
- ○ C) Intelligence
- ○ D) The ability to produce a variety of sounds

Item 5

Which of the following would most weaken the author's claim that chimps are the most intelligent communicators in the animal world?

- ○ A) Through whistling and clicking alone, two dolphins are able to work together to perform coordinated movements.
- ○ B) A wolf's howl can be heard by another wolf from several miles away.
- ○ C) Ants have more developed chemical messages than any other animal.
- ○ D) A honey bee instinctively performs a complicated series of movements that signals the location of a pollen source to the rest of the hive.

Item 6

The author most likely believes that by studying chimpanzee behavior, humans may learn:

- ○ A) that chimpanzees communicate as effectively as humans.
- ○ B) new ways of communication.
- ○ C) how ancestors of humans developed speech.
- ○ D) why chimpanzees can't speak.

Item 7

The author claims that "The modern chimp may be making the first steps toward language" (paragraph 2). Based on the context of this claim in the passage, the author might also agree with which of the following statements?

- ○ A) Modern chimpanzees will one day develop their own spoken language.
- ○ B) Given the right training, modern chimpanzees are capable of speech.
- ○ C) Specific social behaviors of chimpanzees may prevent them from developing a universal language.
- ○ D) Modern chimpanzees are evolving more fluid communication skills.

NEXT

Passage II (Questions 8–16)

Item 8

According to the passage, a universally accepted scientific theory:

- A) cannot be proven wrong.
- B) is not a fundamental truth.
- C) usually replaces a religious belief.
- D) is no better than a religious belief as a predictor of natural phenomena.

Item 9

The author believes that the view that "You can't argue with science" is:

- A) not scientific.
- B) held only by top scientists.
- C) generally correct.
- D) true concerning matters outside of religion.

Item 10

The author mentions the Scopes Monkey Trial in order to support the claim that:

- A) religion and science are contradictory.
- B) the functions of science and religion are often misunderstood.
- C) science will eventually triumph over religion.
- D) when science and religion are in conflict, most people will believe religion.

Item 11

Einstein once said, "Whether you can observe a thing or not depends on the theory which you use. It is the theory which decides what can be observed." This quote best supports the author's claim that:

- A) science is an imperfect description of nature.
- B) science is not based on fact.
- C) religion is more reliable than science.
- D) religion and science are similar.

Item 12

Dawkins claims that "Religion is, in a sense, science; it's just bad science" (paragraph 4). Dawkins' point is that:

- A) religion attempts to answer the wrong questions.
- B) religion does not provide answers.
- C) the answers provided by religion are unreliable.
- D) religious people are less honest than scientists.

Item 13

If during a speech Dawkins said, "The argument that religion and science answer different types of questions is just false," which of the following statements made by Dawkins in the same speech would most weaken his own claim?

- A) Religions throughout history have attempted to answer questions that belong in the realm of science.
- B) Religion is science; it's just bad science.
- C) Science, then, is free of the main vice of religion, which is faith.
- D) Most religions offer a cosmology and a biology, a theory of life, a theory of origins, and a reason for existence.

Item 14

According to the passage, which of the following properly belongs to the realm of science, but NOT to the realm of religion?

- A) Healthy skepticism
- B) Reliable prediction
- C) Close observation
- D) Peer review

Item 15

With which of the following statements might the author agree?

- A) Science proves that God does not exist.
- B) Science proves the existence of God.
- C) God responds to prayer with a gentle guiding hand.
- D) God reveals himself through the lawful harmony of the universe.

Item 16

According to the author, science and religion:

- A) ask the same questions, and provide conflicting answers.
- B) ask the same questions, and provide compatible answers.
- C) ask different questions, and provide conflicting answers.
- D) ask different questions, and provide compatible answers.

Passage III (Questions 17–23)

Item 17

The author of the passage believes that the modern art held in high esteem by today's art critics:

○ A) has a weaker impact on contemporary society than did classical art.
○ B) should not be judged in the same context as classical art.
○ C) makes a clear statement about today's society.
○ D) is a testament to the extraordinary skills of modern artists.

Item 18

The comparison of sculpture and architecture (paragraph 2) best supports the author's claim that:

○ A) modern artists have had to use new technologies in order to stay connected to their audience.
○ B) modern art is more recognizable than classical art.
○ C) art must address the social problems faced by contemporary society.
○ D) function restrains novelty and dictates beauty.

Item 19

The author would most likely agree that truly great works of art:

○ A) comment on important contemporary social issues.
○ B) are beautiful to look at.
○ C) express the inner feelings of the artist.
○ D) stimulate novel thoughts.

Item 20

It has been said that art not only mimics reality, but reality also mimics art. Which of the assertions from the passage would best support this claim?

○ A) Beauty is not in the eye of the beholder, but is an absolute reality to be discovered by the artist.
○ B) Great men in history have been inspired to great deeds by great art.
○ C) No mere child could recreate The Statue of David.
○ D) Classical artwork was carefully planned and crafted.

Item 21

Artwork resembling modern abstract art, but painted by a chimpanzee, recently sold alongside famous works at a prestigious London auction house for over $25,000. Based on this information, the author might agree with which of the following statements?

○ A) Chimpanzees are capable of expressing emotion.
○ B) Some chimpanzees may be great artists.
○ C) Some modern art resembles the scribbling of a chimpanzee.
○ D) Great artwork doesn't require great minds.

Item 22

Picasso is credited with saying "If there were only one truth, you couldn't paint one hundred canvasses on the same theme." This statement best supports which of the following assertions from the passage?

○ A) If we find classical art beautiful, it is because we see hints of perfection in otherwise common and familiar forms.
○ B) The modern artist invites us to share a reality that is uniquely his own.
○ C) There is beauty in truth.
○ D) Upon a closer inspection, we see that the Diskobolus by Miron portrays the discus throw rather than the discus thrower.

Item 23

The passage places the blame for the average person's lack of interest in modern art on:

    I. a lack of talented modern artists.
    II. obtuse subject matter.
  III. the ignorance of the average person.

○ A) I only
○ B) II only
○ C) I and II only
○ D) I, II, and III

STOP

Don't look at the answers yet, just read on.

Passage I

Question 1: From a layman's perspective, the beaver is "communicating" to other beavers. Thus, we know that the word "true" here is going to be important. The author has apparently distinguished "true communication" from our everyday understanding of the word. From question 2 we see that apes and monkeys both "communicate" according to the passage. Apes and monkeys don't have language, so we can assume that "true communication" does not require language. We can get rid of choice B. Choice D seems poor as well, since presumably a beaver in danger would not be emotionless. Of course you might make the argument that all animals lack emotion, but then there is question 2 again, where apes are animals and apes are communicating, so communication is possible for animals. Since the author is interested in communication (a human quality) in animals, it seems likely that the author would also believe that animals can feel emotion (another human quality). So now we are left with choice A or C. The tail slap is instinctive, as per the question, and it seems to be unidirectional. So which one would be a reason that it is NOT "true" communication? We can think of many examples of communication that are unidirectional: television, a smile, a letter, etc... This weakens choice C. Choice A is correct.

Question 2: Common sense tells us that having greater intelligence and being better at producing sound and facial expressions would make us better communicators, so the question is really asking, "At which of these an ape is better than a monkey?" From question stem 5 we see that chimps, which are apes, are "the most intelligent communicators in the animal world," so we know that option III must be part of the answer. Thus choice A is incorrect. We can't be certain about sound or facial expressions, so it is difficult to narrow this one down just yet.

Question 3: This question is basically asking us, "In the wild, which other chimpanzees, if any, does the author think a signing chimpanzee would teach sign language? And would the signing chimpanzee even retain his sign language?" This question is about social interactions within the troop. We don't have enough information to answer it yet.

Question 4: At first glance, all the answers seem to be possible. As usual, it is important to read the question stem carefully. The stem does not ask for "the only reason" why humans developed language and chimps didn't; it is asking for the "most important" reason, and the most important reason "according to the passage." All of the answers may be legitimate reasons why chimps didn't develop language and humans did, but which one does the author believe is the most important? Is this author most concerned with genetics, social relationships, intelligence, or ability to produce sounds? Question 3 clearly lends support to choice B. Question 5 seems to strengthen choice C, since it points out the importance of intelligence in communication. Question 2 mentions sound in an answer choice, but we don't know whether it is the correct answer choice. Genetics seems to have no support from any other question, so choice A seems wrong.

Question 5: This question can be answered with common sense. The question asks about intelligence. Which answer choice has to do with intelligence? Only choice A.

Question 6: Choice A is false according to common sense and based on other questions. For example, question 4 points out that chimpanzees did not develop language while humans did, and question 5 presents chimps as "the most intelligent communicators **in the animal world**," implying that they are still not as skilled as humans. Choice B seems highly unlikely; since it has been established that chimpanzees communicate less effectively than humans, why would humans learn new communication methods from them? Choice D is wrong because the author's interest lies in communication, not in chimps themselves. In other words, when it comes right down to it, he wants to learn about communication, not about chimps. Choice C satisfies this criterion. Notice that this question also emphasizes behavior. The passage is looking more and more to be about communication as it is affected by social interactions. This provides more support for choice B in question 4.

Question 7: It is important to keep your common sense. Does the author really believe that chimps will be speaking one day? No, of course not. Choices A and B are incorrect. That leaves choices C and D. Both are tempting, but choice C is the better answer because the social behavior aspect of choice C fits so neatly with the rest of the questions. Choice C also strongly suggests that the answer to question 4 is B.

We now have enough information to revisit and answer the earlier questions.

Passage I

Question 2 REVISITED: We know that option III is true. The only hint for choosing option I or II, and it is quite a small hint, is the sense in the questions that the passage was concerned with signs, supporting option I, and not really as concerned with sounds, lacking support for option II. It would be difficult to be confident about this without reading the passage, but, hey, that's why you read the passage. Choice B is correct.

Question 3 REVISITED: Now that we understand that the passage is about social behavior as well as communication, and that (according to the answer to question 7) the social behaviors of chimps prevent them from developing a universal language, we know that the chimps are not going to teach all their troop mates to use sign language. Choice C is wrong. There is no evidence in the question stems that the chimp would lose his ability to use sign language, so choice D is unlikely. The question is, "Would the adults teach signing to their offspring?" This is very tough to answer without reading the passage, but there is a hint. What are the "first steps toward language" that the author talks about in question 7? The chimps are teaching their offspring, but not their peers—this is another social behavior standing in the way of language development. Choice B is correct.

Question 4 REVISITED: From questions 6 and 7 we see that the answer must be choice B.

Passage II

Question 8: As an MCAT® student strong in the sciences, you know that choice A is false and that choice B is true. Choice C is possible. Choice D seems unlikely. The answer is probably choice B, but we'll have to come back.

Question 9: Again, as an MCAT® student strong in the sciences, you know that choices B, C, and D are false. Furthermore, choice C is not a good MCAT® answer because it is incredibly vague. Choice A is correct. Now it is easy to go back and answer question 8.

Question 8 REVISITED: In the light of question 9, the correct answer is choice B. Also, since we now know that choice D is wrong, we know that the author is taking a kind of middle ground between science and religion.

Question 10: Choices A and C do not represent the tone that questions 8 and 9 present. They are incorrect. Choice B seems most closely related to the middle ground tone of the questions and answers to 8 and 9. The Scopes Monkey trial refers to the trial of John Scopes for illegally teaching evolution in public school. He was convicted. Obviously,

it was discussed in the passage, so being familiar with it before the MCAT® is unnecessary. The trial was a conflict between science and religion, but it in no way supports the conclusion drawn by choice D. However, it could support an argument that the roles of religion and science are misunderstood. Choice B is correct.

Question 11: Choice B implies that a quote from Einstein is used to support a claim that science is not based upon fact. It also implies that the author believes science is not based upon fact. Notice that this further supports the answer to 9 by ruling out choice B; Einstein was certainly a top scientist, and he believed that science could be questioned.

Because choice D from Question 8 was incorrect, the author probably would find choices B and C to be incorrect as well. The question doesn't draw any connection between religion and science, so choice D seems unlikely. Choice A seems to be a middle ground again and works especially well with the assertion in question 8 that a scientific theory is not a fundamental truth. Choice A is correct.

Question 12: Dawkins is not the author, or he wouldn't have been named in the question. Dawkins must be used to support the author's point. The aggressive, confrontational tone of Dawkins' comment is in strong contrast to the moderate tone of the author as revealed by the questions so far. Still, since this question is about Dawkins, rather than the author, it is difficult to answer without reading more questions. We'll have to come back.

Question 13: This question is a logic problem that can be answered by common sense alone. Choice A most weakens Dawkins' claim. Dawkins claims in the question stem that religion and science don't answer different questions, so they must either answer the same question or no questions at all. Choice A indicates that Dawkins believes that certain questions belong in the realm of science and not in the realm of religion. This means that he believes that religion and science don't answer the same questions. This is a contradiction and weakens his argument. The correct answer is A.

Question 12 REVISITED: From question 13 we see that Dawkins does not believe choice A. Question 12 also seems to indicate that Dawkins believes religion does provide answers, just answers that are somehow not as good as those provided by science. This fits best with choice C. The honesty of religious people is not addressed, leaving no evidence for choice D. Choice C is correct.

Question 14: Choice B fits nicely with choice D in question 8 being incorrect. Skepticism, close observation, and peer review are not addressed by any other question, so choices A, C, and D are not supported.

Question 15: Based upon questions 8 and 9, the author would have difficulty arguing that science proves anything. Choices A and B are incorrect. These answer choices are also weakened by the fact that they are stated much more strongly than the moderate tone of the other questions and correct answers. Choice C might be possible, but choice D goes much better with question 14. Based upon questions 8 and 14, the author seems to feel that science is a reliable predictor. Choice D allows for such predictions (in accordance with "lawful harmony") and for God, while choice C seems likely to interfere with the predictive powers of science.

Question 16: Question 14 tells us that the author believes that science and religion ask different questions. The tone of the questions tells us that he believes the answers are compatible. Choice D for question 15 accounts for both the different questions asked by science and religion and the compatibility of science and religion. Choice D is correct.

Passage III

Question 17: Why does the question include the modifying phrase "held in high esteem by today's art critics"? To what other kind of modern art might the question refer? Is there modern art that today's art critics consider bad? Is there bad modern art? Apparently, the question writer wants to be clear that he is talking only about good modern art and not about bad modern art. Choice A is the only answer that makes sense using this distinction. With this distinction, choice A can be rephrased as "Even good modern art is worse than classical art," while the importance of the distinction is lost with choices B, C, and D. For instance, choice B: "Even good modern art should not be judged in the same context as classical art." Choice C: "Even good modern art makes a clear statement about today's society." Choice D: "Even good modern art is a testament to the extraordinary skills of modern artists." For the MCAT®, it is important to develop this sense or feeling of whether or not the answer choice fits the question stem. Choice A is correct because it fits with the question stem while the other choices do not. Based upon this answer we have learned quite a bit about the author. Now we know that the author has something against modern art and is in favor of classical art. Since choices B, C, and D are incorrect, we can assume that the author thinks it is acceptable to judge modern art and classical art in the same context, that modern art does not make a clear statement about today's society, and that modern art is not a testament to the skills of the modern artist.

Question 18: The question asks about a comparison. The correct answer should address a comparison. Choice D indicates that function behaves in two different ways: 1) It restrains novelty and 2) It dictates beauty. How might this work with sculpture and architecture? How does function apply to architecture? Architecture has a specific function as housing or shelter. Might this function restrain novelty (or new ideas) in architecture? It seems logical. A roof can be made to look differently, but it still must have certain characteristics in order to function like a roof. Might this function also dictate beauty in architecture? Perhaps since the roof is required, what is beautiful in architecture must include a roof. On the other hand, sculpture doesn't seem to have a function in the same sense. Could a comparison to sculpture and architecture demonstrate how function restrains novelty and dictates beauty? It would seem so. Choice D is a possibility. Choices A, B, and C do not address the comparison quite as well. In addition, choices A and B seem to favor modern art, contradicting the negative feel toward modern art in question 17. Choice D seems to be correct, but we cannot be certain yet.

Question 19: The word "truly" is important here. It indicates that the author distinguishes between great works of art and "truly" great works of art. Might that mean that he disagrees with art critics about what is and is not great art? This would support our answer for question 17. Since the author does not seem to be enamored with modern art, and he does seem to like classical art, it is unlikely that he would think that "truly" great art must comment on important contemporary social issues. Choice A is probably out. We will revisit this question after the next question.

Question 20: This question can be answered by common sense. Only choice B answers the question. Only choice B is an example of reality mimicking art. The other choices simply don't address the premise of the question. Choice B is correct. This question is important because it gives us four examples of what the author thinks in the four answer choices (all "assertions from the passage"). Even if we had read the passage, these answer choices would be valuable because they sum up the author's ideas in the question writer's words. What the question writer thinks the author said is even more important than what the author thinks he said. Choice A tells us that the author believes beauty is a reality rather than a matter of opinion. This verifies choice B for question 19.

Question 19 REVISITED: From question 20, choice A, we know that the author believes that beauty is not a matter of opinion. This indicates that choice B in question 19 must be correct.

Question 21: Clearly choices A and B are wrong; this passage is not about chimps, it is about art. Choice D would indicate that the author thinks that modern art by chimps is "great artwork." Instead, common sense and the author's attitude toward modern art in question 17 tell us that the correct answer is choice C.

Question 22: The quote says there is more than one reality and that art is the painter's idea of reality. Only choice B matches the quote. Choice B is correct. Again we have four examples of what the author thinks in the four answer choices. Especially revealing is choice A, which verifies

that the author likes classical art and tells us why. This strongly supports choice B in question 19.

Question 23: From previous questions we know that the author likes classical art more than modern art. Choice A in question 22 tells us that classical art is beautiful because of the true beauty discovered in its common and familiar subject matter, while choice B tells us that the modern artist is sharing his own reality that is "uniquely his own," i.e., not a common familiar subject matter. Therefore the subject matter of modern art must be a key reason that the author finds modern art less beautiful. Choice II must be one of the answer choices. On the other hand, there is no hint that the author has an issue with the talent of the modern artist; he is instead focused on the very nature of modern art. This leaves only choice B.

DON'T FORGET YOUR KEYS

1. Rephrase complex wording in the question stem to find the simple question being asked.

2. Through the question set, stay in touch with the passage and the author: after reading each question stem, restate the main idea and predict an answer.

3. The best answer matches the passage and the question stem.

Answers:					
1. A	5. A	9. A	13. A	17. A	21. C
2. B	6. C	10. B	14. B	18. D	22. B
3. B	7. C	11. A	15. D	19. B	23. B
4. B	8. B	12. C	16. D	20. B	

These exercises are NOT intended to convince you to not read the passage. You should always read the passage. However, the exercises should show you that the questions and answer choices contain a large amount of information. If you achieved a higher score without even reading the passage, you probably haven't been taking advantage of the wealth of information in the question stems and answer choices.

Advanced CARS Skills

4.1 Introduction

This lecture introduces advanced skills that will take your performance to the next level. The previous three lectures introduced foundational skills required for success on the Critical Analysis and Reasoning Skills section of the MCAT®. While reading closely, construct a main idea, get to know your author, and focus on the big picture. While answering questions, stay in touch with the main idea, simplify the question and answer choices, and avoid distractors.

Once these fundamental tools have been mastered, you are ready to move on to advanced skills that will offer further help with achieving a high score on the CARS section. The first skill, recognizing passage archetypes, will allow you to readily identify main and supporting ideas. It will also help you avoid common pitfalls, like feeling overwhelmed by a new concept or endless details. Mastering the second skill, recognizing question archetypes, will help you avoid distractors and hone in on the best answer. The third skill, building a spectrum, will help you identify the author's position and construct the main idea by organizing the ideas presented within a passage.

THE 3 KEYS

1. Use passage types to approach and master each new CARS passage.

2. When reading a CARS question stem, consider the type: use the main idea, parts of the argument, or application of new information.

3. Build a spectrum of opposing ideas and locate the author along the spectrum.

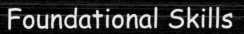

Foundational Skills

- Construct main idea

- Know your author

- Focus on the big picture

Advanced Skills

- Recognize passage archetypes

- Recognize question archetypes

- Build a spectrum

4.2 | Identifying Passage Types

The CARS section is designed to test critical analysis and reasoning skills. The MCAT® uses passages with archetypal structures. Familiarity with these passage types will give you an advantage over students unfamiliar with them. You will be able to more readily identify main and supporting ideas and their relationship, while avoiding common pitfalls.

To demonstrate how knowledge of a passage archetype can be helpful for understanding a written work, consider the five-paragraph essay. A five-paragraph essay is structured according to the following predictable pattern: introductory paragraph, first, second, and third body paragraphs, and concluding paragraph. In the introductory paragraph, readers can expect to find the author's central argument, that is, his or her thesis statement. Then, in each of the three body paragraphs, readers can expect to find an argument or example that supports the central argument presented in the introductory paragraph. In the concluding paragraph, readers can expect both a restatement of the thesis and a summary of the three body paragraphs.

A reader familiar with this pattern can easily find and identify the author's central argument, supporting arguments, examples, and the relationships among them. When looking for supporting arguments or examples, go right to the first or second sentence (the topic sentence) of each body paragraph. When looking for the relationships between supporting arguments, focus on the transitional phrases used in last and first sentences of adjacent body paragraphs. Readers unfamiliar with this pattern will not know where to look.

Passages appearing in the Critical Analysis and Reasoning Skills section are often structured according to an archetype, or pattern. The following are four passage types that commonly appear on the MCAT®: 1. compare and contrast; 2. details, details, details; 3. new topic; and 4. point of view. While not all CARS passages will follow one of these archetypes, it is likely that one or more of these archetypes will appear in the CARS section.

1) Compare and Contrast

In this passage archetype, the author presents two related ideas and explores their similarities and differences. This passage structure is common across a wide variety of disciplines. You could be presented with a passage on two philosophers, two economic theories, two cultures, or two architectural styles, etc. If you encounter this passage type, read for the ways the ideas relate. How are they similar? What are their differences? Make sure that the main idea includes both topics and the way(s) in which they relate to each other. Be prepared to answer questions on their relationship. Consider the author. Which of the two ideas does your author favor?

There is also a common variant on this archetype. Often, at the end of the passage, the author will introduce a third concept or idea that relates to the first two. When this happens, include the third concept in your main idea, emphasizing it to the extent that it was emphasized in the passage. Be prepared to answer questions on how this third idea relates to the first two.

2) Details, Details, Details

This passage archetype is bursting at the seams with details. It may read like a history textbook or an obscure piece of literature. It is full of seemingly disconnected statements, and it may seem boring. This is by design. This passage archetype attempts to lose the interest of the unfocused, fatigued, or untrained test taker, leading him or her to skim sentences or even whole paragraphs. With an animated reading, engage with each component, name its purpose, and identify relationships between components and to the main idea.

This passage type normally has many short paragraphs, each of them presenting a distinct aspect of the main idea. Do not skim or skip any paragraphs. The questions may ask you for about an idea found only in one or two paragraphs.

Remember your CARS strategy and tactics. If you read all the information completely and immerse yourself to remain interested, you will retain details and be able to answer the questions asked. Do not worry about including all of the paragraphs in the main idea. Unify the subtopics as best you can, and pay attention to overarching themes. As always, you should also be able to tell if the author is neutral, as in a textbook, or whether he has an agenda or opinion.

3) New Concept

A CARS passage will often present an idea with which the vast majority of MCAT® test takers are unfamiliar. This commonly occurs in passages presenting legal or ethical issues, though you may also see explorations of concepts from fields, such as philosophy, economics, psychology, etc. In most of these passages, you can find and summarize the major focus of the passage in one to two words, such as laissez faire (economics), utilitarianism (philosophy), non-maleficence (medical ethics), or due process (political science). The main idea will be how the author uniquely expands on this concept. The remainder of this passage will further explain and provide examples. This passage type introduces and explores the unknown topic, and is written assuming the reader brings no previous knowledge. Be careful if you do have background knowledge or bias to leave it out of your reading; it can confuse your ability to follow the author's argument and read for the author's opinion.

Be prepared for the MCAT® to test your understanding of this concept in several ways. You may be asked to simply and succinctly state the author's definition of the new idea, reducing the whole passage to one or two sentences. You may be given new information and be asked to consider it through the lens of the newly-understood idea. They may ask you what would weaken or strengthen the point made in the passage. While these question types occur across the entire CARS section, they are especially common in the "new concept" archetype. As always, a close reading, a strong understanding of the passage topic and a clear main idea will lead you to the correct answer.

4) Point of View

In this passage type, the author has a strong agenda and is attempting to persuade the reader. The author's position may be obvious, or may be very subtle, as though the author does not want to offend. Either way, you will be able to spot a point of view passage by noticing the author's use of emotional or argumentative language. The author may present varied viewpoints from others in the field. The author may agree with some while dismissing others. Read critically and remember what we said in Lecture 2: pretend you are a Harvard professor reading a high school essay written badly. If the author draws a conclusion that seems unfounded or dismisses data without justification, make a mental note. Questions may ask you to consider the author's argument or point out logical weaknesses. You can also expect questions on the author's tone, purpose for writing, or presumed identity.

In the "bait and switch" variant, the author initially supports one point of view, but later critiques that position to reveal an adjusted point of view. When this happens, expect to see questions on the author's true feelings. Read critically: Has the author deliberately presented a weak version of the opposing side, a so-called "straw house" argument, just so he could then oppose it? Did the author do a good job or a poor job of refuting the other side, the counterpoint? Once again, a strong main idea that captures the author's nuanced point of view will guide you through the questions.

Lucky for you, you're prepared for this passage type. You're disciplined and focused, and you think that a detailed analysis of the Bolshevik Revolution or a close reading of War and Peace is fascinating.

Identifying Question Types

Just as the MCAT® models passages after standard archetypes, the MCAT® uses archetypal question stems and answer choices. The previous lecture described typical false answer choice called distractors. This lecture will discuss the following question stem archetypes:

1. **Point of view** questions ask you for the main idea or to distinguish the main idea from other points of view. These questions test "foundations of comprehension" by the AAMC.

2. **Connection** questions test your reading of the argument, asking you to determine the relationships of passage components to one another or to the main idea. The AAMC is testing "reasoning within the text".

3. **Credibility** questions ask you to evaluate the credibility of the author, the argument or the writing. These are also part of "reasoning within the text".

4. **Going further** questions are called "reasoning beyond the text" by the AAMC. These questions bring new information and ask you to apply passage ideas in new contexts (**application**) or to incorporate new information into passage ideas (**integration.**)

TABLE 4.1 > Critical Analysis and Reasoning Skills Tested by the MCAT®

Question Archetype	Skill(s)	Example Question
Point of View	Identifying the author's point of view and/or distinguishing other points of view from it or from one another	The author suggests that French intervention in post-colonial Côte d'Ivoire was justified by:
Connection	Determining the relationships of passage components to one another or to the main idea	Which of the following claims is offered to counter the claim that constructivism poses a threat to legal institutions?
Credibility	Evaluating the credibility of the author and his or her writing	The author's claim that the literary forms available to nineteenth century female writers were ill-suited to the feminine voice is supported by:
Going further	Application: applying passage ideas to new contexts	Which of the following would be LEAST likely to benefit from the software development processes described in the passage?
	Integration: assessing the impact of new information on passage ideas	Suppose that during times of economic downturn, demand for operational analysis decreased. This finding would best support the claim that:

Table 4.1 presents many of the skills tested by the CARS section, along with examples of the question archetypes designed to test them.

As you become more familiar with these question types, you can more easily identify the necessary information to answer the questions. You will be better equipped to eliminate distractors and hone in on the correct answer. A 'going further' question might ask you to apply passage ideas in new contexts. When you identify a going further question, bring to mind the passage idea and apply it in the new context. You can then eliminate answer choices that reference perspectives not included in the passage or that misapply ideas from the passage.

Point of View

Point of view questions generally ask you to identify the main idea as well as to distinguish points of view from one another. Point of view questions might include language similar to the following:

- The passage suggests that _____ might hold the view that:
- According to the passage, _____ would deny the claim that:
- The author most likely believes that:
- The author suggests that:
- According to the author, _____:

As you read, make note of each point of view, especially the author's point of view, the main idea. Consider how the words, tone and arguments used by the author reveal his or her point of view. Compare the author's point of view to each of the other points of view presented in the passage.

Connection

Connection questions invite you to relate passage components to one another and to the main idea. They ask about the relevance of a particular discussion, example, or detail to a broader point made in the passage.

- The example ____ best supports the author's claim that:
- The discussion of ____ is primarily intended to support the author's claim that:
- The example of ____ is most relevant to the author's assertion that:
- What is the intended relevance of the author's comment that ____ to the rest of the passage?
- The opinion that ____ is challenged in the passage by the argument that:

As you read, consider whether each statement supports or undermines, clarifies or obscures a point of view introduced in the passage. Do not focus on details, but rather identify the purpose of the detail and the relationship of details to other passage components.

Credibility

Some questions will require you to assess the credibility of the author and/or his or her writing. A typical credibility question will ask you which of various claims is most or least supported by examples in the passage. Answering this type of question can be as simple as recalling the level of evidence or support the author provided for each answer choice. Did the author write a paragraph providing examples or supporting evidence, or was it just mentioned as a passing comment? Was the evidence concrete and specific or vague?

It is common to see language similar to the following in credibility questions:

- The author offers no supporting evidence for the claim that:

- Implicit in the passage is the assumption that:

- What is the most significant weakness of the passage author's argument?

- Which of the following assertions is not clearly supported by the passage author?

- For which of the following conclusions does the passage offer the most support?

Reading with confidence, even a bit of arrogance, as described in Lecture 1, allows you to judge the strength of the author's argument. As you read, consider how credible you find the arguments to be. Do the conclusions follow from premises, and are the premises substantiated and true? If the author makes an unjustified claim or a piece of the argument seems particularly weak, trust that you have judged correctly.

Going Further

Many questions will ask you to interpret the passage as it currently stands, but some questions require you to go one step further either by applying the main idea to new situations or re-assessing the main idea in light of new information. These questions are of two types – application or integration. Application questions ask you to apply the main idea in a new context. Integration questions ask you to incorporate new information. Your interpretation of the passage must be flexible enough to adjust the main idea as needed to incorporate new information given that may support, challenge, or complicate the author's point. These questions are easy to spot: they will use words like "suppose", "assume", and "would", and will often appear in a two-sentence format where new information is given and a question about that information is asked. The question may explicitly ask what the author would think about the new information.

Application

Application questions ask you to take the author's argument as it currently stands and apply it in a new situation. These questions may explicitly ask what the author would think about a given scenario. Be especially careful here to avoid bringing your own outside information and biases.

Application questions might include language similar to the following:

- If the information in the passage is accurate ___, then . . .

- Given the information in the passage, the author would most likely . . .

- The passage suggests that the author would be most likely to disagree with which of the following statements?

- Suppose ___. Which of the following explanations is most compatible with passage information?

- The author of the passage would be most likely to agree with which of the following opinions?

Integration

An integration question will provide a new piece of information and ask you to determine how, if at all, it affects passage ideas. A classic question of this type asks how the new information affects the author's argument. The answer choices may include strengthening or weakening the argument, not affecting the strength of the argument, or only affecting the argument if some other condition is also met.

Integration questions may use phrasing similar to the following:

- Suppose that . . . This finding would best support the claim that:
- If . . . which of the following conclusions in the passage would be challenged?
- Suppose . . . This new information would most challenge the claim that:
- If . . . then one would expect that:
- Assume . . . This finding:

Use your knowledge of questions likely to appear on the MCAT® to guide your reading of the passages.

Use your knowledge of the questions likely to appear on the MCAT® to guide your reading of passages. As you read, identify and determine relationships among points of view presented in the passage. Determine the author's point of view and the ways in which he or she expresses it. Know how particulars relate to the general. Evaluate the credibility of the author and the claims he or she makes. Assess whether or not his or her conclusions follow from true premises. Has he or she made any unstated assumptions? If you predict what you will need as you read, then you will be ready for any question type, including those that ask you to reason beyond the text.

As you continue your MCAT® preparation, you will encounter each of the question types: point of view, connections, credibility and application questions. With each question, identify the question type to predict the best answer.

The spectrum is a strategy for creating a road map of the passage. With practice, you will become a master at using the spectrum to organize contrasting viewpoints.

4.4 | Constructing the Main Idea: A Practical Approach

This final advanced skill of the Examkrackers method, incorporates many of the skills presented throughout this manual. The spectrum is a particular way of organizing CARS passages. A key component of locating the main idea is taking advantage of contrasting points of view. The continuum of opinions between two opposite ideas can be called a spectrum. The author of each passage will be located somewhere along this spectrum. This section will introduce the spectrum along with an example.

You have probably noticed by now that many, if not most, CARS passages present contrasting ideas. This is particularly evident in passages that follow the point of view or compare and contrast archetypes discussed earlier in this lecture. In fact, every passage type communicates the author's view which always falls along a spectrum of opinions. Using the spectrum as a framing technique allows the test taker to utilize contrast to distinguish nuanced ideas found within the passage. The main idea is often the reconciliation of opposite ends of the spectrum. Sometimes the author presents only one end of the spectrum. In this case, you can build the opposite end.

Examining a familiar passage will demonstrate the usefulness of the spectrum. You may have been constructing a spectrum of ideas without realizing it. As you read the passage, notice the contrasts the author sets up and where the main idea falls between those contrasts. Use the chart on page 121 to gather words and ideas on opposite sides of the spectrum. You will see that some ideas fall at the extremes while others are located toward the middle of the spectrum.

Here is an example of how two contrasting ideas could be presented in a single sentence: Some readers have dismissed Jane Austen's work as lacking in substance, but others have argued that her novels have depth in terms of social critique and characterization.

Passage I

It is roughly a century since European art began to experience its first significant defections from the standards of painting and sculpture that we inherit from the early Renaissance. Looking back now across a long succession of innovative movements and stylistic revolutions, most of us have little trouble recognizing that such aesthetic orthodoxies of the past as the representative convention, exact anatomy and optical perspective, the casement-window canvas, along with the repertory of materials and subject matters we associate with the Old Masters—that all this makes up not "art" itself in any absolute sense, but something like a school of art, one great tradition among many. We acknowledge the excellence which a Raphael or Rembrandt could achieve within the canons of that school; but we have grown accustomed to the idea that there are other aesthetic visions of equal validity. Indeed, innovation in the arts has become a convention in its own right with us, a "tradition of the new," to such a degree that there are critics to whom it seems to be intolerable that any two painters should paint alike. We demand radical originality, and often confuse it with quality.

Yet what a jolt it was to our great-grandparents to see the certainties of the academic tradition melt away before their eyes. How distressing, especially for the academicians, who were the guardians of a classic heritage embodying time-honored techniques and standards whose perfection had been the labor of genius. Suddenly they found art as they understood it being rejected by upstarts who were unwilling to let a single premise of the inherited wisdom stand unchallenged, or so it seemed. Now, with a little hindsight, it is not difficult to discern continuities where our predecessors saw only ruthless disjunctions. To see, as well, that the artistic revolutionaries of the past were, at their best, only opening our minds to a more global conception of art which demanded a deeper experience of light, color, and form. Through their work, too, the art of our time has done much to salvage the values of the primitive and childlike, the dream, the immediate emotional response, the life of fantasy, and the transcendent symbol.

In our own day, much the same sort of turning point has been reached in the history of science. It is as if the aesthetic ground pioneered by the artists now unfolds before us as a new ontological awareness. We are at a moment when the reality to which scientists address themselves comes more and more to be recognized as but one segment of a far broader spectrum. Science, for so long regarded as our single valid picture of the world, now emerges as, also, a school: a *school of consciousness*, beside which alternative realities take their place.

There are, so far, only fragile and scattered beginnings of this perception. They are still the subterranean history of our time. How far they will carry toward liberating us from the orthodox world view of the technocratic establishment is still doubtful.

These days, many gestures of rebellion are subtly denatured, adjusted, and converted into oaths of allegiance. In our society at large, little beyond submerged unease challenges the lingering authority of science and technique, that dull ache at the bottom of the soul we refer to when we speak (usually too glibly) of an "age of anxiety," an "age of longing."

Source: Adapted from T. Roszak, The Making of a Counter Culture. 1969 Doubleday.

One Theme	The Opposite Theme
words from the passage	opposite words
new	old
change	the same

Tradition	The New	Extreme Change
Standards		Defections
Orthodoxy		Innovative
Convention		Revolutions
Absolute		One school of art
The past		The New
		Radical originality
		Change that preserves quality
Continuity		
Science		Alternative Realities
Single valid picture		School of consciousness
Technocratic establishment		Rebellion

Notice that the author talks about change in different ways throughout the passage. Sometimes it's all the way over on the side of extreme change; sometimes it's more towards the middle which the author likes the most- change that preserves the good.

As you read the passage, collect words that represent one opinion and write them into one side of the spectrum, then add its opposite directly across. Notice which side of the spectrum the author favors using language choice. Notice when the author presents an opinion that falls between the two extremes. Often this is the main idea. The author will generally stay on the same side of the spectrum while moving toward the middle.

Many CARS passages are deliberately vague and therefore uncomfortable for the pre-medical student to read, as s/he is accustomed to clear and factual science writing. To identify the main idea in a field of grays, the spectrum allows the student to lay out the black and white extremes, in order to locate the author between them. Remember that CARS practice is medical practice. Patients are human beings whose needs and bodies do not fit into the neat lines created by textbooks. The CARS section rewards your preparation for the inevitable uncertainty in the art of medicine.

4.5 | Building the Spectrum Step by Step

Creating a spectrum while reading a passage requires some practice. It may be awkward at first, but just like identifying the main idea, it will get easier with time and will dramatically improve your ability to answer the questions correctly. The following skills are required for the spectrum technique:

1. Restating the material;

2. Identifying contrasts; and

3. Using your "lens"

These skills are described further below. Each will be demonstrated in the context of portions of a CARS passage, much like in the close reading of a passage presented in the Main Idea Lecture.

Restating the Material

Restating the material is a key skill for building a spectrum and gaining a deep understanding of CARS passages. To use the spectrum, restate the author's language in your own words. This allows for greater comprehension and recollection of the passage, which, in turn, improves your ability to answer the questions. In addition, coming up with your own simple word or phrase to describe preceding information provides a lens through which to view the rest of the passage.

Restating the Material: An Example

Philosophers Immanuel Kant and David Hume both spent their professional careers searching for a universal principle of morality. Considering that they began their searches with seemingly irreconcilable ideas of where to look, the similarity in the moral systems they constructed is surprising. ...

Hume decided at the outset that a moral system must be practical, and maintained that, since reason is only useful for disinterested comparison, and since only sentiment (emotion) is capable of stirring people to action, the practical study of morality should be concerned with sentiment. Hume begins with the assumption that whether something is judged moral or praiseworthy depends on the circumstances. He says, "What each man feels within himself is the standard of sentiment." ...

Kant and Hume were different but arrived at a similar end.

Hume wanted a practical system of morality based on sentiment. He believed that morality was relative.

Restating the ideas of the passage in short phrases or sentences as you go along, as described in the previous section, makes it easier to organize these ideas according to their similarity or dissimilarity from one another.

Identifying Contrasts

Identifying contrasts simply means recognizing contrasting pieces of information when they occur in the passage. Find ideas that fall on opposing sides. As you read, ask yourself whether new information contradicts ideas that the author presented earlier in the passage. Contrasting ideas may be presented early on or towards the middle and end of the passage. The author may choose to introduce both ideas together, or talk about one idea at length before bringing up a contrasting idea. An important tool in identifying contrasts is taking note of transitional words and phrases, as described in the Main Idea Lecture. Pay attention to words like "but" and "yet." They provide a hint that the author is about to change gears and may introduce a contrasting idea.

If only one perspective is found in the passage, you can project the opposite idea to lay out the spectrum. If no pair of contrasting ideas can be identified, the author is focusing on only one viewpoint without considering alternatives. Similarly, if a pair of contrasting ideas does exist but only one is followed by supporting evidence or examples, the passage is shown to be one-sided, giving a clue as to the author's opinion. For example, if the author mentions the merits of Freud's psychoanalytic technique but then dives into a three paragraph exploration of the contrasting ideas of Jung, you can bet that the author is more interested in Jung.

Identifying Contrasts: an Example

Anticipate contrasts to come between Kant's and Hume's approaches. Anticipate similarities in the moral systems they constructed.

Note the phrase "By contrast." Hume set out to create a practical system of morality based on sentiment. Hume = Subjective
By contrast, Kant set out to create a theoretical system of morality based on reason. Kant = Objective.

Philosophers Immanuel Kant and David Hume both spent their professional careers searching for a universal principle of morality. Considering that they began their searches with seemingly irreconcilable ideas of where to look, the similarity in the moral systems they constructed is surprising. ...

Hume decided at the outset that a moral system must be practical, and maintained that, since reason is only useful for disinterested comparison, and since only sentiment (emotion) is capable of stirring people to action, the practical study of morality should be concerned with sentiment. Hume begins with the assumption that whether something is judged moral or praiseworthy depends on the circumstances. He says, "What each man feels within himself is the standard of sentiment." ...

By contrast, Kant begins by assuming that, while some time should be devoted to studying practical morality ("ethics"), it is also valuable to have an absolute system of morality based solely on reason, to be called "metaphysics". That forms the core of his laborious exploration of pure logic, called Grounding for the Metaphysics of Morals.

SPECTRUM 4.3 > Hume vs. Kant

Hume's Morality = Subjective	Kant's Morality = Objective
Practical (stirring to action)	Theoretical
Sentiment	Reason
Relative- depends on circumstances	Absolute- does not depend on circumstances
Ethics	Metaphysics

One reader's spectrum is likely to differ from another reader's spectrum. Here is one framework into which the contrasts between Hume and Kant can be organized.

Using Your Lens to Revise and Refine

Finally, read new material in the passage using the "lens" of your earlier understanding of the passage. Each new sentence in a passage relates to those that came before in some way. As you restate sentences and paragraphs, articulate their relationships to other passage components.

By now you have probably noticed that passages in the CARS section often do not follow a straightforward path. The author may jump around from one point to the next without a clear transition, or talk at length about one topic before switching to another and leaving the old one behind. Reading new sentences through the lens of what you read before makes confusing passages easier to understand; it allows you to organize new information according to earlier concepts; and it keeps you focused on the main idea.

You are likely to see the same pair of contrasts repeated multiple times with distinctive wordings. Test takers who do not read with an eye to constructing a spectrum, using previous material to make sense of new material, may be caught off guard and think that they are seeing new or confusing information. With the help of your spectrum and the ability to read through the lens of what came before, you will unmask these new information when it is just a new way of saying the same thing. You can use this restatement to continue building the spectrum.

Because passages are filled with twists and turns, you may find that the pair of contrasts you use at the start of the passage does not work the whole way through. That's ok! If not, look for a new pair of contrasts to continue building a new spectrum.

Using Your Lens: an Example

Philosophers Immanuel Kant and David Hume both spent their professional careers searching for a universal principle of morality. Considering that they began their searches with seemingly irreconcilable ideas of where to look, the similarity in the moral systems they constructed is surprising. ...

Hume decided at the outset that a moral system must be practical, and maintained that, since reason is only useful for disinterested comparison, and since only sentiment (emotion) is capable of stirring people to action, the practical study of morality should be concerned with sentiment. Hume begins with the assumption that whether something is judged moral or praiseworthy depends on the circumstances. He says, "What each man feels within himself is the standard of sentiment." ...

By contrast, Kant begins by assuming that, while some time should be devoted to studying practical morality ("ethics"), it is also valuable to have an absolute system of morality based solely on reason, to be called "metaphysics". That forms the core of his laborious exploration of pure logic, called Grounding for the Metaphysics of Morals.

For both authors, the problem of subjectivity threatened to prevent unbiased analysis of morality. So both invented systems of "moral feedback," in which the philosophic actor tries to imagine the results of his actions as if someone else were performing them. Still, the final evaluation of the action's worth must, in the end, be subjective. Kant's ultimate standard of morality is the "categorical imperative". It is phrased, "[To follow your] duty, act as if the physical act of your action were to become a universal law of nature." This means that, before one does anything, one should forget one's own motives for a moment, and ask if he would want everyone to do as he does. If the answer is no, then his subjective desire is different from his objective assessment, and the action is contrary to duty.

Hume says that moral actions are those that create agreeable sentiments in others, as well as in oneself. You can therefore judge what kind of sentiments your actions may cause others to feel by imagining someone else performing that action, and thinking about what kind of sentiments it would inspire in you. To make both of these constructions possible, there is a notion of some kind of uniformity in people's reason or emotion in both works; Kant's reason for using pure logic was precisely to bypass empirical differences between people and individual circumstances, and ... he has the belief that people using only logic must inevitably reach the same conclusions about the morality of their own actions. Hume also admits that "the notion of morals implies some sentiment common to all mankind." ...

Some Marxist theorists have speculated that Marx would tar both Kant and Hume as "bourgeois" philosophers. Answering why is an extremely difficult question. ... It may lie in this sentence from Marx's Manuscripts of 1844: "The interests of the capitalist and those of the workers are therefore, one and the same, assert the bourgeois economists." ... In the directly preceding passage, Marx explained how capitalists try to mask the class struggle and exploitation inherent in capitalist production, by monopolizing cultural institutions to establish hegemonic control over the working class. This is why, he explains, workers are actually conditioned to be grateful to the factory owner for allowing them to produce goods, only to have these taken away and sold. Based on these writings, Marx would probably see any system that sought out a universal theory of morality as ignoring the opposing economic classes in society, and easily adapted to give the workers a false perception of the unitary interest of them and their oppressors.

Hume responded to the problem of subjectivity by suggesting the use of sentiment to evaluate actions. This is consistent with his belief that sentiment should guide morality.

Both Hume and Kant assume some type of uniformity among individuals. Kant assumes uniformity of reason. Hume assumes uniformity of sentiment. This is a new contrast that can be placed along our existing spectrum.

Marx objected to the assertion that the interests of the capitalists and the workers are the same. He probably would see systems of universal morality as likewise ignoring the differing interests of capitalists and workers. The contrast between universal morality and the differing interests of capitalists and workers is a new contrast that cannot be placed along our existing spectrum. A second spectrum is needed.

Hume's Morality	Kant's Morality
Practical (striving to action)	Practical is not sufficient
Sentiment	Reason
Relative-depends on circumstances	Absolute -does not depend on circumstances
Ethics	Metaphysics
System of moral feedback	
choice	Duty
agreeable	imperative
Uniform sentiment	Uniform reason

Note how consistently applying the old spectrum to new information allows you to follow the author's shifting ideas and interests.

SPECTRUM 4.5 > Hume and Kant vs. Marx

Hume and Kant	Marx
Universal morality	Differing interests of capitalists and workers

Remember, you may have to construct more than one spectrum if the author attends to multiple pairs of contrasts within the passage.

Notice that the author argues that despite beginning with seemingly irreconcilable premises, Kant and Hume arrive at similar conclusions, both of which assume some notion of uniformity among individuals. Marx, he suggests, would maintain that the differing interests of capitalists and workers oppose such uniformity.

In many cases, the author's viewpoint will fall along one or more spectra. You may find it helpful to indicate the placement of the author's viewpoint with an asterisk. The spectrum will allow you to clearly state his or her point of view.

The author here seems to prefer Hume over Kant based both on the enthusiasm of language and the amount of writing devoted to Hume. The author also seems to conclude by favoring Marx over both Hume and Kant.

Getting Comfortable with the Spectrum

Just like finding the main idea, developing a spectrum takes practice. At first it will be time-consuming. Start by developing the individual skills required while reading each passage. As you read, practice restating sentences and paragraphs. Make a mental note of each viewpoint introduced by the author, and consider its relationships to the other viewpoints presented in the passage.

Then, take as much time as you need to construct a spectrum. Take note of which skills you found most challenging. Was it restating the material, identifying contrasts, or revising and refining? With practice, the spectrum will become a useful shortcut for understanding the passage and answering the questions. Eventually this tool for organizing the passage will become second nature, and it will greatly enhance your ability to find the main idea and answer the questions.

DON'T FORGET YOUR KEYS

1. Use passage types to approach and master each new CARS passage.

2. When reading a CARS question stem, consider the type: use the main idea, parts of the argument, or application of new information.

3. Build a spectrum of opposing ideas and locate the author along the spectrum.

STOP!

DO NOT LOOK AT THESE EXAMS UNTIL CLASS.

30-MINUTE IN-CLASS EXAM FOR LECTURE ii

Passage I (Questions 1-7)

Neuro-Linguistic Programming (NLP) is a controversial theory about the connections between thought, language, and behavior. NLP involves attempting to improve people's communication skills by teaching them about the relationship between eye-movements and thought. Proponents of NLP claim that when right-handed people look up to their right, they are likely to be visualizing a "constructed" (i.e., imagined) event, while when they look up to their left they are likely to be visualizing a "remembered" memory (i.e., an event that has actually happened to them).

A recent experiment was performed to assess the validity of NLP eye movement as an indicator of lying. As part of the study, participants were first given the experimenter's cellular phone. They were then instructed to go into a private office, hide the phone in either their pocket or bag, and return to the briefing room. When asked what they did inside the office, participants either lied or told the truth, according to whether they had been assigned to the lying or not-lying group. No significant differences were observed in participants' eye movements between the lying and not-lying conditions.

In a second experiment, one group of participants was informed of the patterns of eye movement that NLP practitioners believe to be associated with lying while a control group was not. Both groups were presented with video clips and asked to assess whether the speaker was lying. They were also asked to rate their levels of confidence on a scale from 1 (not at all confident) to 7 (very confident). The results are displayed in Table 1.

	NLP-training condition (N=21)	Control condition (N=29)	p value
Mean correct	16.33	16.59	0.81
Mean confidence	4.65	4.58	0.67

Table 1. Mean number of correct judgments and rated confidence with and without NLP training

This passage was adapted from "The Eyes Don't Have It: Lie Detection and Neuro-Linguistic Programming." Wiseman R, Watt C, ten Brinke L, Porter S, Couper S-L, Rankin C. *PLoS ONE*. 2012. 7(7) doi:10.1371/journal.pone.0040259 for use under the terms of the Creative Commons CC BY 3.0 license (http://creativecommons.org/licenses/by/3.0/legalcode).

1. The findings described in the passage support the conclusion that:

   A. only trained practitioners can effectively use NLP to detect lies.
   B. NLP training is not effective at detecting lying.
   C. NLP training is inconsistent in effectively detecting lies.
   D. NLP training increases confidence among lie detectors.

2. Which of the following is an element of the experimental design that could pose an ethical concern?

   A. Some participants were asked to lie, which could lead to distress.
   B. Deception was used to mask the purpose of the study.
   C. The owner of the cellular phone was deceived.
   D. Some participants in the lying group may be more proficient at lying than others.

3. If experimenters modified the experiment so that participants in the first experiment were informed of NLP techniques prior to their participation in the experiment, how might this affect the data collected?

   A. Accuracy in collected data would be decreased by introducing systematic error.
   B. Accuracy in collected data would be decreased by introducing random error.
   C. Precision in collected data would be decreased by introducing systematic error.
   D. Precision in collected data would be decreased by introducing random error.

4. Researchers studying NLP were interested in the ability of NLP practitioners to develop their skills over time. In a follow-up experiment, researchers studied the subjects in the NLP-trained group from the second experiment and administered additional NLP testing at regular intervals over the course of two years. This experimental design is best classified as a(n):

   A. experimental study.
   B. cross-sectional study.
   C. cohort study.
   D. case-control study.

5. The researchers conducted a follow-up study of NLP to test the hypothesis that there are some situations in which NLP is effective. What is the greatest impediment to studying this hypothesis?

   A. The hypothesis would require a large number of experiments.
   B. The hypothesis is not falsifiable.
   C. The findings of the passage experiments disprove this hypothesis.
   D. Testing the hypothesis would require deception.

6. What would be the best test of significance to assess the findings of the second experiment?

   A. Chi-squared test
   B. Linear regression
   C. T-test
   D. A test of significance would not be appropriate in this instance.

GO ON TO THE NEXT PAGE.

7. According to the design of the experiments described in the passage, which of the following can be classified as independent variables?

   I. Rated confidence
   II. NLP instruction
   III. Lying or telling the truth

   A. I only
   B. II only
   C. II and III only
   D. I, II, and III

Passage II (Questions 8-14)

Stress describes the state of an organism when, under the influence of internal or external stimuli, the dynamic equilibrium of the organism is threatened. Stimuli can include combinations of physical or mental forces. The adaptive response to stress activates the components of the sympathoadreno-medullary (SAM) system, releasing key peripheral mediators, including the catecholamines epinephrine and norepinephrine.

Catecholamines work in concert with the autonomic nervous system to regulate the cardiovascular, pulmonary, hepatic, skeletal muscle, and immune systems. Excessive catecholamine signaling is known to have cytotoxic effects on the heart, stomach, and brain. A recent study investigated the effects of SAM activation on liver toxicity in movement-restrained mice, which are known to experience psychological and physical stress. Blood samples were collected every 30 minutes from immobilized mice over a period of six hours. Samples were analyzed for levels of *aspartate transaminase* (AST), a marker for hepatocyte apoptosis. Results of the experiment are shown in Figure 1.

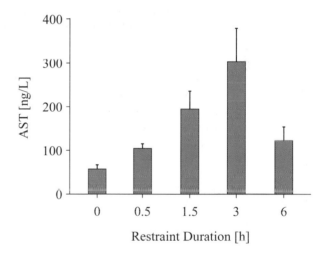

Figure 1. Mean AST concentrations (ng/L) in blood drawn at specific time points, measured in hours (h), during the restraint stress procedure. Values at each time point were tested for significance against initial blood levels (restraint duration 0). Error bars = standard deviation.

The experimenters also tested the efficacy of several compounds in preventing liver toxicity during restraint-induced stress. The restraint experiment was repeated using mice randomly assigned to pre-treatment with one of four different drugs. Liver tissue was then collected and analyzed for cell death markers following restraint treatment. Among the tested drugs, only the compound prazosin significantly lowered apoptosis to levels comparable with unrestrained animals.

This passage was adapted from "The Role of Alpha-1 and Alpha-2 Adrenoceptors in Restraint Stress-Induced Liver Injury in Mice." Zhu Q, Gu L, Wang Y, Jia L, Zhao Z, Peng S, Lei L. **PLoS ONE**. 2014. 9(3) doi:10.1371/journal.pone.0092125 for use under the terms of the Creative Commons CC BY 3.0 license (http://creativecommons.org/licenses/by/3.0/legalcode).

8. Which of the following statistical tests would be best suited to analyze the data collected in the second experiment described in the passage?

   A. T-test
   B. ANOVA
   C. Tollens test
   D. Linear regression

9. Suppose that the mean AST levels at 0 and 3 hours depicted in Figure 1 were found to be significantly different, with a p value of 0.01. Which of the following best explains the meaning of this finding?

   A. There is a one percent chance the alternate hypothesis is correct; the difference between groups cannot be due to random chance.
   B. There is a one percent chance the alternate hypothesis is correct; the difference between groups could be due to random chance.
   C. There is a one percent chance the null hypothesis is correct; the difference between groups cannot be due to random chance.
   D. There is a one percent chance the null hypothesis is correct; the difference between groups could be due to random chance.

10. The researchers described in the passage performed a third experiment to investigate whether daily antioxidant intake could mimic the protective effects of prazosin. In this experiment, mice were given food containing high quantities of glutathione, a known antioxidant, for two weeks before repeating the restraint-induced stress procedure and examining liver tissue for toxicity. Tissue samples were compared with those of untreated and prazosin-treated mice. Which of the following best describes the role of the prazosin-treated group?

   A. Positive control
   B. Negative control
   C. Independent variable
   D. Dependent variable

11. Which of the following is best represented by Figure 1?

   I. The central tendency of each data set
   II. The most common value in each data set
   III. The dispersion of each data set

   A. I and II only
   B. I and III only
   C. I only
   D. I, II, and III only

12. Which of the following statistical tests was most likely used to analyze the data depicted in Figure 1?

   A. One-tailed t-test
   B. Paired t-test
   C. Unpaired t-test
   D. Chi-squared test

13. Which of the following best explains why the second experiment described in the passage involved random assignment to experimental groups?

   A. To ensure significance is found between groups
   B. To increase subjectivity
   C. To neutralize the influence of variability within the subject population
   D. To eliminate bias by ensuring that all data is continuous rather than categorical

14. Suppose the researchers described in the passage also found a statistically significant relationship between body fat percentage and stress-induced liver damage. Given the passage information, which of the following could **NOT** be possible?

   A. A correlational test proved that hepatocyte apoptosis is dependent on body fat percentage.
   B. High body fat percentages were correlated with lower risk of hepatocyte apoptosis.
   C. Low body fat percentages were correlated with lower risk of hepatocyte apoptosis.
   D. A chi-squared analysis revealed significant deviation from expected liver toxicity at extremely low body fat percentages.

Passage III (Questions 15-21)

Rechargeable batteries are composed of electrochemical cells whose reactions are electrically reversible. Recent research has focused on the use of lithium/sulfur cells in rechargeable batteries. These cells are composed of a lithium anode, a carbon-sulfur cathode, and an electrolytic solution through which lithium ions pass from the anode to the cathode. The cathode in this battery is in liquid form. When lithium arrives at the cathode, it reacts with sulfur as shown in Reaction 1. Before forming the final product, a number of aqueous lithium polysulfide (PS) intermediates are passed through as shown in Reaction 2.

$$2\,Li^+ + S^{2-} \rightarrow Li_2S$$

Reaction 1

$$Li_2S_{8(aq)} \rightarrow Li_2S_{6(aq)} \rightarrow Li_2S_{4(aq)} \rightarrow Li_2S_{2(s)} \rightarrow Li_2S_{(s)}$$

Reaction 2

Performance of the lithium/sulfur cell is affected by the properties of these PS intermediates. When PS dissolves into the liquid electrolyte, it is able to more readily react with non-conductive sulfur. Reducing the electrolyte volume/sulfur weight (E/S) ratio affects cell performance in two ways: it suppresses Reaction 2, which prevents lithium sulfide from precipitating, and it also increases the solution's viscosity. Researchers sought to determine the E/S ratio that would result in the highest capacity retention, meaning maintained capacity over the course of multiple cycles, in the lithium/sulfur cell. They looked at how battery capacity changed per cycle in lithium/sulfur cells that had E/S ratios of 5, 10, and 15. Results are shown in Figure 1.

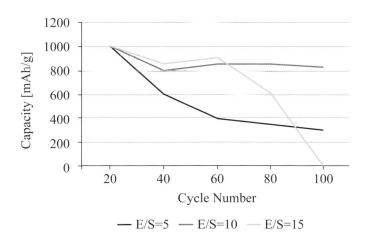

Figure 1. Capacity retention relative to cycle number

This passage was adapted from "Improved Cyclability of Liquid Electrolyte Lithium/Sulfur Batteries by Optimizing Electrolyte/Sulfur Ratio." Zhang, Sheng. *Energies*. 2012. 5(12) doi:10.3390/en5125190 for use under the terms of the Creative Commons Attribution 3.0 License (http://creativecommons.org/licenses/by/3.0/legalcode).

15. Why does the solution with an E/S ratio of 10 best maintain charge capacity?

A. It has a higher rate of Reaction 2 than the solution with an E/S ratio of 15 and lower viscosity than the solution with an E/S ratio of 5.

B. It has a lower rate of Reaction 2 than the solution with an E/S ratio of 15 and lower viscosity than the solution with an E/S ratio of 5.

C. It has a higher rate of Reaction 2 than the solution with an E/S ratio of 15 and higher viscosity than the solution with an E/S ratio of 5.

D. It has a lower rate of Reaction 2 than the solution with an E/S ratio of 15 and higher viscosity than the solution with an E/S ratio of 5.

16. Given only the results presented in Figure 1, which additional E/S ratio would the researchers most likely choose to test?

A. 4
B. 16
C. 9
D. None of the above

17. When designing the study, it was likely most important for the researchers to control for which of the following properties of the electrolyte solvent?

A. Molar mass
B. Density
C. Polarity
D. Volume

18. Researchers noted that the voltmeter they were using to measure charge capacity showed a reading of 10mV even when disconnected. This error is most likely to affect the measurements':

A. accuracy.
B. precision
C. accuracy and precision.
D. type of measurement scale.

19. According to Figure 1, which E/S ratio has the worst long term cycling efficiency?

   A. E/S = 5
   B. E/S = 10
   C. E/S = 15
   D. E/S = 5 and E/S = 15 are equally inefficient.

20. Researchers repeated the described experiment ten times and noted at which cycle charge capacity dropped below 50% for E/S = 5 cells and E/S = 15 cells. A two-tailed t-test comparing these datasets returned a p value of 0.007. Which of the following describes a conclusion that researchers could appropriately draw from these results?

   A. E/S = 5 cells have significantly longer-lasting capacity than E/S = 15 cells.
   B. E/S = 15 cells have significantly longer-lasting capacity than E/S = 5 cells.
   C. There is no significant difference between E/S = 5 and E/S = 15 capacity.
   D. More information would be necessary to draw any of the above conclusions.

21. Suppose the researchers later find that E/S ratio is closely correlated with conductivity and that conductivity affects capacity retention. Which of the following best describes the implications of this finding?

   A. Conductivity is a confounding variable that threatens internal validity.
   B. Conductivity is a confounding variable that threatens external validity.
   C. Conductivity is a biased variable that threatens internal validity.
   D. Conductivity is a biased variable that threatens external validity.

STOP. IF YOU FINISH BEFORE TIME IS CALLED, CHECK YOUR WORK. YOU MAY GO BACK TO ANY QUESTION IN THIS TEST BOOKLET.

STOP.

30-MINUTE IN-CLASS EXAM FOR LECTURE 1

The digital revolution has manifested itself in a range of cultural changes that are in many ways far more radical than the ones unleashed by the invention of the printing press over five hundred years ago, and they have made their presence felt far more swiftly. While those earlier changes took centuries before their impact was fully realized, the digital revolution has redefined our communicative world in decades. And whereas the invention of moveable type preserved the basic form of the codex, the digital revolution has altered the most fundamental ways that it is possible to think about the materiality of writing, and about the relation between books and texts.

That is the upside. But if the extraordinarily rapid and wide-ranging changes unleashed by the digital revolution have shaken up our most entrenched assumptions about important forms of cultural production and reception in critically exciting ways, it is equally true that it is hard to think of a time when the humanities were so badly besieged on any number of levels, the most serious of which has been a jarring shift in research priorities towards market-driven applied knowledge: a retrenchment that has foregrounded all over again the question of how to make the case for the value of the humanities.

History repeats itself, but never in quite the same way. The single most important aspect of this history may be the fact that the humanities emerged in their modern form during an age not unlike our own, in which leading activists resisted any vision of reform that was not driven by a central recognition of the importance of applied knowledge. For utilitarians such as Thomas Love Peacock (a poet himself in earlier days), the poet was "a waster of his own time, and a robber of that of others," whose cultivation of poetry had been "to the neglect of some branch of useful study," in stark contrast with the tendency of "the thinking and studious" to draw on "the materials of useful knowledge" in order to prepare for "the real business of life."

Scientists within and outside of universities have been equally outraged by what they regard as an unprecedented attack on the idea of curiosity-driven abstract research. In December 2012, hundreds of leading scientists in lab coats marched to protest being muzzled by a government that is mistrustful of any sort of research that is not in step with their business agenda. Five months later, John McDougall, the businessman who serves as President of Canada's National Research Council, made headlines by insisting that "innovation is not valuable unless it has commercial value." McDougall's comments were part of an announcement of a broader shift in the NRC's focus towards research the government deems "commercially viable."

The crisis that forces us to make the case for the humanities today in the face of similar pressures to focus on "useful knowledge" that is suited to "the real business of life" can best be answered with a clearer understanding of the ways that ideas about the humanities were forged in the crucible of this spirit of intellectual reaction which defined itself in terms of the unique importance of more "serious" forms of knowledge. For early

nineteenth-century theoreticians, the arts constituted a central aspect of a larger struggle for social progress, but like today, these arguments were themselves sharpened by the need to challenge a utilitarian emphasis on the primacy of applied knowledge.

This passage was adapted from "'Imagining What We Know': The Humanities in a Utilitarian Age." Keen, P. Humanities. 2014. 3(1) doi:10.3390/h3010073 for use under the terms of the Creative Commons CC BY 3.0 license (http://creativecommons.org/licenses/by/3.0/legalcode).

22. Based on the information presented in the passage, which of the following changes would the author consider the best remedy to the current state of the humanities?

   A. An understanding that the materiality of writing need not affect the content that it conveys
   B. An increase in public sector funding for the basic sciences
   C. A recognition that applied research can be better contextualized through the lens of the humanities
   D. A hearkening back to the primacy of applied knowledge

23. Which of the following is **LEAST** supported by information presented in the passage?

   A. The digital revolution has changed the nature of the humanities.
   B. Studying the humanities makes for a more well-rounded person.
   C. There is a historical precedent to the current changes in the humanities.
   D. Research funding is harder to acquire for research in the humanities.

24. How would Thomas Peacock most likely view a biologist studying the mechanism of a particular class of ion pumps?

   A. The scientist is engaged in a valuable enterprise that benefits society.
   B. The pursuit of knowledge for knowledge's sake is a pointless endeavor.
   C. The scientist ought to spend more time studying the humanities.
   D. The scientist should instead study business.

25. It is reasonable to infer from the language used in the passage that the author believes which of the following about John McDougall's statements?

   A. McDougall raises legitimate concerns about the financial solvency of certain kinds of research.
   B. McDougall supports the plight of leading scientists facing budgetary constraints.
   C. McDougall is misinformed about the commercial viability of certain kinds of research.
   D. McDougall has misaligned priorities regarding research funding.

26. Which of the following statements best articulates the author's views on the role of academia outside of the humanities?

   A. Academia outside of the humanities is a more practical course of study.
   B. Academia outside of the humanities is more financially burdened than the humanities.
   C. Academia outside of the humanities is a less worthy pursuit than the humanities.
   D. The author does not express an opinion about academia outside of the humanities.

27. Which of the following statements, if true, would most weaken the author's argument?

   A. Research in the humanities is better funded now than it has ever been.
   B. The digital revolution had little effect on the humanities.
   C. The humanities have not lost any ground to the basic sciences.
   D. The situation of the utilitarians was markedly different from that of the humanities today.

28. Which passage topic could be considered a more "serious" form of knowledge, as defined in paragraph 5?

   A. "entrenched assumptions" in paragraph 2.
   B. "market-driven applied knowledge" in paragraph 2.
   C. "the humanities" in paragraph 2.
   D. "curiosity-driven abstract research" in paragraph 4.

Passage II (Questions 29-35)

In the Bible, when Jesus Christ was queried by skeptical Israelites on how Christians could continue to pay taxes to support the (pagan) Roman governors of Israel, he counseled, "Render unto Caesar what is Caesar's; render unto God what is God's." The basic meaning of this guidance was that Christians may practice their faith while coexisting with the secular government. Later Christian theorists followed this example, often urging peaceful coexistence even with governments which violated every precept of Christian teachings, in accordance with the teachings of Jesus that were laid out in the New Testament as the foundation of the Christian religion.

The early Catholic bishop (St.) Augustine of Hippo and the Protestant dissident leader Martin Luther both advocated submission to the rule of tyrants, employing the analogy of a *dual* city or government, where earthly rule is often oppressive, yet is balanced by the assurance of brotherly love in the kingdom of heaven.

According to Luther, true Christians should be willing to suffer persecution, without seeking to resist it by the anti-Christian methods of taking up arms in violent revolt, or seeking redress in the courts of the unbelievers. Luther even took the analogy so far as to suggest that it is the Christians themselves who most benefit from harsh secular laws, which protect *them* from exploitation and persecution by false Christians and heathen. In fact, when commenting on popular "Christian" uprisings, Luther lays more blame on self-righteous Christian rebels (such as various German peasant rebels of the age) than upon their oppressors, teaching that, regardless of their rulers' faults, rebels immediately cease to be Christians upon taking up arms, and incur further displeasure from God by blasphemously arrogating His name and scriptures for an un-Christian cause. Luther claims that this is furthermore exacerbated because what the rebels often want is material benefit rather than religious freedom. According to Luther, it is the role of God alone to punish rulers, and rebels' usurpation of that authority for themselves adds another sin to the list of charges against them; they effectively revolt against God's justice.

St. Augustine would have agreed. His *Confessions* and other theological writings maintained that God grants earthly rule to Christians and pagans alike, but that His inscrutable will is always just. In the case of a revolt, Luther claimed, *both* sides inevitably incur divine punishment, since "God hates both tyrants and rebels; therefore He sets them on each other." Luther's vision of God raising up the peasants to punish their tyrants perfectly matches Augustine's frequent portrayal of the Germanic "barbarians" who finally sacked Rome as the brutal instruments of God, sent to crush the corrupt Romans' arrogance. Augustine never considers the individual fate of these living tools, but Luther maintains that God sends the devil to stir them up with lies, and afterwards they go to eternal torment.

Both of these theologians would hold that uprisings generally occur for the wrong reasons (i.e. worldly ambitions), because no tyrant can keep a true Christian from salvation, which should be all Christians' only concern in life. For Luther, salvation lies in faith emanating from personal understanding of Biblical teachings, and "it is impossible that anyone should have the gospel kept from

GO ON TO THE NEXT PAGE.

him...for it is a public teaching that moves freely." In Augustine's understanding, salvation is granted through the mercy of God, who sends hardship and death to test men's faith. The true Augustinian Christian would maintain his faith through any ordeal, and even if his body perishes, God will save him for his conviction.

29. Which of the following statements, if true, would most directly *challenge* the principles of Martin Luther?

    A. The Bible's Old Testament refers to a period before the birth of Jesus.
    B. The Bible alone contains only a small part of what Jesus intended for his followers.
    C. The German "barbarians" who sacked Rome had been previously converted.
    D. Augustine's understanding of salvation granted through the mercy of Christ was flawed.

30. Some theologians believe that killing and violence are acceptable when used in self-defense. An appropriate clarification of the passage would be the stipulation that:

    A. both Luther and Augustine would have disagreed with this belief.
    B. both Luther and Augustine would have agreed with this belief.
    C. only Augustine might have agreed with this belief.
    D. only Luther might have agreed with this belief.

31. If the information in paragraph 4 is correct, one could most reasonably conclude that, compared to Luther, Augustine was:

    A. much more reasonably inclined.
    B. more prepared to define God's will.
    C. less eager to send people to eternal torment.
    D. less willing to announce God's final judgment on those who had sinned.

32. The author's attitude toward the theories of Augustine and Luther in the passage is most accurately described as:

    A. disapproving.
    B. mistrustful.
    C. neutral.
    D. favorable.

33. Which is the most likely meaning of the passage statement that "The true Augustinian Christian would maintain his faith through any ordeal, and even if his body perishes, God will save him for his conviction" (paragraph 5)?

    A. This Christian would end up in heaven because of his beliefs.
    B. God would save this Christian for judgment at the end of the Christian's ordeal.
    C. God would save this Christian from his ordeal and judge him.
    D. It was not necessary for this Christian to die for him to be convicted.

34. The author's primary purpose in the passage is apparently:

    A. to clarify the differences between the ways in which the early Catholics and Protestants dealt with persecution.
    B. to justify the persecution of early Christians by secular governments.
    C. to consider the similarities between the ways in which the early Catholics and Protestants dealt with persecution.
    D. to question the passive practices of the early Catholics and Protestants when faced with persecution.

35. What is the most serious apparent weakness of the information described?

    A. While implying that Christians may coexist with a secular government, it differentiates between Catholics and Protestants.
    B. While implying representation of Augustine and Luther, its conclusions are based primarily on information according to Luther.
    C. While implying representation of all Christian theorists, only Augustine and Luther are mentioned.
    D. While implying agreement between Augustine and Luther, their attitudes were clearly opposed.

GO ON TO THE NEXT PAGE.

Passage III (Questions 36-42)

Of all the bizarre and melancholy fates that could befall an otherwise ordinary person, Mary Mallon's has to be among the most sad and peculiar. Like millions before and since, she came to this country from Ireland, seeking a better life. Never "tried" in any sense, instead, she was forced by public health officials to live for a total of 26 years on a tiny island in the East River, isolated from and shunned by her fellow humans. And, while she was not the only one of her kind, her name became synonymous with disease and death. She was Typhoid Mary, and her story really begins on Long Island.

In the summer of 1906, Mallon was working as a cook for a wealthy New York banker, Charles Henry Warren, and his family. The Warrens had rented a spacious house in Oyster Bay, "in a desirable part of the village," for the summer. From August 27 to September 3, six of the eleven people in the house came down with typhoid fever, including Mrs. Warren, two daughters, two maids and a gardener. Two investigators were unable to find contaminated water or food to explain the outbreak. Worried they wouldn't be able to rent the house unless they figured out the source of the disease, the owners, in the winter of 1906, hired George Soper, a sanitary engineer.

Soper soon dismissed "soft clams" and other potential contaminants as the cause and began to focus on the family. He later wrote, "It was found that the family had changed cooks about three weeks before the typhoid epidemic broke out ... She remained with the family only a short time, leaving about three weeks after the outbreak occurred ... [and] seemed to be in perfect health." Soper became convinced that this woman was a healthy carrier of the disease, and, in so doing, was the first to identify a healthy typhoid carrier in the United States. Although his deduction was undoubtedly brilliant, his handling of Mallon was not.

Soper tracked Mallon down to a home on Park Avenue in Manhattan where she was a cook. Appearing without warning, Soper told her she was spreading death and disease through her cooking and that he wanted samples of her feces, urine, and blood for tests. In a later description, Soper wrote, "It did not take Mary long to react to this suggestion. She seized a carving fork and advanced in my direction. I passed rapidly down the narrow hall through the tall iron gate."

Convinced by Soper's information, the New York City health inspector in March 1907 carried Mallon off, screaming and kicking, to a hospital, where her feces did indeed show high concentrations of typhoid bacilli. She was moved to an isolation cottage on the grounds of the Riverside Hospital, between the Bronx and Rikers Island.

She stayed there for three years, in relative isolation. It was during that time that she was dubbed Typhoid Mary. Mallon despised the moniker and protested all her life that she was healthy and could not be a disease carrier. As she told a newspaper, "I have never had typhoid in my life and have always been healthy. Why should I be banished like a leper and compelled to live in solitary confinement?" After a short period of freedom in which Mallon failed to comply with the health inspector's requirements, she was eventually sent back to North Brother Island, where she lived the rest of her life, alone in a one-room cottage. In 1938 when she died,

a newspaper noted there were 237 other typhoid carriers living under city health department observation. But she was the only one kept isolated for years, a result as much of prejudice toward the Irish and noncompliant women as of a public health threat.

36. The author probably mentions that Mallon was "never 'tried' in any sense" (paragraph 1) in order to:

    A. demonstrate the power of the wealthy at that time.
    B. provide a comparison with people who have actually committed a crime.
    C. illustrate the persistence of Soper's investigations.
    D. support the claim that she deserved at least a hearing.

37. According to the passage, the first two investigators were unable to find the cause of the outbreak (paragraph 2). The information presented on typhoid makes which of the following explanations most plausible?

    A. They focused too closely on the "soft clams" that Soper later discredited.
    B. Typhoid is not really passed through contaminated food or water.
    C. They never considered that typhoid could be carried by a healthy person.
    D. By this time, Mallon was no longer employed by the Warren family.

38. The author's argument in the last paragraph that Mallon's isolation was "a result as much of prejudice ... as of a public health threat" is most weakened by which idea in the passage?

    A. Mallon's primary occupation was as a cook.
    B. Mallon did not believe that she was a carrier of the disease.
    C. Mallon would not abide by the health inspector's requirements.
    D. Mallon actually was the source of the typhoid outbreak in the Warren home.

39. Which of the following statements is the most reasonable conclusion that can be drawn from the author's description of the typhoid outbreak in the house at Oyster Bay?

    A. The Warren family did not hire Soper.
    B. The two investigators were hired by the Warrens.
    C. The Warren family hired Soper.
    D. The owners were anxious to sell the house.

GO ON TO THE NEXT PAGE.

40. Passage information indicates that which of the following statements must be true?

   A. Mallon had probably not infected anyone prior to the Warren family.
   B. Mallon was almost certainly not washing her hands prior to preparing the Warren's meals.
   C. Being labeled 'Typhoid Mary' by the press was the primary reason for her confinement.
   D. The health inspector was doubtless prejudiced toward the Irish.

41. According to passage information, Mallon worked for the Warren family for approximately:

   A. two weeks.
   B. three weeks.
   C. five weeks.
   D. six weeks.

42. The contention in the last paragraph that in "1938 when [Mallon] died, ... there were 237 other typhoid carriers living under city health department observation. But she was the only one kept isolated for years" can most justifiably be interpreted as support for the idea that:

   A. Mallon was unfairly treated by the city health department.
   B. Mallon's isolation might have stemmed from the health department's early ignorance of the disease.
   C. the "other" 237 typhoid carriers were all kept isolated at one time or another.
   D. the "other" 237 typhoid carriers were much like Mallon.

STOP. IF YOU FINISH BEFORE TIME IS CALLED, CHECK YOUR WORK. YOU MAY GO BACK TO ANY QUESTION IN THIS TEST BOOKLET.

STOP.

30-MINUTE IN-CLASS EXAM FOR LECTURE 2

Polling research shows that the ideal speaking voice should be clear and intelligible, of moderate volume and pace, and inflected to suggest the emotions expressed. To suggest credibility, the voice's tone should be pitched as low as is naturally possible. A low pitch is desirable because it is popularly associated with truth-telling. However, an artificially lowered voice can sacrifice intelligibility, which is irritating to listeners. Thus, speakers should experiment to find their optimal level, which will be at their lowest intelligible pitch. To deepen the pitch, speakers should make an extra-deep inhalation before speaking, and then exhale fully as they speak.

Habits to be avoided (because they irritate most listeners) include monotony, mumbling, grating, pretension, high-pitched whining, and breathiness. Among the best practitioners of mainstream vocal "propriety" are famous news anchors, like Walter Cronkite, Dan Rather, and Jane Pauley, for whom vocal image is a key component of their job success. However, everyone who communicates should be aware that their voice is a critical component of their audience's perceptions of them, comprising about 38% of the overall impression imparted by their presentation. (By comparison, appearance accounts for about 50% of the speaker's impact, and the quality of content accounts for a mere 6%.)

For those not born with naturally pleasant voices, or worse still, those with naturally unpleasant ones, speech training can be invaluable in improving impressions. No voice teacher is necessarily required, since practice alone can produce significant improvements. However, some special equipment is needed. Because talking always causes cranial resonance, which distorts the speaker's hearing, no one can hear what his voice really sounds like to a listener. Thus, some sort of tape recorder or other feedback is a virtual necessity.

Speaking begins with breathing, since speech is just exhaled air that sets the vocal cords to resonating. If insufficient air is inhaled before speaking, the words formed must necessarily be strained and breathless. Diaphragmatic breathing results in a deeper voice than upper-lung breathing. People tend to stick out their chests and inhale shallowly with the upper lungs, resulting in a high-pitched voice, which must also be rapid to avoid running out of breath before the sentence ends. In diaphragmatic breathing, the lower abdomen moves out, inflating the bottom two-thirds of the lungs fully, but the shoulders do not rise. To practice switching from shallow breathing to deep, diaphragmatic inhalations, it helps to lie on the floor and breathe naturally, since diaphragmatic breathing is natural when prone. Increasing lung capacity will also deepen the voice and permit longer sentences without pausing. One method to increase lung capacity is to inhale fully, then count out loud slowly, while enunciating each number clearly, aiming for a count of 60.

Loudness, or volume, is distinct from pitch, though the remedy for overly soft-spoken people is similar. They can manage to speak louder by first inhaling more deeply, which allows them added lungpower to project their sentences. Alternately, they can pause more often and say fewer words in every breath, thus leaving more air power for each. There are those who speak too softly not because of improper breathing, but due to psychological factors: they may be shy and not wish to be obtrusive, or may not hear that their words are too soft to be intelligible at a distance. For them, one useful exercise is to recognize the five basic volume levels (whisper, hushed, conversation, loud, and yelling) by practicing speaking a word in each of these modes.

43. According to the passage information, which of the following would be most likely if a person who was talking to you attempted to make their voice sound unusually low?

   A. You might think that they were lying.
   B. They could be irritated with you.
   C. They might well sound monotonous.
   D. You could find them difficult to understand.

44. The author most likely believes that one of the main purposes of speaking during a face-to-face meeting should be to:

   A. convey a favorable impression.
   B. effectively transmit your ideas.
   C. gain leverage.
   D. communicate as naturally as possible.

45. In the second paragraph, the author provides a list of "habits to be avoided." Which of the habits would the suggestions in this passage not help a speaker to curb?

   A. Monotony
   B. Breathiness
   C. Pretension
   D. High-pitched whining

46. The term "ideal speaking voice," as used in the first paragraph, refers implicitly to a voice that is:

   A. the most pleasant to listen to.
   B. the most persuasive.
   C. the least irritating.
   D. the most natural.

47. Passage information indicates that a person speaking in a high-pitched voice might be doing all of the following EXCEPT:

   I. Breathing with their upper lungs
   II. Breathing deeply
   III. Lying

   A. I only
   B. II only
   C. III only
   D. I and III only

GO ON TO THE NEXT PAGE.

48. Which of the following assertions is most clearly a thesis presented by the author?

   A. Speakers can gain by improving their speaking voices.
   B. The tone of the ideal speaking voice should be pitched as low as possible.
   C. What you are saying is more important than how you are saying it.
   D. Emotional inflections can be an irritating aspect of a speaker's voice.

49. The ideas discussed in this passage would likely be of most use to:

   A. a doctor.
   B. a journalist.
   C. a radio show personality.
   D. a television commentator.

Passage II (Questions 50-56)

A great deal of international conflict arises from border disputes. Throughout history, particularly along borders which have been "artificially" defined, rather than utilizing more natural pre-existing cultural and geographical demarcations, there has been a constant ebb and flow as nations have sought to consolidate their borders and their security. However, with ever-increasing economic disparity between many bordering countries, these conflicts have changed and now center more around issues of immigration. Such situations are prevalent today in countries such as New Zealand, the Colombian-Peruvian border, and the U.S.'s Mexican border. These instances exemplify the problems caused by such disputes.

Presently, New Zealand's conflict stems from illegal immigration into its territory, mostly from the Chinese island-province Fujian. Fujian is situated on China's southern coast, near Taiwan. Many Fujianese immigrants use New Zealand, because of its location, as a stepping-stone to their final goal, the U.S. Their transport is usually a smuggling boat's hold, where living conditions are inadequate and sometimes dangerous, with insufficient food, sanitation, and ventilation. Within the past year, U.S. officials found three Chinese immigrants in a smuggling boat's sealed cargo container, dead from suffocation. Recently, New Zealand attempted to deal with these aliens by enacting new immigration laws which hasten the process required to deport them.

The reasons for the Chinese immigrant's journey stems from both "push" and "pull" factors relative to the countries of origin and destination. For example, the Fujianese feel compelled ("pushed") to leave because of the area's low standard of living. The poor wages, bad housing, and lack of political freedom can also be seen as "pull" factors, due to the idea that the Fujianese understand that life would be better in other countries. The U.S. and New Zealand offer much higher wages, a better standard of living, and political freedom. These push and pull factors are powerful incentives. What keeps New Zealand from experiencing an even more profound illegal immigration problem is that the immigrants often do not settle there.

The border issue between Colombia and its neighbors is another illustration of international conflict. Colombia lies along a corridor from South to Central America. This region has historically been politically unstable, partially due to regional narcotics trafficking, and the wars this engenders. Colombia, itself, is notorious for its export of drugs, especially cocaine. This reputation forces neighboring countries to strengthen patrols over adjoining borders. Recently, Peru deployed additional soldiers to its border with Colombia. Although Peruvian President Fujimori denied any diplomatic problems and stated his troops were there "to guarantee the sovereignty and integrity of Peruvian territory," their mission is both to keep guerrillas and drugs out of Peru. Though understandable, this has in turn pushed Colombia to respond in kind with more Colombian border troops facing Peru. This brinksmanship seriously depletes resources from these needy countries which might be better spent elsewhere.

Traditionally, these two countries might have been attempting to secure their borders from invading countries, or even seeking to expand their own territories and acquire additional resources.

GO ON TO THE NEXT PAGE.

However, Ecuador and Peru are protecting their borders from rogue drug traffickers and guerillas, not Colombia's government. Neither side is attempting to acquire new territory, but rather to secure and protect that which they already hold.

50. The author's discussion of "push" and "pull" factors in paragraph 3 most accurately implies that:

    A. "pull" factors compel someone to leave, while "push" factors induce someone to come.
    B. "pull" factors induce someone to come, while "push" factors also induce someone to come.
    C. "push" factors require someone to leave, while "pull" factors also compel someone to leave.
    D. "push" factors compel someone to leave, while "pull" factors induce someone to come.

51. Given the information in the passage, if "'artificially' defined" borders (paragraph one) were eliminated throughout the world, which of the following outcomes would most likely occur?

    A. People would naturally immigrate to areas with higher standards of living.
    B. Nations would encounter less traditional border strife.
    C. Nations would require greater border security measures.
    D. People would live more harmoniously.

52. Which of the following assertions does the author support with an example?

    A. Transportation methods used by illegal immigrants are sometimes dangerous.
    B. Peru and Colombia are seeking to expand their own territories.
    C. New Zealand has enacted laws that hasten deportation proceedings.
    D. The mission of the Peruvian troops is to keep guerillas and drugs out of Peru.

53. The passage as a whole suggests that in order for a nation to slow the exodus of its inhabitants to other countries, it must:

    A. become more attractive to those who are leaving.
    B. abandon the traditional methods of guarding borders.
    C. respond in some way to the conflicts arising from border disputes.
    D. answer the challenges set forth by adjoining countries.

54. If the passage information is correct, what inference is justified by the fact that virtually no immigration from West Berlin to adjoining East Berlin occurred, over the 40 years before the period described?

    A. Crossing the heavily guarded borders between West and East Berlin was very dangerous.
    B. It was understood that life would be better in East Berlin.
    C. The inhabitants of both 'Berlins' were happy to remain where they were.
    D. The economic conditions of West Berlin were much more favorable than those of East Berlin.

55. The author implies that which of the following is not one of the reasons that Peruvian President Fujimori deployed soldiers to its borders with Colombia?

    I. Fujimori is attempting to keep drugs out of his country.
    II. Fujimori fears that Colombia is seeking to expand its territories.
    III. Fujimori is probably concerned that Colombia wants to acquire additional resources.

    A. I only
    B. II only
    C. III only
    D. II and III only

56. It seems likely that New Zealand may be suffering less from immigration issues than the United States for which of the following reasons?

    I. The U.S. offers higher wages than New Zealand.
    II. New laws enacted in New Zealand allow faster deportation proceedings.
    III. Immigrants often do not settle in New Zealand.

    A. II only
    B. III only
    C. II and III only
    D. I, II, and III

GO ON TO THE NEXT PAGE.

Passage III (Questions 57-63)

Perhaps the greatest problem with the law of personal injury is its uncertainty about its own purpose—does it exist to compensate victims fully, or to deter careless wrongdoers fully? It must choose, because these two aims are mutually exclusive: tort awards cannot *fully* compensate and *correctly* deter, as long as there are administrative costs involved in obtaining an award. Assume a plaintiff's lawyer charges a 30% contingency fee upon winning a case (or the equivalent flat fee). If the plaintiff is awarded 100% of the damages suffered, she only receives compensation for 70% of her injuries. If she is paid in full, then the defendant is paying 130% of the actual harm caused, and is over-deterred.

In reality, compensation tends toward inadequacy, and not just because of administrative costs. There is no compensation unless the plaintiff proves "negligence," meaning a person may cause any amount of harm, but be excused from paying because she acted "reasonably" rather than carelessly. The hurdle of proving negligence also tends toward inadequate deterrence, because even negligent injurers escape liability if plaintiffs cannot collect convincing proof of negligence.

On the other hand, in a few cases, both compensation and deterrence are exorbitant, especially when a single jury award tries to be both. Consider the following permutation on actual events. A tanker passing through a residential neighborhood leaks acrylonitrile, destroying several homes and poisoning one. Angry residents sue the company for designing its tanker cars negligently. At trial, the company's counsel—a good economist, but a poor lawyer—admits safer tankers were available, but the cost is prohibitive. After extensive cost-benefit analyses, he says, the company found it cheaper just to pay victims for their losses, as it now offers to do. Sound fair? The company would be lucky to escape punitive damages! Remember, these have been applied where judges deemed that even full compensation is inadequate deterrence; generally when the plaintiff's conduct is seen as malicious. However, they may also be awarded when there is "a conscious and deliberate disregard of others." In this case, the company's cost-benefit analysis is economically "correct" and justifiable: if the new tanker costs more than it saves, it is inefficient. On the other hand, how many juries—or even judges—will see this very analysis as anything but a cold and calculating balancing of profits against the costs of human life? If (arbitrary) punitive damages are granted, plaintiffs emerge overcompensated, and defendants pay out of proportion to harm. Since repeated punitive awards are allowed, the company may be forced to buy the expensive tankers. This is unfortunate, because it results in a waste of resources.

Tort law, gradually realizing the difficulty of proving negligence, has moved towards allowing recovery with ever less proof of negligence. Potentially, the most promising development in tort (personal injury) law has been the advent of strict liability, which waives plaintiffs' need to prove the defendant's carelessness in certain instances where the carelessness is obvious, or could have resulted from no factor other than negligence. Unfortunately, the *application* of strict liability is severely constrained by legal doctrine, which limits its application to a small range of "unusually hazardous activities."

Sometimes, the criteria for imposing strict liability seem arbitrary. For example, the law permits strict liability only when the expected damage—a product of risk and probable harm—is high. Yet it is equally appropriate when the damage is *slight*. Consider the same tanker spilling toxic chemicals along a 200-mile stretch of farmland. Imagine the total cost of decontamination is $1,000,000, but the costs are borne by 150 small farmers. In this scenario, the total damage is high, but comes to only $6,667 per plaintiff. Since just proving negligence may cost more, few will actually sue. The same applies for small harms; there is neither compensation nor deterrence, because plaintiffs bear the loss, and defendants effectively have no incentive to prevent small harms.

57. Suppose that a woman spilled hot McDonald's coffee in her lap and successfully sued for several million dollars. How would the author most likely respond?

   A. This case does not reflect that compensation is usually insufficient.
   B. This case is a good example of just the right amount of compensation.
   C. This case does not reflect that deterrence is costly.
   D. In this case, the woman was malicious.

58. Which of the following assertions is the most effective argument *against* the author's opinion that personal injury law cannot satisfactorily compensate and deter "as long as there are administrative costs involved in obtaining an award" (paragraph 1)?

   A. These administrative costs are inconsequential.
   B. Attorneys are a necessary part of the judicial system and should be compensated for their work.
   C. The administrative costs should be added to the compensation received by the plaintiff.
   D. The administrative costs should be subtracted from the compensation received by the plaintiff.

59. The passage indicates that its author would **NOT** agree with which of the following statements?

   A. Tanker companies are a good example of defendants who are under-deterred.
   B. Negligence on the part of the defendant is generally not difficult for the plaintiff to prove.
   C. The costs associated with suing and defending against suits can be tremendous.
   D. In many situations, over-deterrence results in primarily economic ramifications.

60. Assume that since the 9-11 terrorist attacks on the World Trade Center (WTC) buildings, all lawsuits have been settled by the WTC insurance companies, who have now mandated that they will no longer insure any building in the world that is over five stories tall. The author's comments suggest that this situation could reasonably be interpreted as evidence that:

   A. the insurance companies were over-deterred.
   B. the insurance companies were under-deterred.
   C. the plaintiffs were under-compensated.
   D. the plaintiffs were overcompensated.

GO ON TO THE NEXT PAGE.

61. Suppose that a study found that police agencies routinely set aside large amounts of money in their yearly budgets, which they expect to pay out in lawsuits against their agency. Which of the following statements is an assumption of the author about the effects of lawsuit awards that would be called into question?

   A. Simply proving negligence can be a very costly process.
   B. Many people will not sue because the process is too costly.
   C. If a plaintiff receives full compensation and administrative costs, the defendant is over-deterred.
   D. Depending upon the size of the award, a defendant police agency might not be deterred at all.

62. Which of the following conclusions can justifiably be drawn from the experience of the tanker company's counsel mentioned in the passage?

   A. Good economists make for poor attorneys.
   B. Costs should never be considered prohibitive where safety is concerned.
   C. Toxic materials should not be shipped through residential neighborhoods.
   D. Honesty is not always the best policy for an attorney.

63. In the fourth paragraph, the author argues that "Potentially, the most promising development in tort (personal injury) law has been the advent of strict liability." These beliefs imply that:

   A. the use of strict liability has become increasingly popular for defendants.
   B. the uses of strict liability should remain limited in scope.
   C. the author approves of waiving the requirement for proof where carelessness is evident.
   D. the author approves of compensation where carelessness is evident.

STOP. IF YOU FINISH BEFORE TIME IS CALLED, CHECK YOUR WORK. YOU MAY GO BACK TO ANY QUESTION IN THIS TEST BOOKLET.

STOP.

30-MINUTE IN-CLASS EXAM FOR LECTURE 3

In Western cultures, gender identity is presumed to be a corollary of assigned sex, with sex assignment determined primarily by visual inspection of the genitalia. People for whom this assumption is incorrect may desire hormone therapies or surgeries aimed at modifying their bodies so that they more closely align with their preferred gender identity. At present, accessing such treatments requires a diagnosis of gender dysphoria as specified in the DSM-5 [the official handbook of psychiatric disorders], which emphasizes the "distress that may accompany the incongruence between one's experienced or expressed gender and one's assigned gender." The fact that gender dysphoria exists in the DSM is an admission on the part of psychologists that our society has clearly defined gender roles that contribute to what is generally considered "normal."

A recent case history of gender dysphoria described "Chris," a female-assigned-at-birth patient who identified more closely with the male gender and stated a wish to be addressed by male pronouns. It is important to stress, when looking for causal factors for Chris's disorder, that Chris was in no way confused about his identity and was described as a well-adjusted individual. Basic defects in personality can thus be ruled out as causes of his uneasiness with his assigned sex. One must then ponder the age-old question of society as the cause.

The notion of gender identity is so heavily dependent on societal norms that, in this case, many psychologists may believe society is the culprit. The mere labeling of some behaviors as "masculine" and others as "feminine" may have created the criteria for Chris's experience to be labeled as deviant or abnormal. In another culture, where the labeling is different, would Chris have even felt the need to identify as distinctly male? Along the same lines of thinking, would the incongruity even be considered a "disorder" in another culture?

Evidence varies regarding the two sides of the issue. Upbringing and/or some biochemical processes may account for the etiology of the disorder, indicating that it is not simply due to societal labels. Indeed, it may seem convincing to argue that Chris strongly identified with males very early in his life, and that this was reflected in his interest in "male" activities. Yet one could also argue that certain activities were labeled male, and Chris molded his interests to include them so that he would be considered "male." It is virtually impossible to unravel which came first, the labeling of his favored activities as "male" or his interest in them. Almost certainly, there is a complex interaction between the two.

Remaining, however, is the question of treatment for Chris. He expresses a desire for hormone treatment to lessen his experience of gender dysphoria. One might ask if this is really necessary, since he is already well adjusted. Part of what we strive for as psychologically healthy individuals is an acceptance of ourselves in a "natural" state. It is sometimes the case that, through psychotherapy, one learns that one may not necessarily have to change oneself as much as one's perception of self. The effect of hormone treatment on Chris' happiness cannot be foretold with complete certainty.

In conclusion, it is interesting to note that Chris' desire to have the physical characteristics of a man is considered part of a "disorder," while a small-breasted woman's desire for breast implants would usually be construed as a desire to increase her

femininity and not be labeled as such. Perhaps Chris is somewhere on a male-female continuum and is pushing himself toward the end of the spectrum in our neatly constructed gender binary that is closest to his identity.

This passage was adapted from "Healthcare Experiences of Gender Diverse Australians: A Mixed-methods, Self-report Survey." Riggs DW, Coleman K, Due C. *BMC Public Health.* 2014. 14(230) doi:10.1186/1471-2458-14-230 for use under the terms of the Creative Commons Attribution License 2.0 (http://creativecommons.org/licenses/by/2.0).

64. The passage suggests that its author would probably disagree with which of the following statements?

    A. It is possible that Chris participated in "male" activities in order to be considered male.

    B. It is possible that Chris naturally participated in "male" activities.

    C. Chris was not confused about his identity.

    D. Every culture has defined gender roles.

65. Implicit in the passage is the assumption that:

    I. one should be happy in one's "natural" state.
    II. one can be well-adjusted, yet unhappy with one's "natural" state.
    III. one's perception of self is most important.

    A. I only
    B. II only
    C. III only
    D. I and III only

66. The author of the passage would be most likely to agree with which of the following ideas?

    A. A DSM-5 'disorder' may not actually be a disorder at all.

    B. The DSM-5 is a poor descriptor of abnormal behavior and desires, since it is easily influenced by societal norms.

    C. Some DSM-5 'disorders' are simply an attempt to characterize socially abnormal behavior and desires.

    D. Behavior and desires must fall within the parameters of the DSM-5 to be considered normal by society.

67. The author hints that the fact that Chris is well-adjusted indicates that his "uneasiness with his assigned sex" (paragraph 2):

    A. is a problem which should be overcome through psychiatry.
    B. is influenced by the culture he lives in.
    C. can be overcome through surgery.
    D. is a basic personality defect.

GO ON TO THE NEXT PAGE.

68. Suppose it were discovered that antidepressant prescription medication allows Chris to become somewhat more comfortable with his "natural state. Would this discovery support the author's argument?

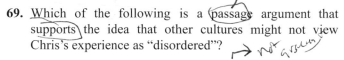

 A. Yes; it confirms it.
 B. No; it does not affect it.
 C. No; it weakens it.
 D. No; it disproves it.

69. Which of the following is a passage argument that supports the idea that other cultures might not view Chris's experience as "disordered"?

 A. Other cultures do not strictly assign gender according to the inspection of genitalia at birth.
 B. Societally determined labeling can determine what is viewed as abnormal behavior.
 C. Socially constructed gender roles have precluded Chris from being as well-adjusted as he might have been in another culture.
 D. Chris may have intentionally sought out activities that our society views as "gendered."

70. The author's attitude toward "our" societal norms is most accurately described as:

 A. favorable.
 B. neutral.
 C. distrustful.
 D. disapproving.

Passage II (Questions 71-77)

Instrumental rationality is exclusively concerned with the search for efficient means and, consequently, is not concerned with assessing the ends pursued. This form of rationality has become dominant in post-Enlightenment liberal democratic capitalist societies.

For classical liberals, individuals were defined as rational pursuers of self-interest not defined by any form of substantive communal bonds. Given this, individuals needed freedom from interference by the state to pursue their self-interest, as well as the provision of rules for competition to reduce the risk of losing private property. Freedom and the provision of "rules of the game" to regulate competition were the most efficient means for individuals to pursue rational self-interest. Beyond the provision of such rules and the raising of taxes to pay for their enforcement, the state had no legitimate right to impose norms or control behaviors.

Whereas a "thick" conception of politics would regard individuals as being defined by their ties to others in a community and the norms of those communities, the classical liberal conception of politics is a "thin" conception, where the activity of politics is reduced down to providing rules to regulate competition. In other words, the "thin" liberal approach to politics is an expression of instrumental rationality.

One problem identified with "thin" liberalism is the condition of anomie – a sense of normlessness – that comes with the domination of instrumental rationality, which evacuates meaning from the world and replaces it with formal, bureaucratic process. The cognitive ethic of the Enlightenment shifted focus from the authority of the clerics to the inner abilities of individuals to know the world, and the post-Enlightenment re-examination of all associations desacralized and disestablished everything substantive. This helped the scientific revolution but evacuated meaning from the world.

Ernest Gellner's proffered solution to anomie argues for a "constitutional religion" analogous to a constitutional monarchy. This solution prudently accepts an incoherent worldview. On the one hand, domains such as science are based on rational questioning with no sacred sources of knowledge, such as clerical authority. On the other, the need for meaning and cohesion should be based on a "pre-industrial mode of legitimation" which treats religion with "a limited seriousness" and does not let religion "interfere with serious cognitive and productive business."

Against this, Robert Bellah argues that a clearly identifiable civil religion, constructed by political elites, already exists, because the authority of political figures is historically based on something "higher" than the self-interest of voters or politicians. If the norms of this civil religion had real traction with the citizenry and were applicable to key domains of public life, citizens might be motivated to learn about the activities of the elites controlling those key domains. This would not be a desired outcome for those elites, because it would make the pursuit of self-interest potentially less efficient. For it to be instrumentally rational for the political elite to construct such a religion, it would have to be the case that the religion would not motivate the citizenry to become active in public life.

GO ON TO THE NEXT PAGE.

So how to lessen the influence of the political elites? Perhaps the answer to this question lies with John Dewey, who envisages democracy as an ethical way of life, where an active citizenry values participation in public life as an end in itself and holds elites to account. Central to this vision is an on-going critical dialogue where reasons are entwined with emotions and norms. Democracy as an ethical way of life could be constructed by changing the educational system to base learning on questioning and valuing public affairs, with this being complemented by what Dewey takes to be a natural tendency in people to sociability and the building of communal ties.

This passage was adapted from "Democracy versus the Domination of Instrumental Rationality: Defending Dewey's Argument for Democracy as an Ethical Way of Life." Cruickshank J. *Humanities*. 2014. 3(1) doi:10.3390/h3010019 for use under the terms of the Creative Commons CC BY 3.0 license (http://creativecommons.org/licenses/by/3.0/legalcode).

71. Based on the information in the final paragraph, John Dewey's conception of "democracy as an ethical way of life" is an example of:

  A. classical liberalism.
  B. a "thick" approach to politics.
  C. instrumental rationality.
  D. a "thin" approach to politics.

72. Which statement, if proven true, would provide the best support for the passage author's argument?

  A. Societies with high levels of anomie have traditionally been most vulnerable to civil war and collapse.
  B. Societies with strong social norms have traditionally been most vulnerable to civil war and collapse.
  C. Most liberal democracies do not struggle with anomie.
  D. John Dewey has also argued against the creation of a civil religion.

73. Which of the following best explains the meaning of the passage author's statement that "[Gellner's proffered solution] prudently accepted an incoherent worldview" in paragraph 5?

  A. Anomie is best combated through the establishment of a "constitutional religion."
  B. Post-enlightenment re-examination of the world helped the scientific revolution.
  C. The needs of a cohesive society call for a different set of norms than the needs of scientific progress.
  D. The advancement of both science and society depend on the restoration of clerical authority.

74. Robert Bellah's claim that "a clearly identifiable civil religion, constructed by political elites, already exists" would be most strongly challenged by which assertion?

  A. Historically, citizens of Western democracies have accepted their own self-interests as the source of political authority for elected officials.
  B. Classical liberalism is actually an example of a "thick" approach to politics.
  C. The U.S. educational system currently does not base learning on questioning and valuing public affairs.
  D. Most modern democracies ascribe political authority to the service of some greater good.

75. Which of the following statements, if true, best explains why the passage author considers the "thin" approach to politics an example of instrumental rationality?

  A. The "thin" approach is concerned with the use of social norms to promote certain behaviors.
  B. The focus of the "thin" approach is only on the ties, responsibilities and power relations with others in a community.
  C. The focus of the "thin" approach is only on the provision of efficient means for individuals to realize self-interest.
  D. The writers of the US Constitution believed in both instrumental rationality and the "thin" approach to politics.

76. Suppose a new scientific technique for easily altering traits like hair color and height before birth was developed. Based on passage information, Ernest Gellner would most likely respond to this development by arguing that:

  I. Science should continue to investigate such areas without undue concern for the moral or ethical implications.
  II. Moral concerns should end this line of scientific inquiry.
  III. Society should adopt a set of cohesive but not overly intrusive norms to determine how this technology should be used.

  A. I only
  B. II only
  C. I and II only
  D. I and III only

77. Based on the information in paragraph 2, classical liberals would most likely support which of the following?

  A. Tax incentives for individuals who donate money to certain charities
  B. A law prohibiting fraudulent investment practices by bankers
  C. The abolishment of all laws regulating interactions between individuals
  D. The establishment of a constitutional religion

GO ON TO THE NEXT PAGE.

Passage III (Questions 78-84)

From its very beginning, the New York City Opera production of "Mephistopheles" deserves high marks for visual excellence. It begins with an audiovisual show featuring stars, religious images projected onto swirling mist, and very, very loud brass winds, intended for drama and only slightly corny.

The scene then shifts to Hell, where a naked, disheveled Mephisto, singing from his broken throne, sarcastically apologizes for not being up to Heavenly standards of singing, providing the proof that harmony is still a longer way off in some places than in others. In the director's vision, the characterization of Mephisto is akin to Milton's rebellious, but somewhat sympathetic anti-hero, a dissident angel who dares to fight a vastly superior power to preserve his vision of the world. Accordingly, this production features a Mephisto who is flippant but clever, blasphemous but thought provoking, and possessed of both sympathy and contempt for human weaknesses. He strikes a balance between his boldness and his cowering before Heaven.

A chorus presents the essential plot of Faust, reduced from its several incarnations. When the angels point out the mortal Dr. Faust, as God's incorruptible servant on earth, the devil Mephisto promises to turn him from God through temptation. Thus, this version presents temptation as essentially a wager, or struggle, between God and the Devil (which, at one time, was a remarkably blasphemous notion, as it contradicted the dogma that God is all-powerful over evil). As the divine host departs, Mephisto regains his mocking manner, singing, "It's nice to see the Eternal Father talking with the Devil—in such a human way!"

Mephisto tempts Faust in the middle of a country fair thronged with revelers, which is meant to symbolize the worldly pleasures. This symbolism hearkens back to the ancient morality play *Vanity Fair*, which also featured a bazaar extolling sins. Mephisto, garbed in virtue as a gray robed beggar monk, finally announces himself to be Mephisto. In a good aria, much of which is delivered while dancing or rolling on the ground, the devil again introduces himself sympathetically as God's constructive critic, one who "thinks of evil/ but always achieves the good," singing menacingly of how he wages an eternal dissent against God:

> "Light has usurped my power,
>
> seized my scepter in rebellion;
>
> I hurl forth this single syllable—NO!"

In this version of *Faust*, it is Faust who seizes the devil's bargain: Mephisto must furnish him with a single moment so lovely it deserves to last forever.

In Scene II, Faust is transformed into a younger man, who courts the young woman of his dreams, a commoner named Margaret. At this point, the play devolves into stock characters and slapstick. Faust and Margaret sing very forgettable arias about the supremacy of feeling over reason, a theme which is not really congruent with the Faust myth. The shallowness of the libretto's throwaway lyrics is compounded by Margaret's emotionless singing.

Those who read the book know the next scene as the Witch's Sabbath on Walpurgis Night, though the libretto itself offers little explanation for the abrupt change of scene. Mephistopheles now appears as the leader of hedonistic sinners, calling them with the aria "Come on, onward, onward." Again, the portrayal of his character is less evil than rebellious and hedonic; he recognizes the power of mankind's pursuit of earthly pleasures, singing, "Here is the world, round and empty" while holding the globe. It is unclear whether it is his effort, or human nature itself, which is responsible for sin. At one point, he laments *mankind's* cruelty and cunning, concluding, "How I laugh when I think what's in store for them! Dance on; the world is lost."

78. Assume that several others who had attended the same opera were interviewed. If they remarked that Margaret sang with tremendous passion, these remarks would weaken the passage assertion that:

   A. Mephisto had rendered her irresistible to Faust.
   B. the lyrics which she sang were "throwaway."
   C. the young woman of Faust's dreams sang without emotion.
   D. the young woman of Faust's dreams was a commoner.

79. On the basis of the passage, it is reasonable to conclude that:

   A. Faust lost his soul to the devil.
   B. the "country fair thronged with revelers" was not in the book.
   C. the operatic interpretation differed from the book.
   D. the author did not enjoy the performance.

80. According to the passage, the author felt that the New York City Opera production of "Mephistopheles":

   A. was plagued with a poor characterization of Mephisto.
   B. suffered from noticeable weaknesses beginning in Scene II.
   C. was enhanced by Dr. Faust's singing.
   D. could have been improved in Scene III.

81. The passage seems to indicate that the author most enjoyed:

   A. the music of the opera.
   B. the singing of the opera.
   C. the plot of the opera.
    D. the images of the opera.

82. Which of the following does the author suggest was a component of the original "Faust myth" (paragraph 5)?

   I. Reason triumphing over feeling
   II. A more evil Mephisto
  III. A more powerful God

   A. I only
   B. II only
   C. III only
   D. II and III only

83. According to the passage, through what primary means is the fundamental plot transmitted to the audience?

   A. Through visual imagery
   B. Through Faust's musings
   C. Through the chorus
   D. Through Mephisto

84. Regarding the devil's bargain with Faust, the passage strongly implies that:

   A. it is Faust who got the better deal.
   B. it is the devil who got the better deal.
   C. in other versions, the bargain was with Margaret.
   D. in other versions, it is Faust who does the bargaining.

STOP. IF YOU FINISH BEFORE TIME IS CALLED, CHECK YOUR WORK. YOU MAY GO BACK TO ANY QUESTION IN THIS TEST BOOKLET.

STOP.

30-MINUTE IN-CLASS EXAM FOR LECTURE 4

Helping individuals make decisions that promote their own welfare, without limiting their freedom of choice, is one of the hallmarks of "libertarian paternalism." Paternalism is often considered a serious threat to the autonomy and choice of an individual, and is associated with perceived authoritarian policies. Libertarian paternalism, however, aims to provide a framework where individuals make decisions that benefit themselves and society, whilst still maintaining a range of available options. In other words, by changing the "choice architecture" for decision making, individuals can be "nudged" into making the right choices.

The premise for this approach is based on behavioral economics, which has characterized the decision making processes and the biases that may lead to "reasoning failure." These biases can result in choices that negatively impact welfare, which is particularly relevant to medical practice where patients are often required to weigh the risks of survival, toxicity, and quality of life when making treatment decisions. Under these circumstances, patients may be influenced by an array of emotions, such as fear and grief. Studies of cancer patients have found that demands for particular treatments do not come from a neutral evaluation of risks and benefits but rather from a perception of hope even when faced with a high likelihood of major toxicity and low benefit. Further inconsistencies in decision making may arise from previous experiences, particularly if these have been unpleasant.

Informed decision making requires the provision of comprehensive and objective information. This can be problematic because patients may struggle with probabilities, over-estimating their level of risk of disease and the potential benefits of treatment. It has been argued that too many options can have negative consequences by resulting in individuals using heuristics (rules of thumb) to counter the numerous choices on offer, leading to suboptimal decisions. Individuals may suffer from "myopia" where they are not able to imagine decisions that will impact them in the future, specifically not anticipating how their preferences may change over time.

Critics of nudge policies suggest that they do not unbias individuals' decision making, but rather utilize these biases to trick them into certain decisions. They contend that the use of such mechanisms impacts individuals' autonomy as they are not fully in control of their actions, and that there should be greater transparency. Freedom of choice is a core tenet of the libertarian paternalism philosophy, but opponents claim that there remains incongruity between the "nominal freedom of choice" and the "effective freedom of choice." For example, auto-enrolled opt-out schemes (e.g. organ donation) result in only a small proportion of people leaving the scheme, due to exploitation of their status quo bias.

It may be that using paternalism and autonomy as the two overriding principles is overly simplistic. Some critics of medical paternalism have suggested that it is perhaps more accurate to consider nudge techniques a form of "manipulation," a term meant to evoke images of the advertising industry. While many clinicians are quick to dismiss the comparison, the similarities in technique are undeniable and raise some interesting ethical issues. Many proponents of libertarian paternalism have replied that, in medicine at least, the use of nudge policies should be transparent and publicly defensible. For example, a clinician might acknowledge to a patient that he or she was delivering the information in a specific way by saying, "I am giving you the information in this way to help you understand why I think this is the best course of action." This approach is ideal and effective: if the motivation is for the patient's benefit and the clinician is open about the way he or she delivers information, claims of manipulation can be refuted and patient autonomy maximized.

This passage was adapted from "'Nudge' in the clinical consultation - an acceptable form of medical paternalism?" Aggarwal A, Davies J, Sullivan R. *BMC Medical Ethics*. 2014. 15(31) doi:10.1186/1472-6939-15-31 for use under the terms of the Creative Commons CC BY 2.0 license (http://creativecommons.org/licenses/by/2.0).

85. Which of the following ideas established by the passage author is **LEAST** supported by evidence?

    A. Patients do not always think optimally when making medical decisions.
    B. Libertarian paternalism has become the unyielding dominant philosophy in modern medical ethics.
    C. Medical paternalism and the advertising industry employ the same techniques.
    D. Clinicians can make efforts to maintain patient autonomy.

86. Why does the passage author most likely give the example of "opt-out" programs in paragraph 4?

    A. To demonstrate how opt-out programs can improve medical decision making.
    B. To show that the appearance of autonomy does not guarantee actual autonomy.
    C. To give an example of patients with no freedom of choice.
    D. To explain the similarities in tactics between clinicians and advertisers.

87. Based on passage information, critics of medical paternalism would most likely respond to news that billions of dollars per year could be saved if clinicians downplayed the effectiveness of a powerful but often unnecessary new treatment by:

    A. Supporting this practice because the money saved is significant enough to outweigh the loss of autonomy.
    B. Opposing this practice because the money saved is significant enough to outweigh the loss of autonomy.
    C. Supporting this practice because it utilizes patients' biases.
    D. Opposing this practice because it utilizes patients' biases.

GO ON TO THE NEXT PAGE.

88. Which of the following best describes the relationship between "nudge policies" and libertarian paternalism described in the passage?

   A. Nudge policies are techniques used to fight libertarian paternalism.
   B. Nudge policies are techniques that fall within the philosophy of libertarian paternalism.
   C. Nudge policies are unrelated to libertarian paternalism.
   D. Nudge policies can maintain patient autonomy when clinicians explain why they present information in a certain way.

89. Suppose a new chemotherapy drug is developed that has the potential to extend one out of every ten thousand cancer patients' lives by up to four months. The drug costs $125,000 per year, and has horrific side effects that can lead to prolonged hospitalization. The passage author would most likely respond to this news by arguing that clinicians should:

   A. Focus on informing patients of the side effects and costs of the treatment.
   B. Prescribe the treatment in all cancer cases.
   C. Provide patients with all known information on the drug so they can decide their treatment options.
   D. Refuse to prescribe the drug to any patient under any circumstances.

90. It is likely that the critics of nudge policies object to their "[utilization of] …biases" (paragraph 4) for all of the following reasons EXCEPT:

   A. They are overly manipulative.
   B. They exploit a symptom of the problem rather than unbiasing the patient.
   C. They are ineffective.
   D. They rob the patients of their freedom of choice.

91. Which assumption, if proven false, would most weaken the case for medical paternalism?

   A. Clinicians are generally better informed of the optimal medical decision than patients.
   B. Patients are generally better informed of the optimal medical decision than clinicians.
   C. All patients are poor medical decision makers.
   D. Nudge techniques are ineffective at changing behavior.

Passage II (Questions 92-98)

The question of human overpopulation and its relationship to human carrying capacity – the planet's limited ability to support its people – has been controversial for over two centuries. In 1798 the Reverend Thomas Malthus hypothesized that population growth would exceed the growth of resources, leading to periodic reduction of human numbers by either "positive checks," such as disease, famine, and war, or "negative checks," by which Malthus meant restrictions on marriage. This "Malthusian view" was rapidly accepted and remained popular until fairly recently.

Malthus's worst fears were not borne out in the century following his death in 1834—food production largely kept pace with the slowly growing global population. However, soon after 1934, the global population began to rise steeply as antibiotics, vaccines, and technology increased life expectancy. By the 1960s, concerns of a mismatch between global population and global food supply peaked.

But the 1970s surprised population watchers. Instead of being a period shadowed by calamitous famine, new crop strains (especially grains such as rice and wheat) caused a dramatic increase in the global production of cereals, the main energy source in the global diet. Despair turned into cautious optimism. By the end of the decade, the public health community felt sufficiently empowered to proclaim "Health for All by the Year 2000." Average life expectancy continued to zoom upwards almost everywhere.

But the tremendous successes of the era had a pernicious effect: this rise in life expectancy coincided with fading concern about overpopulation, reaching a nadir with the election of US President Ronald Reagan in 1980. Unlike his predecessor, Richard Nixon, Reagan considered concerns about global population size to be "vastly exaggerated." In the same year, the US surprised the world by abdicating its previous leadership in the effort to promote global family planning. This reversal has since proved disastrous in many disciplines outside of public health.

As foreign aid budgets fell, the Health for All targets began to slip from reach. Instead, international agencies promoted structural adjustment programs, health charges for patients, and the "trickle down" effect as the best ways to promote development. It is plausible that a fraction of the public who remained concerned about Third World development thought that these economic policies deserved a chance. Less charitably, the new economic policies also allowed people already financially comfortable to give up concern for Third World development because the new orthodoxy asserted that market deregulation, rather than aid, was the royal road to development.

The harvest that market deregulation and generally high birth rates have sown in many Third World countries is now clear. Health for All, if recalled at all, is now seen as absurdly optimistic. The failure of development is most obvious in many sub-Saharan countries, where life expectancy has fallen substantially. But life expectancy has also fallen in Haiti, Russia, North Korea, and a handful of other nations.

Among the multitude of causes that can be identified for declines in either total population or life expectancy,

GO ON TO THE NEXT PAGE.

overpopulation is hardly considered, except by "dissidents" such as Maurice King. Amid the many different explanations for the horrific 1994 Rwandan genocide, the possibility of a Malthusian check is scarcely mentioned. There is even less discussion entertaining the possibility that the sub-Saharan epidemic of HIV/AIDS may also be a check. King refers to the silence on overpopulation as the "Hardinian Taboo," after the ecologist Garett Hardin, who described the proscriptions used to avoid confronting the need for population control. Whatever the cause of the scarcity of modern academic analysis, the related issues of human carrying capacity and overpopulation deserve fresh consideration.

This passage was adapted from "Human Carrying Capacity and Human Health." Butler CD. *PLoS Med.* 2004. 1(3) doi:10.1371/journal.pmd.0010055 for use under the terms of the Creative Commons CC BY 3.0 license (http://creativecommons.org/licenses/by/3.0/legalcode).

92. Which of the following ideas concerning foreign aid is most strongly implied by the information in paragraph 4?

    A. The Health for All targets were always doomed to fail.
    B. Selfishness among citizens of wealthy nations probably contributed to the global decline in foreign aid.
    C. Reagan-era development strategies were largely unpopular in Third World countries.
    D. The failure to reach the Health for All targets should be blamed on the "already financially comfortable."

93. Which of the following statements, if true, would most *weaken* the author's arguments concerning carrying capacity and overpopulation?

    A. Vaccines contributed more to increased life expectancy in the 20th century than antibiotics.
    B. Malthus's views were widely criticized at the time of their publication.
    C. Historical population reduction is fairly uncommon.
    D. Historical population reduction is most common when resources exceed population demands.

94. Which of the following passage assertions is **LEAST** supported by evidence within the text?

    A. "This reversal has since proved disastrous in many disciplines outside of public health."
    B. "The harvest that market deregulation and generally high birth rates have sown in many Third World countries is now clear."
    C. "Malthus's worst fears were not borne out through the century following his death in 1834."
    D. "But the tremendous successes of the era [the 1970s] had a pernicious effect."

95. Assume that a new strain of rice is developed that can be harvested in half as much time as traditional rice. The passage author would most likely respond that:

    A. This development should solve the problem of carrying capacity and overpopulation.
    B. The Malthusian viewpoint is no longer relevant to the analysis of global population levels.
    C. This development will simply mask the increasing risk of overpopulation until it has grown even higher.
    D. This development represents a new "positive check."

96. Based on the information in the first paragraph, which of the following would the author most likely consider a modern-day "negative check"?

    A. The rise of national vaccination programs.
    B. Widespread famine among sub-Saharan nations.
    C. Escalating violence in the Middle East.
    D. Growing rates of birth control usage.

97. The passage author most likely believes the Rwandan Genocide and AIDs crisis are:

    A. Examples of the dangerous consequences of excessive foreign aid.
    B. Less serious than population declines in Haiti, Russia, and North Korea.
    C. Widely recognized "positive checks."
    D. Unacknowledged consequences of overpopulation.

98. The author's use of quotation marks around the word "dissidents" in paragraph 6 is most likely meant to convey which of the following?

    A. A literal military conflict.
    B. An ironic reversal of fortune for a once widely accepted theory.
    C. The author's disappointment with current overwhelming support of the Malthusian theory.
    D. The author's disdain for Maurice King and his views.

Passage III (Questions 99-105)

The end of the colonial era saw the birth or rebirth of many nations, especially in Africa and Asia. Not only did these events transform the face of the globe, they also had an immediate impact on archaeology. Nations wishing both to legitimize their own existence and to foster feelings of national pride began to define their own past and paid tribute to the achievements of their ancestors. Such feelings were especially strong in those countries where the colonial rulers had consistently subordinated the history of local peoples to that of the conquerors. In Rhodesia, as it was then called, the British were unable to accept the hypothesis that the magnificent structures at Great Zimbabwe were built by "mere natives" and it was not until several generations of archaeologists brought accumulated evidence to bear on the subject that Great Zimbabwe became known to the world as a uniquely African development.

Hunger on the part of these people to establish their cultural ancestry, and to right the historical balance, led to the expenditure of large sums of money on the creation of national antiquities services and on the training of local archaeologists. In some cases archaeological artifacts appeared on postage stamps or in souvenir shops, while the sites themselves became rallying places and even national shrines. The new state of Israel used the imposing fortress of Masada as the location where new recruits were sworn in to the army, for it was there that the Jewish Zealots had held out with great bravery against the occupying Roman armies.

Many states poor in natural resources have come to realize that their archaeological heritage is also an important financial asset, providing them with attractions for tourists. The past becomes an invisible export and a powerful tool for public relations. Here archaeology is well and truly out of the ivory tower and stands amidst many attendant temptations – both ideological and financial. If the past is not quite as glorious as might be wished, perhaps it would be a good idea to manipulate the facts; if, on the contrary, other carefully selected "facts" prove useful in the battle for hearts and minds, they can be embellished; if the monuments are not quite picturesque enough, perhaps they should be improved.

The misuse of the past for political ends is also widely recognized as a problem. The political importance of the past is immense. Thus archaeology and history are not purely scholarly pursuits – knowledge for knowledge's sake – but are intrinsically powerful weapons in ideological discourse and indoctrination. The perversions of archaeology and history for propaganda are worth studying in their own right, once their true nature has been recognized, because they give us important insights into how people and nations wish to be seen and, in some cases, what their ideals and objectives are.

We may never know exactly how the past was, but it is relatively easy to show how the past was not. Hypotheses can be shown to have a better, or worse, fit to data. Debates over interpretations will continue; this is how research proceeds. But when we leave the even playing field of the observational sciences, and begin to make strident connections between the past and present, we are on our way down the slippery slope of ideology and self-interest. This is not to say that it is inappropriate that peoples take pride in their past, but simply that we should not labor to glorify our ancestors in the face of evidence to the contrary.

This passage was adapted from "Prehistory as Propaganda." MacDonald KC, Hung FYC, Crawford H. *Papers from the Institute of Archaeology*. 1995. 6 (1995) for use under the terms of the Creative Commons CC BY 3.0 license (http://creativecommons.org/licenses/by/3.0/legalcode).

99. In the second paragraph, the author's reference to "these people" refers to:

    A. British colonial powers
    B. Builders of the Great Zimbabwe in Rhodesia
    C. Nations wishing to legitimize their own existence
    D. Israeli army recruits

100. Which of the following assertions in the passage is **LEAST** supported with explanation or examples?

    A. Historic sites become rallying places and national shrines.
    B. Archaeology is a tool for nations wishing to legitimize their own existence.
    C. The misuse of the past for political ends is a widely recognized problem.
    D. The past can be an invisible export and a powerful tool for public relations.

101. Which of the following conclusions is most strongly implied by the passage?

    A. Political gain is often the motivating force behind developing historical sites for tourism.
    B. Manipulating knowledge about archaeology is more important among oppressed people than among their oppressors.
    C. Academic archaeology more accurately represents prehistory than popular archaeology.
    D. Objectivity in archaeology is threatened by a variety of motivations.

102. For which archaeological practice would the author of the passage be **LEAST** likely to advocate?

    A. DNA analysis to determine genetic identity of prehistorical peoples
    B. Speculation on the uses of various objects unearthed through archaeological digging
    C. Identifying the geographic origin of objects through chemical analysis
    D. Independent dating of archaeological objects

GO ON TO THE NEXT PAGE.

103. Which of the following is most likely to represent the author's opinion about archaeological artifacts appearing on postage stamps and in souvenir shops?

    A. Such practices cheapen the field of archaeology.
    B. Archaeology is a more effective tool of propaganda when used by a culture on itself rather than as a tool for the conquerors against the conquered.
    C. It shows that archaeological artifacts can become potent symbols of national pride and unity.
    D. These items are beneficial because they provide a way for archaeology to get out of the ivory tower.

104. Which practice relating to newspaper journalism is **LEAST** analogous to the attendant temptations described in paragraph 3 of the passage?

    A. Embellishing a story to make it more interesting to the reader
    B. Re-publishing an old story to remember the past
    C. Publishing sensationalized stories to sell more newspapers
    D. Omitting sections from an interview to change the meaning of the quotations

105. Suppose that a country chosen to host the Olympics decides to beautify several national historic sites to be even more extravagant than their original conditions before the games begin. Based on the information in the passage, which is the most likely logic behind the restoration project?

    A. Historical artifacts can be leveraged for gains in finances and public relations.
    B. Restoration emphasizes national pride and unity.
    C. The selected changes provide insight into how the nation wants to be seen by the world.
    D. Archaeologists cannot know exactly how the past was.

STOP. IF YOU FINISH BEFORE TIME IS CALLED, CHECK YOUR WORK. YOU MAY GO BACK TO ANY QUESTION IN THIS TEST BOOKLET.

STOP.

ANSWERS & EXPLANATIONS

FOR
30-MINUTE IN-CLASS EXAMINATIONS

ANSWERS FOR THE 30-MINUTE IN-CLASS EXAMS

Lecture 1	Lecture 2	Lecture 3	Lecture 4	Lecture 5
1. B	22. C	43. D	64. D	85. C
2. A	23. B	44. A	65. B	86. B
3. A	24. B	45. C	66. C	87. D
4. C	25. D	46. A	67. B	88. B
5. B	26. D	47. B	68. C	89. A
6. C	27. A	48. A	69. B	90. C
7. C	28. B	49. C	70. D	91. A
8. B	29. B	50. D	71. B	92. B
9. D	30. A	51. B	72. A	93. D
10. A	31. D	52. A	73. C	94. A
11. B	32. C	53. A	74. A	95. C
12. B	33. A	54. D	75. C	96. D
13. C	34. C	55. D	76. D	97. D
14. A	35. B	56. C	77. B	98. B
15. B	36. B	57. A	78. C	99. C
16. C	37. C	58. B	79. C	100. C
17. C	38. C	59. B	80. B	101. D
18. A	39. A	60. A	81. D	102. B
19. C	40. B	61. C	82. A	103. C
20. D	41. D	62. D	83. C	104. B
21. A	42. B	63. C	84. D	105. A

MCAT® CRITICAL ANALYSIS AND REASONING SKILLS

Raw Score	Estimated Scaled Score
21	132
20	131
19	130
18	129
17	128
15-16	127
14	126
12-13	125
11	124
9-10	123
8	122
6-7	121
5	120
3-4	119
1-2	118

EXPLANATIONS FOR 30-MINUTE IN-CLASS EXAM ii

1. **B is correct.** Both experiments show that NLP provides no benefit over pure guessing in assessing whether someone is lying. There is no stated comparison between trained and untrained practitioners, so choice A is incorrect. It is possible that trained practitioners would be able to effectively use NLP, but this cannot be shown by the experiments described in the passage. Both studies showed that NLP had no effect, so there was no inconsistency, making choice C incorrect. D is incorrect based on the results shown in Table 1: confidence was almost exactly the same in both groups, and the given p value is very large. The p value cutoff for statistical significance can vary between experiments, but p = 0.67 would never be considered significant (p = 0.67 means that there is a 67% probability that the difference between groups is due to chance)!

2. **A is correct.** The correct answer must both be an element of the experimental design and pose an ethical concern. Choice A meets both of these requirements. Being forced to lie can be distressing, and causing participants to be distressed should be minimized whenever possible. Choice B could be a good answer, except that there is no evidence in the passage that deception was used. In any event, deception is sometimes necessary for the experiment, and can be acceptable if participants are briefed afterwards and are not unduly impacted by the deception. For these reasons,choice B is not as good of an answer as choice A. As the experimenter, the owner of the cellular phone must know what is going to happen and therefore is not being deceived; C is incorrect. Choice D is incorrect because it refers to the expected variance between subject participants, rather than an element of the experimental design, and has no ethical implications.

3. **A is correct.** This modification to the experiment constitutes systematic error by biasing outcomes in one direction. Participants who were informed of NLP techniques would be likely to modify their behavior to mask potentially revealing eye movements. Note that it isn't really necessary to understand exactly how the modification would change participants' behavior to realize that systematic error, rather than random error, would result. By definition, random error is random and could not be induced by a particular experimental modification (outside of the factors that normally cause random error, such as the use of faulty equipment). Choices B and D can be eliminated. Systematic error is associated with accuracy, not precision, making A the correct answer.

4. **C is correct.** TThe situation described is a cohort study. In a cohort study, one population is followed over the course of time. There is no manipulated variable, so this isn't an experimental study design, making choice A incorrect. A cross-sectional study examines a sample at a single point in time, so choice B can be eliminated. A case-control study follows two sample populations, not just one, so choice D is incorrect.

5. **B is correct.** The hypothesis is phrased in such a way that it would be impossible to prove wrong, or falsify. Imagine that NLP is never effective. This would make falsifying the hypothesis presented an impossible task: it would require testing the efficacy of NLP in every situation imaginable (of which there are an infinite number of possibilities!) in order to show that it is NOT effective in any situation. Rather than simply requiring a large number of experiments, no number of experiments would make it possible to falsify the hypothesis, so B is a better choice than A. Since the hypothesis cannot be disproven, the findings of the passage experiments cannot possibly disprove it; C is incorrect. There is no indication that deception would be required to test the hypothesis, making D incorrect.

6. **C is correct.** A t-test can be used to compare the means of two groups when the dependent variable is continuous. As the graph presents the mean for both the number correct and rated confidence for two groups, a t-test would be most appropriate to compare the means for each of the variables. A chi-squared test cannot be used because both variables are not categorical; a linear regression cannot be used because both variables are not continuous. D can be eliminated because there is no plausible reason not to use a test of significance for the results; furthermore, p values are reported in Table 1, so it is clear that a statistical test can be used!

7. **C is correct.** Independent variables are those that are manipulated by experimenters. In the first experiment, participants were told whether to lie or not to lie. Thus lying vs. not lying was the independent variable, while pattern of eye movement was the dependent variable. Choice III is therefore true, eliminating answer choices A and B. In the second experiment, NLP training was the independent variable: the experimenters assigned participants to training and non-training groups. Number of correct judgments about and rated confidence were the variables measured by the

experimenters and were thought to possibly vary according to the independent variable. In other words, they were the dependent variables. Choice I is false while II is true, making C the correct answer.

Passage II (Questions 8-14)

8. **B is correct.** The passage states that the second experiment involved comparing apoptosis levels among four different experimental groups. Analyzing this data would require a statistical test capable of comparing several data sets to each other. T-tests are only powered to make comparisons between two groups, so a t-test would not be adequate for this type of experiment; choice A can be eliminated. The lecture explains that correlation and regression analyses are useful when both the independent and dependent variables are represented as continuous rather than categorical data. In the passage experiment, however, the independent variable (which drug the mouse received) is categorical, meaning linear regression is not the optimal test; choice D can be eliminated. A Tollens test is a reaction used in organic chemistry, and is a distractor answer choice here; C can also be eliminated. Recall from the lecture that ANOVA is the preferred statistical test for comparing multiple data sets, making B the best answer choice.

9. **D is correct.** This question tests your understanding of what a p value represents; the specific time points in Figure 1 are not important. Recall from the lecture that a p value indicates the likelihood that a difference between data sets was obtained by random chance alone. This is also known as the null hypothesis. A p value of 0.01 means there is a one percent chance $(0.01 = \frac{1}{100} = 1\%)$ that this null hypothesis is true, meaning the correct answer must be choice C or D. Remember that no matter how small the p value, there is always *some* possibility that the result is due to random chance, even if it is incredibly small. There is no statistical test that can tell with total certainty that the null hypothesis must be incorrect. For this reason, choice C can be eliminated and choice D is the correct answer.

10. **A is correct.** This question stem contains some helpful clues. It states that the experimenters are testing some new independent variable to try and mimic the effects of prazosin. This implies that the effects of prazosin are already known. The independent variable in this scenario is the presence of glutathione in the mouse's food, and the dependent variable is the level of liver toxicity. Neither of these refers to the prazosin group, so choices C and D can be eliminated. Furthermore, the variables refer to aspects of each group that are being manipulated or studied, not the groups themselves. Both choices A and B refer to types of control groups. Recall from the lecture that a negative control is a group in which no effect is expected. This is most similar to the untreated mice, described in the passage – no treatment effect is expected if there is no treatment. This makes choice B incorrect. The prazosin group is a positive control, since the researchers already know what effect should be expected from prazosin treatment.

11. **B is correct.** The legend for Figure 1 states that each bar represents the mean for the values collected at that particular time point. Recall that the mean describes the central tendency of a data set. Answer choice I is correct. Note that because choices A, B, C, and D all contain choice I, you can assume it must be correct. The most common value in any data set is known as the mode. Figure 1 does not depict any mode, so answer choice II is untrue, eliminating choices A and D. The legend also states that the error bars in Figure 1 represent one standard deviation. Standard deviation is a descriptive statistic used to indicate the dispersion of a data set, making III true and choice B correct.

12. **B is correct.** The passage states that the experimenters compared mean AST values at each time point to the initial values to test for significance. Since they are not analyzing distributions of entire data sets, it is unlikely that a chi-square test is being used, making choice D incorrect. Note that chi-square tests are almost always used to compare an observed distribution to an expected (e.g. normal) distribution. The one-tailed t-test is useful when experimenters are only trying to investigate a difference in one direction. In other words, if the passage researchers had performed the first experiment knowing from past research that AST levels would only decrease after stress induction, a one-tailed t-test would be ideal. There is no information in the passage to indicate this is the case, however, so choice A is not the optimal answer. Since only choices B and C remain, the correct answer must be either a paired or unpaired t-test. The lecture states that paired t-tests are ideal when there is a natural partner in the comparison group. In this experiment, since samples were drawn from the same animal at several time points, each piece of data has a natural partner: the initial value from that mouse. For this reason, a paired t-test would be more powerful, and choice B is the correct answer.

13. **C is correct.** Random assignment is a powerful tool that researchers use to ensure that all groups are equivalent so that experimental observations can be attributed only to manipulations of the independent variable. Ideally, this process removes a subjective element (assigning subjects to groups) from experimental design, so choice B can be eliminated. Since random assignment ensures that significant effects do not come from biased experimental groups, it should not guarantee that significant differences are found – this depends only on the phenomenon being studied and the experimental procedure – so choice A is also incorrect. Although random assignment should eliminate bias, it does not do so by forcing results to be continuous. The second half of choice D is thus irrelevant to the topic. Random assignment attempts to control for within-group variability by distributing that variability randomly across all groups. For this reason, choice C is the best answer.

14. **A is correct.** Note that the question stem only tells you that a relationship was found between two variables; it says nothing about the specifics of that relationship. For this reason, it is possible that either high or low body fat could be correlated with lower risk of liver damage. This means that either choice B or C could be true, and both answer choices can be eliminated. This is a somewhat uncommon example of two answers that appear to contradict each other both being true or false. It is also possible that a chi-square test could reveal a break from the expected liver damage levels at extreme body fat percentages, so choice D should be eliminated. One of the limitations of correlation tests is that they cannot describe the causality of a statistical relationship. This means that a correlation can never prove that one variable depends on another, making A untrue and the correct answer.

Passage III (Questions 15-21)

15. **B is correct.** The passage states that lowering the E/S ratio *decreases* the rate of Reaction 2. Choices A and C both state that a lower E/S ratio has an *increased* reaction rate, so both can be eliminated. The passage also states that lowering the E/S ratio *increases* the viscosity, meaning that the battery with an E/S of 5 has a higher viscosity than the battery with an E/S ratio of 10. Thus D can be eliminated and B is correct.

16. **C is correct.** The figure indicates that the optimal E/S ratio is somewhere between 5 and 15, as the battery with an E/S ratio of 10 is more efficient than either of the end points. Recall that the goal of the experiment was to find an optimal E/S ratio. The researchers can expect that batteries with E/S ratios of 4 or 16 would similarly be inferior to the E/S ratio of 10, so researchers would not want to test either of these values. However, it is possible that another value between 5 and 10 or between 10 and 15 would be even more efficient. Choice C provides an E/S ratio falling in one of these ranges, and thus is the correct answer.

17. **C is correct.** As described in the passage, the electrolyte solvent serves as a medium for ion movement. If the solvent were polar, it could react with either the lithium ions or lithium polysulfides that were being released into it, interfering with the reactions that are of interest in the experiment. No passage information indicates that molar mass, density, or volume could affect the experimental conditions.

18. **A is correct.** The scenario described in the question stem provides an example of systematic error: all of the readings will be about 10mV higher than the true value. As a result, accuracy is compromised. However, all readings of a repeated measure should still agree with each other as well as they would if the equipment were not flawed, so precision is not affected. Choices B and C can be eliminated, and choice A is correct. Choice D is a nonsense error; the type of measurement scale would not be affected by measurement error.

19. **C is correct.** This question could be restated as: "Which E/S ratio has the lowest capacity when all the cycles have been completed?" The E/S = 15 cell appears to maintain capacity retention well at first, but as time progresses it short circuits while the other two cells continue to recharge and discharge to some degree.

20. **D is correct.** The t-test returned a p value of 0.007. The threshold of significance is most often set at $p = 0.05$ or 0.01, so this relatively low p value indicates significant differences between the groups, eliminating choice C. The results in Figure 1 suggest that the capacity of E/S = 5 cells drops below 50% in fewer cycles than does the capacity of E/S = 15 cells. However, there is no way to know from the information given if the other trials in the experiment returned the same results. Because it is unknown whether E/S = 5 or E/S = 15 cells had a greater average number of cycles to 50% capacity, neither choice A nor choice B are appropriate assumptions. Therefore the answer must be choice D. Notice that the question stem contains a clue to the answer by using the term "two-tailed t-test." Recall that a two-tailed t-test makes no assumptions about the direction of the relationship between two groups. Therefore it would both test to see if the results of E/S = 15 are greater than those of E/S=5 and whether the results of E/S = 5 are greater than those of E/S = 15. Without more information, the direction of the significant results cannot be concluded.

21. **A is correct.** A confounding variable is a variable that is correlated with the independent variable (in this case, E/S ratio) and has a causal effect on the dependent variable (capacity retention). This is exactly the situation being described in the question stem, limiting the possible answer choices to A and B. (C and D are distractors; "biased variable" is not a term that you need to know for the MCAT®). Internal validity refers to whether a causal relationship between the independent and dependent variable can be justifiably concluded from an experiment. It can be greatly affected by confounding variables, which may give the appearance of a causal relationship where none actually exists. External validity refers to the generalizability of results from a sample to a wider population, and is determined by factors like whether or not the characteristics of the sample are representative of those of the population. Choice A is therefore the best answer.

EXPLANATIONS TO IN-CLASS EXAM FOR LECTURE 1

Passage I (Questions 22-28)

22. **C is correct.** This answer can best be arrived at through process of elimination. Though nothing in the passage directly suggests that choice C is the best answer, it aligns with the general arguments that the author is making and choices A, B, and D can be eliminated because they contradict passage information. Choice A draws from the first paragraph, but the author believes this is an "upside," so it does not need to be remedied. Furthermore, this reference is tangential to the overall argument of the passage and thus is unlikely to be the correct answer to a question that speaks directly to the author's main point. Choice A can be eliminated. The author is primarily arguing in favor of the humanities; even though he or she draws a parallel between the humanities and the (basic) sciences in acknowledging the "unprecedented attack on the idea of curiosity driven abstract research", there is nothing to suggest that increasing science funding would help the humanities. The "primacy of applied knowledge" is exactly what the author is opposed to, as this comes at the expense of the humanities, making choice D incorrect.

23. **B is correct.** While choice B is commonly used as an argument in support of the humanities, this argument is not brought up in the passage. This is an example of a statement meant to appeal to test-takers who try to apply outside knowledge rather than relying on the passage. Choice A is supported by the first paragraph and is a major point of the passage, so choice A is wrong. The third paragraph provides extensive support for choice C, so C can be eliminated. While budgetary constraints are not directly indicated as a reason that the humanities are "besieged," there are numerous allusions to a shift in research priorities, which can reasonably be inferred as affecting research funding. Out of the choices given, choice B is least supported by the passage and is the best answer.

24. **B is correct.** Thomas Peacock's remarks indicate that he fails to recognize the merits of any endeavor that does not produce a tangible benefit to society (and that Peacock is exactly the sort of person the author finds him or herself at odds with when making a case for the humanities). Because the study of this ion pump has no stated objective aside from increasing understanding (it would be categorized as basic science, rather than applied science), Peacock would fail to recognize how it is a worthy use of time and resources, making A incorrect. As the humanities have no tangible benefit, and especially considering Thomas Peacock's abhorrence of poetry, he would not advocate study of the humanities, making choice C incorrect. While choice D could be a reasonable answer, we have no way of knowing whether Thomas Peacock would consider studying business "useful knowledge." The use of the word "business" in D is different than that in the passage: Peacock intends "the real business of life" to refer broadly to the study of the tangible and salient issues of the day. Given B as an answer choice, choice D can be eliminated.

25. **D is correct.** McDougall is arguing against the author's position and in favor of research that "has commercial value", a value that the humanities lacks. The author does not recognize that the concerns about non-commercially directed research is a valid concern, making choice A incorrect. Choice B is not supported in the passage either. The author never directly challenges the commercial viability of different kinds of research, but does argue in favor of challenging an emphasis on "the primacy of applied knowledge", making choice D correct and choice C incorrect.

26. **D is correct.** While the author does draw a comparison with scientists within and outside of universities in paragraph four— i.e., people who are involved in academia outside the humanities— he never passes judgment on these scientists beyond acknowledging that they find themselves in a similar situation as academics within the humanities. Likewise, despite threats that focus on applied research as encroaching on the turf of the humanities, the author never passes judgment on those performing the applied research.

Choice A runs counter to the overall point of the passage, which defends the value of the humanities, and thus cannot be an expression of the author's views; choice A can be eliminated. Paragraph four indicates that scientists who pursue basic research receive less funding than those who carry out applied research, but this is a difference in funding between different areas of academia outside of the humanities; no comparison is made with funding for the humanities. This makes choice B incorrect. Choice C could seem consistent with the author's opinions, but it is a distortion of the passage argument. The author argues for the value of the humanities but does not devalue other areas of study. This leaves choice D as the correct answer. This answer may not "feel good" because the author does refer to academia outside the humanities in the passage, but it is a better answer than any of the other choices.

27. **A is correct.** The author's major argument is that the humanities are under attack by those who value applied research more highly and thus direct funds toward that type of study, rather than the humanities and other non-applied academic areas. The assertion in choice A is the exact opposite of this argument; if the humanities were better funded now than ever, it would be difficult to believe that they are under attack. If choice A were not an option, choice B could be a good choice. The author starts the passage by discussing the digital revolution and indicating that it has impacted the perceived value of the humanities. However, the digital revolution is not directly relevant to the author's central argument, which specifically refers to funding of the humanities. Choice B is therefore not as good of an answer as choice A. Choice C refers to the *basic* sciences, not the applied sciences. The author implies that the basic sciences are in the same position as the humanities, so he or she would not expect them to be in competition with the humanities. Choice C can be eliminated. Choice D refers to the comparison drawn in paragraph three to a similar historical attack on the humanities. However, even if this proved not to be an analogous situation, this would not challenge the author's thesis, which is concerned with the *current* state of the humanities.

28. **B is correct.** Answering this question requires an understanding of the fundamental opposing concepts discussed in the passage: study that does not have a specific application, particularly the humanities, versus applied study. If necessary, look back at paragraph 5 to review the meaning of "serious" knowledge. As you would probably expect, the phrase refers to applied study like that valued by Peacock. The correct answer will be an example of applied study. Choice B jumps out as a prototypical example of applied research and is the best answer. "Entrenched assumptions" refers to assumptions about humanities that changed as a result of the digital revolution. This is a distractor choice that cannot easily be defined as "serious" or non-serious knowledge, so choice A is incorrect. The humanities is exactly the opposite of "serious" forms of knowledge, making choice C incorrect. Choice D is likewise an example of a course of study that would not be considered to be "serious;" it is the type of research that has been losing funding due to the increased value placed on "serious" knowledge like the type described in choice B. Choice D can be eliminated. Notice that choices B and D directly conflict with each other, so it is likely that they could not both be "serious" forms of knowledge, and thus one must be the correct answer.

Passage II (Questions 29-35)

29. **B is correct.** The passage mostly discusses similarities between the ideas of Luther and Augustine, but since the question stem refers only to Luther, you can guess that the correct answer will speak to one of the few differences in their thinking. Two differences were pointed out in the passage: Luther argues that people who participate in violent rebellion will go to "eternal torment," while Augustine does not consider their fate; Luther's vision of salvation focuses on Biblical teachings, while Augustine focuses on God's mercy. Choice B speaks directly to Luther's views on salvation. If the Bible is fundamentally incomplete, knowledge of its teachings may not be sufficient for salvation. Choice A is similar to B; if it were established that the Biblical teachings referred to by Luther were from before the time of Jesus, whose teachings were "the foundation of the Christian religion," Biblical teachings could not be the key to salvation of Christians. However, according to the passage, it is the "New Testament" that is the basis of Christianity. The fact that the "*Old*" Testament referred to in choice A comes from before the time of Jesus is therefore not surprising, and does not challenge Luther's theory of salvation. Choice A can be eliminated, and B is a better answer. Choice C is incorrect, since Luther argued that God hated rebels of all kinds; whether or not they had been "converted" is irrelevant to their fate. Choice D has little bearing on the principles of Martin Luther. If anything, this information would strengthen Luther's ideas and principles; if Augustine's understanding of salvation is flawed, it may be more likely that Luther's alternative vision is correct.

30. **A is correct.** Choices C and D can immediately be eliminated because the passage emphasizes the two theorists' agreement on issues of violence and rebellion. There is no passage information to suggest that they would have different opinions on violent self-defense. In fact, they both strongly believe that rebels do not have the right to use violence against the people who are oppressing them. The scenario of self-defense is quite similar to the discussion of rebellion in the passage, so you can conclude that both Luther and Augustine would disagree with the use of violence for self-defense. This makes choice A the correct answer.

31. **D is correct.** A quick glance back at the passage shows that paragraph 4 is where the similarity in Luther's and Augustine's opinions about violent "instruments of God" is discussed. Also in this paragraph, one of the few differences between Luther and Augustine's ideas is indicated: Luther specifies that those who use violence will go to "eternal torment," while Augustine does not make any comment on their fates. Choice A can be eliminated because it is a fuzzy value judgment based solely upon personal opinion. Unless the passage itself provides direct evidence regarding the "reasonableness" of someone's inclinations or ideas, this type of answer is a poor choice. Choice B is the opposite of what is indicated in the passage: since Luther considered the fate of rebels while Augustine did not, Augustine is arguably LESS prepared than Luther to define God's will. Choice C is not a reasonable conclusion, although it may seem attractive to the test-taker, particularly given that "Augustine never considers the individual fate of these living tools, but Luther maintains that … they go to eternal torment." However, neither of the theologians is "sending people to eternal torment." According to the passage, it is God who decides who is "sent" to hell, not Luther or Augustine. Choice D is similar to C, but more correctly defines the role that Luther or Augustine might play as theologians in relation to God. The theologians can only "announce" what God has decided, and Augustine is less willing than Luther to do so.

32. **C is correct.** This type of question must usually be gleaned from the overall impression given by the author as the passage is read. "Going back" to the passage is not likely to be helpful. The reader must ask if there were any derogatory, sarcastic, praiseworthy, or other type of information or words used that provide clues to the author's attitude. If the passage did not try to persuade or argue, then it is probably neutral. This is the case in the correct passage. There is no indication that the author has a particularly negative (disapproving or mistrustful) or positive (favorable) view of the theologians discussed. The author does not seem to be attempting to convince the reader to agree with one theologian or the other, or to agree or disagree with both theologians. This makes choice C the best answer.

33. **A is correct.** Unfortunately, passages and sentences are not always provided in their clearest form. The tortured syntax of this sentence begs for clarification, particularly where the word "conviction" is used in its less common meaning of "belief." The wrong answer choices for this question play on other possible meanings of "conviction." However, answering the question correctly does not require an understanding of the exact meaning of the word. It is simply necessary to recognize that the key idea of paragraph 5 is how Christians can reach "salvation." The claim in the question stem quote that "God will save him," is a reference to salvation. Choice A nicely summarizes the meaning of the quote in the question stem, which could itself be restated as: "The true Christian would maintain his faith through any ordeal, and even if he physically died, God will save him because of his belief." Choice B might also seem tempting, but it can be eliminated because salvation, not judgment, is the focus of the last paragraph of the passage. Choice C is wrong because the passage clearly suggests that God will not save Christians *from* their earthly ideals, but rather will save them *after* they have already suffered. Furthermore, this answer mistakenly equates "for his conviction" with "for his judgment." Finally, choice D can be eliminated for multiple reasons. First, the quote states that his "body perishes"—ie, the Christian must die before salvation. Secondly, though this answer is not completely clear, it seems to mistakenly equate "for his conviction" with "finding him guilty" (convicting him). Incorrect answer choices may repeat words from the question stem to appeal to the test-taker.

34. **C is correct.** On this type of question the "primary purpose" usually means the answer choice that accurately restates important passage information. Generally, three are inaccurate and one is accurate. However, if two answer choices are accurate, one will clearly be more all-encompassing (primary) than the other. The reference to Catholics and Protestants may seem out of the scope of the passage, but Augustine was a Catholic bishop while Luther was a Protestant leader. For the purposes of this question, you could replace "Catholics" with Augustine and "Protestants" with Luther. As with some of the previous questions, the key to finding the correct answer is considering the similarities and differences between Luther and Augustine. Choice A can be eliminated because there seem to be no differences in the passage regarding the way in which the early Catholics and Protestants dealt with persecution. The only differences were in their understandings of how to achieve salvation and pronouncing God's judgment on others. Choice B should "feel" like a mismatch with the passage. The author is fairly neutral and would probably not be interested in "justifying" persecution. Choice C is the opposite of choice A, correctly pointing out that Catholics and Protestants were quite similar in how they dealt with persecution, a major concern of the passage. This makes choice C the best answer. Choice D, similarly to choice B, is wrong because of the author's neutrality. The author is not questioning Catholic and Protestant practices, but explaining the reasoning behind them in a rather objective manner.

35. **B is correct.** This type of question is not necessarily the value judgment that it might first seem to be. At least two of the answer choices will inaccurately restate conclusions or passage information. Of the remaining two, one will obviously weaken the passage, while the other may even strengthen it. In this case, choices A and D can immediately be eliminated because the passage does NOT differentiate between Catholics and Protestants, and all the information provided indicates that the attitudes of Augustine and Luther were quite similar. Choice C can be eliminated because there is no indication or "claim" in the passage of representing all theorists. Process of elimination leaves B as the correct answer. The majority of the passage discusses Luther; even the paragraph that starts with the sentence "St. Augustine would have agreed," immediately returns to Luther's ideas. The passage does not even come close to equally representing the two Christian theorists and is therefore weakened when attempting to use both men's theories in support of the topic.

Passage III (Questions 36-42)

36. **B is correct.** Though the privilege of the wealthy is an underlying theme of the passage, there is no evidence that the "wealthy" and their power had anything to do with Mallon's confinement. The health inspector was the person most directly influential in Mallon's confinement; choice A can be eliminated. By contrast, choice B is in line with the author's obvious opinion that Mallon's treatment was unjust. This is evidenced in the first and last sentences of the passage: "Of all the bizarre and melancholy fates that could befall an otherwise ordinary person, Mary Mallon's has to be among the most sad and peculiar," and "But she was the only one kept isolated for years, a result as much of prejudice toward the Irish and noncompliant women as of a public health threat." Choice D is similar, but goes a step too far. Although the author seems to believe that Mallon was not fairly treated, there is no suggestion that she should have received a "hearing." Finally, choice C is not a plausible answer choice because the quote comes from paragraph 1, before Soper is even mentioned.

37. **C is correct.** Choice A uses a direct quote from the passage to appear more plausible, but the passage only briefly mentions soft clams. A major point of the passage is that Mallon was a healthy carrier of the disease, and that Soper "was the first to identify a healthy typhoid carrier in the United States." Since Soper's investigation and discovery occurred after the "first two" investigators came to the Warren house, it is likely that the investigators had not considered a healthy carrier. This makes choice C the best answer. All passage information supports the assertion that typhoid is passed through contaminated food or water, particularly since Mallon seems to have been spreading disease through her cooking, so choice B is incorrect. Choice D can also be eliminated because no timeframe is given regarding the "two investigators." Furthermore, since Soper was the first person to identify a healthy typhoid carrier in the United States, it is unlikely that the two investigators would have suspected Mallon had she been even directly interviewed by them. C is the better answer.

38. **C is correct.** Note that the correct answer must satisfy two criteria. It must:

    1. be an idea in the passage, and

    2. weaken the author's argument by providing a legitimate reason that Mallon could be considered a "public health threat."

    The answer that most directly portrays Mallon as a health threat is choice C. The passage states that she was forced to return to isolation after she "failed to comply with the health inspector's requirements." If she did not follow the rules that were set in place to prevent her from spreading disease, she was likely a public health threat. None of the other answer choices provides such concrete evidence of the danger that Mallon presented. Although she was initially a cook, if she had followed the requirements (which presumably would have precluded her from preparing meals), she would not have been a threat. Furthermore, the passage never directly states that cooking was Mallon's "primary occupation," which makes this more of an assumption than a passage idea. Choice A can be eliminated. Choice B is a passage idea, but does not weaken the author's argument to the extent that choice C does. Mallon could have followed the requirements despite not believing that she was a carrier, in which case she would not have been a public health threat. Similarly, choice D does not weaken the author's argument to the extent that choice C does because Mallon could have followed the requirements and avoided being a risk to any more people.

39. **A is correct.** This question may require looking back at the passage, but you may find that reading the passage with interest allowed the details to stick with you. If you do need to look back, the best place to start is by resolving the question of whether the passage indicates who hired Soper. A quick glance at the passage would allow both choices A and C to be eliminated if there was not enough information to determine who hired him. The passage states that "the owners" hired Soper. Since the Warrens were renters, not owners, C can be eliminated and A is correct. The other answer choices can also be eliminated based on passage information. No information is given about who hired the two investigators, so choice B can be eliminated. Finally, the passage states that the owners were interested in *renting* the house, not selling it, so choice D is also incorrect. This is a less common "detail" question.

40. **B is correct.** This question demonstrates the importance of paying careful attention to the wording of the question stem. The correct answer is not just implied or indicated by the passage; it *must* be true according to the passage. The best answer choice will likely contain softeners, rather than extreme language. Answer choice D can be eliminated for this reason. The passage implies that prejudice towards the Irish was a factor in Mallon's confinement, but there is no evidence that it *must* be true that the health inspector was *doubtless* prejudiced. Similarly, there is no indication that the nickname given to Mallon *must* have been the *primary* cause of her confinement. In fact, she was given the nickname while already in isolation, so it likely did not contribute at all. Choice C can be eliminated. The language of choice A is less definitive, but the information given about Mallon's life before working for the Warrens is far too limited to determine whether or not she had infected anyone previously. Finally, choice B is not directly stated, but the passage does say that Mallon's feces "did indeed show high concentrations of typhoid bacilli." The only plausible mechanism for the spread of typhoid to the Warren family is that the bacilli were being transferred from the feces to Mallon's hands, to the food she prepared, and then to those becoming sick. Also notice that this answer choice leaves some room for error by saying that Mallon was *almost* certainly not washing her hands. Choice C is the best answer.

41. **D is correct.** Finding the answer to this question requires attention to the information about Mallon that led Soper to consider her as a possible source of the outbreak. According to Soper's own words describing Mallon's tenure in Oyster Bay, as quoted in paragraph 3, "It was found that the family had changed cooks about three weeks before the typhoid epidemic broke out ... She remained with the family only a short time, leaving about three weeks after the outbreak occurred." Since Mallon worked for the Warrens for three weeks before the outbreak and three weeks after, she must have been there for at least six weeks. Thus choice D is the correct answer.

42. **B is correct.** Choice C can be eliminated because there is not enough information to conclude that *any* of the 237 other typhoid carriers were kept isolated at any point, let alone *all* of them. Choice D must also be incorrect: since the quote in the question stem focuses on a way in which Mallon was *different* from all the other typhoid carriers—her lengthy isolation—it is not likely to provide support for the idea that she was similar to them. Choosing between A and B is more difficult. Choice B is a better answer for two reasons. First, it includes a "softener": Mallon's isolation *might have* been due to early ignorance. Second, a major factor in Mallon's treatment was that she was the first known healthy carrier of typhoid. Decades later, at the time of her death, hundreds of other carriers had been identified, indicating a greater understanding of the disease and its spread. Thus, choice B is a justifiable interpretation of the quote. Choice A is possibly implied, but is not as well justified as choice B. "Fairness" requires a comparative analysis of some sort. Mallon was the first of her kind to be identified; her treatment cannot meaningfully be compared to that of the typhoid carriers discovered decades later.

EXPLANATIONS TO IN-CLASS EXAM FOR LECTURE 2

Passage I (Questions 43-49)

43. **D is correct.** It is most likely that an unusually low speaking voice would be difficult to understand. The author states in paragraph 1 that "[A]n artificially lowered voice can sacrifice intelligibility." That you might think that they were lying is not the most likely answer. The key is "unusually low." Though a speaker who was lying might be aware that in order to successfully lie, or "suggest credibility, the voice's tone should be pitched as low as is naturally possible" (paragraph 1), this is a much more "tortured" answer choice. In other words, in contrast to the straightforward nature of choice D, this answer requires several assumptions that are outside the scope of the question, making choice A incorrect. That they could be irritated with you would not be most likely. First, it is lack of "intelligibility" that is irritating. Second, it is the listener who is irritated, not the speaker, making choice B incorrect. There is no passage link between monotony and pitch. Monotony has to do with inflection, not pitch, making choice C incorrect.

44. **A is correct.** The author most likely believes that one of the main purposes of speaking, during a face-to-face meeting, should be to convey a favorable impression. Almost the entire passage is about conveying favorable impressions, not ideas or concepts. The author admits in paragraph 2 that "the quality of content accounts for a mere 6%" of the overall impression given by the speaker, making choice B incorrect. There is no support within the passage for the notion that one of the main purposes of speaking is to gain leverage, making C incorrect. It is also unlikely that the author believes that one should communicate as naturally as possible, since the whole point of the passage is to improve upon one's natural speaking voice. For instance, the author would not be a proponent of communicating "as naturally as possible" if you naturally 1) were shy, 2) spoke with a high-pitched whine, 3) were "breathy," etc. Thus choice D is incorrect.

45. **C is correct.** Notice that, of the four answer choices, choice C differs in "kind" from the other choices. In other words, if you had a list of only these four choices with a new question asking, "Which one of the following items doesn't belong with the others?" you would still likely choose "pretension." Though we may make some assumptions, the passage does not convey how "pretension" is conveyed. Since the symptoms of "pretension" are not defined, there is little in the way of help which can be gleaned from the passage for the person who suffers from it. This answer can also be arrived at by process of elimination. There is information within the passage that would help a speaker curb "monotony." In the first sentence of the passage, the author suggests that speech should be "inflected to suggest the emotions expressed." In other words, developing the ideal speaking voice includes inflecting one's voice to avoid monotony. Choice A can be eliminated. The entirety of paragraph 4 provides information to help a speaker curb breathiness, eliminating choice B. The author suggests ways of lowering the voice to the lowest intelligible pitch, which would also presumably eliminate "high-pitched whining," so choice D is wrong.

46. **A is correct.** That the ideal speaking voice is the most pleasant to listen to is the answer most strongly implied, both in the first paragraph and in the passage as a whole. The author gives us our first clue in paragraph 1 when describing a voice which might "sacrifice intelligibility, which is irritating to listeners. Thus, speakers should experiment to find their optimal level, which will be at their lowest intelligible pitch." At this point, we might assume that, thus, the "optimal level" or ideal speaking voice is the "least irritating" (choice C). However, overall, the implication of the passage is seeking to be the best, not (forgive the tortured syntax) the "least" worst of the worst, making choice A correct and choice C incorrect. We can surmise that since "the quality of content accounts for a mere 6%" (paragraph 2) of the overall impression given by the speaker, "most persuasive" is not a characteristic of the ideal speaking voice, making choice B incorrect. As discussed in the answer explanation for question 44, the passage does not imply that the ideal speaking voice is the most natural, making choice D incorrect.

47. B is correct. The fourth paragraph of the passage is devoted to the avoidance of high-pitched, breathy speech. The author describes techniques to breathe more deeply, and thus prevent the breathiness and high pitch that result from shallow breathing. Thus a person speaking in a high-pitched voice cannot be breathing deeply, and choice II must be included in the correct answer. Choice B is the only one that includes II, so it must be correct. Notice that the same logic that makes answer choice II correct makes I necessarily incorrect, so choices A and D could be eliminated. Also, the first paragraph of the passage associates low pitch with truth-telling. Based on this information, it is reasonable to think that someone with a high-pitched voice might be lying. Answer choice III must be wrong, providing further evidence that choices C and D can be eliminated.

48. A is correct. That speakers can gain by improving their speaking voices is clearly a thesis presented by the author—in fact, improvement of one's speaking voice is the major idea of the passage. This thesis is presented through the negative aspects associated with having a "poor" speaking voice, such as "irritating" the listener; through the examples of "famous news anchors" who had great speaking voices; and through statistics within the passage: "everyone who communicates should be aware that their voice is a critical component of their audience's perceptions of them, comprising about 38% of the overall impression imparted by their presentation" (paragraph 2). Thus choice A is the best answer. Choice B does not "feel" like a thesis; while much of the passage concerns pitch, this idea is not as central as the idea expressed in choice A. Furthermore, the passage does not say that the tone should be pitched *as low as possible*. It should be as low as is intelligible, but pitching the voice too low can be unintelligible and irritating to listeners. Choice B can be eliminated. Choice C clearly contrasts with the author's point of view; in fact, it is an antithesis of the author's position. The author points out that only a small percentage of how a speaker is perceived has to do with the content of speech, while the quality of speech ("how you are saying it") is far more important. Since the whole point of the passage is to improve one's speaking voice, while the content of speech is not addressed at all, choice C must be wrong. Choice D cannot be correct because it is not even stated by the author, let alone presented as a thesis.

49. C is correct. The ideas in the passage focus on the "ideal speaking voice," so the question could be restated as, "For which of the following professionals is an ideal speaking voice most important?" All of the professionals indicated by the answer choices could likely benefit somewhat, but the passage will be *of most use* to just one of them. The ideas discussed in this passage would likely be of most use to a radio show personality, whose career is defined by his or her speaking voice. Thus choice C is the best answer. Choices A and B can be eliminated, as the speaking voice of a doctor or journalist is not as important as is that of a radio show personality. Despite the author's use of "famous [television] news anchors," which might make choice D seem attractive, it is clear that television relies at least somewhat, if not just as much, on visual components and appearance as it does on the speaking voice. However, beyond mentioning that "appearance accounts for about 50% of the speaker's impact" in paragraph 2, there is no further discussion of these ideas within the passage. Nor is any advice given for improving one's "appearance." Thus, this passage would not be as completely useful to a "television commentator" as it would to a radio show personality, making choice D incorrect.

Passage II (Questions 50-56)

50. D is correct. As the names imply, "push" factors compel someone to leave, while "pull" factors induce someone to come. The passage presents negative push factors that compel people to leave, and positive pull factors that compel people to come to other countries. Even if you did not have a strong understanding of the distinction between push and pull factors, you could at least eliminate choices B and C, which state that both types of factor have the same effect. The passage clearly presents push and pull factors as separate phenomena, even though they have the same effect of encouraging immigration.

51. B is correct. Nations would be most likely to encounter less traditional border strife if "artificially defined" borders were eliminated. The key here is "traditional" border strife. In contrast to the immigration problems that are the predominant focus of the passage, this type of strife is characterized by nations/states "attempting to secure their borders from invading countries, or even seeking to expand their own territories and acquire additional resources" (paragraph 5). Why would traditional border strife be minimized by the abolishment of artificially defined borders? Because nations would instead be separated by natural "geographical" boundaries (such as wide rivers, mountain ranges, and oceans), or by cultural boundaries. This makes choice B the best answer. Though the author says that people do tend to immigrate to areas with higher standards of living, there is no reason to believe that elimination of artificially defined borders would increase or decrease this natural tendency, making choice A incorrect. That nations would require greater border security measures is not the most likely to occur. "Geographical" boundaries would provide natural borders that would not require security, making choice C incorrect. That people would live more harmoniously is certainly possible. However, compared to choice B, this answer is vague and unsupported by the passage. Thus choice D can be eliminated.

52. A is correct. Answering a question like this may require going back to the passage. The correct answer must actually be a passage assertion and must be supported by an example. Incorrect answers either are not stated in the passage or are simply stated without any type of example. The assertion that transportation methods used by illegal immigrants are sometimes dangerous is supported with an example: "[w]ithin the past year, U.S. officials found three Chinese immigrants in a smuggling boat's sealed cargo container, dead from suffocation" (paragraph 2). Choice B is not even an assertion in the passage; the passage states that "neither side is attempting to acquire new territory." Thus B is incorrect. Choice C is a passage assertion, but is stated with no supporting example. Similarly, choice D is taken practically verbatim from the passage, but is not accompanied by an example.

53. A is correct. This answer speaks to one of the major ideas in the passage discussion of immigration: that poor conditions in the native country "push" the immigrant, while higher standards in an adjoining country "pull" the immigrant. Presumably, by becoming "more attractive to those who are leaving," a nation would remove push factors and slow the leaving of its inhabitants. Though "more attractive" is somewhat vague, it encompasses a variety of possible changes such as higher pay, better standards of living, better political system, more political freedom, etc. Thus choice A is the best answer. That nations should abandon the traditional methods of guarding borders is not suggested by the passage as a whole. We don't even really know what the "traditional methods of guarding borders" refers to. "Traditional" refers to the types of borders that countries shared, not the methods by which they were guarded. Even if there was a clear definition of these supposed "traditional methods," it seems unlikely that *reducing* border security would *decrease* the rate at which people cross the borders to leave the country. For all these reasons, choice B is incorrect. That nations should respond in some way to the conflicts arising from border disputes is not suggested by the passage as a whole. In addition, the discussion of "border disputes" is presented separately from the discussion of immigration and is not connected to the tendency of countries' inhabitants to stay or leave. This makes choice C incorrect. That nations should answer the challenges set forth by adjoining countries is not suggested by the passage as a whole. This too really has no concrete connection to inhabitants leaving or staying. One might infer that by "challenges," this answer refers to "economic challenges" and rising to meet the standards of the more attractive neighboring country. However, this is a stretch. "Challenges" might just as well mean challenges to war, or sporting challenges, making D incorrect.

54. D is correct. Since the question stem refers to the *lack* of immigration between two areas, the correct answer will likely refer to a lack of push and/or pull factors. Based on passage information, it is justifiable to infer that there was no push factor of bad economic conditions in West Berlin, which, if present, would have motivated emigration to East Berlin. This makes D the best answer. Examining choice A, there is no passage information to support the premise that a "very dangerous" situation would prevent immigration. On the contrary, the example of the suffocated Chinese immigrants indicates that danger would not stop a motivated person from attempting to immigrate. Furthermore, border security was not central to the passage discussion of the factors that motivate immigration. For these reasons, choice A is incorrect. The inference that it was understood that life would be better in East Berlin is not justified by the new "fact"; actually, it is directly contradictory. If life were thought to be better in East Berlin, presumably this would be a pull factor that would spur immigration from West Berlin to East Berlin. Thus choice B is incorrect. The inference that the inhabitants of both 'Berlins' were happy to remain where they were is not justified by the new "fact." The use of the word 'happy' is simplistic and should alert you that this is probably not the best choice. In addition, the question stem does not say whether or not there was immigration from East Berlin to West Berlin, so there is no basis to infer that the inhabitants of East Berlin were happy to remain where they were. For both these reasons, choice C can be eliminated.

55. D is correct. This is quite a difficult question, and the wording is important. The question requires an implication of the author's (*the author implies* which of the following is not one of the reasons…), not the absence of an implication (the author implies that Peruvian President Fujimori deployed soldiers to its borders with Colombia for all of the following reasons EXCEPT). Also notice that the question requires only an *implication*, not an assertion, statement, argument, or any other more definitive indicator.

That Fujimori is attempting to keep drugs out of his country *is* implied in paragraph 5 as one of the reasons the soldiers were deployed, and is therefore incorrect, eliminating I and answer choice A. In paragraph 5, the author states that "*Traditionally*, these two countries might have been attempting to secure their borders from invading countries, or even seeking to expand their own territories and acquire additional resources." This quote involves both choices II and III. The statement that *traditionally* territory expansion and resource acquisition would have been likely goals of the two countries implies that in the present day these are *not* of concern to Fujimori. Thus, the author implies that neither would be a plausible reason behind Fujimori's deployment of troops. This makes II and III correct, making choice D the best answer. Again, the word *implies* in the question stem is critical. Some might argue that only choice II is correct, given that expanding territories is addressed again in the final sentence while resource acquisition is not. However, the single mention of these two issues as processes that would have occurred in the past is enough to *imply* that neither is a concern for Fujimori in the present.

56. **C is correct.** In paragraph 2, the author states that, "recently, New Zealand attempted to deal with these aliens by enacting new immigration laws, which hasten the process required to deport them." This makes it "likely" that new laws, enacted in New Zealand, allow faster deportation proceedings, making II correct and thus eliminating B. The idea that immigrants often do not settle in New Zealand not only "seems likely," but also is provided in the passage as a reason in paragraph 3: "what keeps New Zealand from experiencing an even more profound illegal immigration problem is that the immigrants often do not settle there." This makes III correct, and eliminates choice A. There is no passage support for the notion that the U.S. offers higher wages than New Zealand, making I incorrect and eliminating D.

Passage III (Questions 57-63)

57. **A is correct.** Remember that the author emphasizes in the second paragraph that, "In reality, compensation tends toward inadequacy." He gives several reasons, one of which is the "hurdle" of proving negligence. The question stem indicates that in this case the compensation was not inadequate. For one thing, it is hard to argue that millions of dollars is "inadequate"; for another, the question stem says that the woman "*successfully* sued," indicating that the compensation was satisfactory for the plaintiff. Thus, the author would not believe that the woman's case was reflective of most other torts, making choice A the correct answer. Although we can determine that the compensation was not inadequate, we have no way of knowing if it was "just the right amount," making choice B incorrect. Choice C is wrong because whether deterrence is costly is way outside of the scope of the passage. The only information we have regarding the cost of deterrence is for the defendant. We cannot determine whether or not McDonald's would experience this deterrence as costly, or whether the passage author would consider it costly. Furthermore, the focus of the question is on the woman's compensation, not the deterrence of the defendant. For these reasons, choice C can be eliminated. There is no indication in either the question or the passage that the woman was malicious, making choice D incorrect.

58. **B is correct.** This type of question is often best answered by process of elimination. Choices C and D can quickly be eliminated because they were each already answered in the passage. The author responds to the idea that the administrative costs should be added to the compensation received by the plaintiff in paragraph 1: "If she is paid in full [i.e. administrative costs are added to the full compensation], then the defendant is paying 130% of the actual harm caused, and is over-deterred." An effective argument cannot be one that has already been addressed and defeated by the author; choice C is wrong. The author also responds to the idea that the administrative costs should be subtracted from the compensation received by the plaintiff in paragraph 1: "If the plaintiff is awarded 100% of the damages suffered, she only receives compensation for 70% of her injuries" (paragraph 1). This cannot be the best argument because it is answered already in the passage, making choice D incorrect. Looking at the two options that remain, choice A can be eliminated because it seems clear that the substantial costs—of about 30% of awards—cannot be considered "inconsequential." Process of elimination leaves choice B as the best answer. First, one must realize that the author has essentially defined "administrative costs" as "attorney's fees" in paragraphs 1 and 2. Then, one must ask if it is reasonable to argue that attorneys should be compensated for their work. It is reasonable to argue that anyone should be compensated for their work (we are not saying how much or how little), and thus, yes, it is reasonable that attorneys should be compensated for their work. Finally, unlike some of the other answer choices, this argument is one that the author has not responded to in the passage. For all these reasons, choice B is correct. Notice that it is not a particularly effective argument—it does not really solve the issue presented in the question stem—but it is clearly *more* effective than the other three choices and thus is the best answer.

59. **B is correct.** The correct answer will be a statement that the author would disagree with, as indicated by passage information. Answer choices that the author would agree with can be eliminated. In addition, if it is impossible to determine whether or not the author would agree, the answer choice can be eliminated.

    The author refers multiple times to the "hurdle" or "difficulty" of proving negligence, and presents "strict liability" as a development in tort law in response to this problem. Thus the author would definitely disagree with choice B, making it the correct answer. Choice A can be eliminated because there is no way to extrapolate from the fictionalized story about one tanker company to determine the author's views on "tanker companies" in general. There is also no basis from which to judge whether the author would agree or disagree with the idea that the costs associated with suing and defending against suits can be tremendous. The only dollar amounts provided are in the last paragraph, and the idea of "tremendous" costs is relative. Thus choice C is incorrect. The author would probably agree with the idea that in many situations, over-deterrence results in primarily economic ramifications. The author states in paragraph 3 that over-deterrence "results in a waste of resources." For this reason, choice D is incorrect.

60. **A is correct.** Much like with question 57, this question requires the test-taker to understand that deterrence and compensation are two related but distinct issues. The question stem only provides information about actions on the part of the insurance companies, and does not make any reference to the compensation received by the plaintiffs. Thus, it is not possible to make any inference or interpretation regarding compensation, and choices C and D can be eliminated. The situation described in this question can best be interpreted as evidence that the insurance companies were over-deterred. After settling the lawsuits from the WTC torts, the insurance companies have mandated a very extreme policy by anyone's estimation, presumably due to "over-deterrence." This makes choice A the best answer. It would not be reasonable to infer that the insurance companies were under-deterred. "Under-deterrence" results in defendants "effectively having no incentive" to change or prevent future harms. Thus choice B is incorrect.

Notice that with a poor understanding of the author's concepts from the passage, choice D might seem to go hand-in-hand with choice A; it might seem just as "correct." It is not. For example, there might have been so many plaintiffs that rather small compensatory damage awards simply overwhelmed the insurance companies. We have no way of knowing based upon the information provided. It is conceivable for over-deterrence and under-compensation to occur simultaneously, to the benefit of no one.

61. **C is correct.** The correct answer must satisfy two criteria. It must 1) be an assumption of the author about the effects of lawsuit awards, and 2) be called into question by the given supposition. Much like in the previous question, answer choices that refer only to the plaintiffs are suspect. Choice A is not an assumption of the author; proving negligence is said to be difficult, but there is no reference to cost. Furthermore, this answer choice refers only to the plaintiffs and thus would not be called into question by the given scenario. For these reasons, choice A is wrong. That many people will not sue because the process is too costly is an implication of the author's since the idea was brought up in an example in paragraph 5, though the word "many" makes it highly questionable. More importantly, the statement in choice B is not called into question by the question stem scenario. The supposition clearly states that the "set aside" money is not for defending against lawsuits, but in order to "pay out" the awards. Furthermore, as with choice A, the best answer to this question will reference deterrence and/or defendants, not just plaintiffs. Choice B can be eliminated. Looking at choice C, the idea that the defendant is over-deterred if a plaintiff receives full compensation and administrative costs is very clearly an assumption of the author's (paragraph 1). Further, this statement is called into question by the supposition. If the police agency "routinely" sets aside/budgets the money it will have to pay out in awards, then it seems that this is just a business-as-usual approach. The author's definition of over-deterrence results in a "change" due to the "incentive to prevent [harm]." Thus choice C is the correct answer. Choice D must be incorrect for multiple reasons. The author never refers to police agencies specifically, so the statement is not an assumption of the author. Furthermore, if it were an assumption of the author, it would be supported— not called into question— by the question stem scenario.

62. **D is correct.** The conclusion that honesty is not always the best policy for an attorney can be justifiably drawn from the experience of the counsel (i.e., attorney). The author has already informed the reader that the tanker lawyer is a "poor lawyer." Thus, his actions would not be an example for others to follow. The author emphatically (!) announces that the company would be lucky to "escape punitive damages" because the attorney, a "poor lawyer," was overly honest— he "*admits* safer tankers were available." Based on this example, it can be concluded that attorneys should not always be honest. Thus D is the best answer. Choice A may seem attractive because of the author's reference to "the company's counsel — a good economist, but a poor lawyer" (paragraph 3). However, there is no indication that being a good economist is what made this person a poor attorney. This is a good example of how an incorrect answer choice may repeat a passage phrase in order to seem more plausible. Choice B cannot be correct because it does not answer the question that was asked. The question does not concern the tanker incident in general, but rather the tanker company's counsel. Choice C is incorrect for the same reason: it is outside the scope of the question that was asked.

63. **C is correct.** This question hinges on an understanding of what "strict liability" is. The passage defines strict liability as a process whereby plaintiffs do not need to prove negligence, which has been established as a difficult task, in cases where it is already obvious. The correct answer will reflect the author's approval of this process. Choice A is incorrect because, although the author views strict liability as "promising," there is no indication in the passage that the use of strict liability has become increasingly popular. Choice B is opposite to what is implied by the quote. If strict liability is such a "promising development," its uses should *not* remain limited in scope. The practice described by choice C— "waiving the requirement for proof where carelessness is evident"— is a summary of strict liability. This answer choice could be restated as, "The author approves of strict liability." This is exactly in line with the quote given in the question stem, making C the best answer. Choice D is possibly a true statement about the author, but is not implied by the given quote and thus does not answer the question. Strict liability involves the process of proving negligence, not the determination of compensation.

EXPLANATIONS TO IN-CLASS EXAM FOR LECTURE 3

Passage I (Questions 64-70)

64. D is correct. The author would disagree with the statement that every culture has defined gender roles. The word "every" is what makes this a bad answer choice; the author would agree that "some" or even "many" cultures have defined gender roles. In the first sentence of the paragraph, the author states that "Western cultures" assign gender based on genitalia. This leaves open the possibility that many non-Western cultures do not have such rigid gender roles. The author also alludes to *other* cultures where Chris might not have felt the need "to identify himself as distinctly male." The culture/society wherein Chris lives is clearly defined as "our" culture/society, implying that there are others.

This answer choice can also be arrived upon through process of elimination, since the author clearly would *not* disagree with the other answer choices. Answer choices A and B correspond to the "two sides of the issue" discussed in paragraph 4, which the author concludes probably both contribute to the formation of a gender identity that is incongruent with one's assignment at birth. Thus both are statements that the author would agree with, and these answers can be eliminated. Notice that the phrase "it is possible" is what enables the author to agree with both statements even though they are opposites. The author states that "Chris was in no way confused about his identity," making C incorrect. Even if you did not remember this exact quote, you could intuit that the author would agree that Chris is not confused; the author is supportive of Chris's preferred pronouns and gender identity, and seems interested in exploring Chris's experience rather than questioning it.

65. B is correct. As in the previous question, the wording here is important. The author does not imply that one *should* be happy in a "natural" state. The author states that psychotherapy may sometimes allow people to be happy in their natural state, but there is no value-judgment-type "should" or "should not" implication that would justify choice I. Furthermore, the author seems to have no problem with the idea that Chris would want hormone treatment to alter his "natural" state. Thus choice I is incorrect and choices A and D can be eliminated. Answer choice II provides an accurate description of the author's overall view about Chris, who is well-adjusted but wants to change his "natural" state. It can be inferred that Chris wants to change his natural state because he is unhappy with it, particularly since the passage also indicates in paragraph 5 that hormone treatment may affect Chris's "happiness." Thus choice II is correct, and B must be the answer. Although it is not necessary to address choice III to narrow the answer choices down to B, you could also determine that III is not correct. That one's perception of self is most important is not implied. This assumption is defined by the quote from the passage that "through psychotherapy, one learns that one may not necessarily have to change oneself as much as *one's perception of self*" (paragraph 5). There is no indication or implication in the passage that this is "most important," or *more* important than *changing* the "natural state" to fit our perception of self, making III incorrect for similar reasons that choice I is incorrect. Notice the tentative wording of the quote ("may not necessarily") in contrast to the strong connotation of "most."

66. C is correct. This is a difficult question, but it is fairly easy to narrow the answers down to two possibilities. Choice D can be eliminated because behavior falling *"within"* the parameters of the DSM-5 is considered *abnormal*, not normal. Furthermore, it is societal norms which the author believes have determined the DSM parameters, not the other way around, another reason that D is incorrect. Choice B can also be eliminated because it clearly takes the author's choice a step too far. Though it seems that the DSM is influenced by societal norms, there is no indication that it is "easily" influenced, or that overall it is a "poor descriptor" of abnormal behavior. It may actually be a very accurate descriptor of behavior that society has deemed abnormal, making B incorrect. Selecting between choices A and C is more difficult, but C is the better answer. Choice A is vague and simplistic compared to choice C, and thus is not as well supported by the passage. The author does argue that in another culture, Chris's disorder *might* not even be a disorder. However, the author still seems to consider Chris's experience to be disordered, at least within "our" society. For example, the author tries to elucidate the "causal factors for Chris's disorder," indicating that he or she considers Chris to have a disorder. Choice C is a better answer because it restricts itself to "*some* disorders" and because it specifically refers to the social influence on DSM categorization, a major point of the passage.

67. **B is correct.** Choice A can be eliminated because, as was also important for answering question 65, there is no value-type "should" judgment in the discussion of psychiatry as a possible treatment for Chris. Choice C is also incorrect because the author never discusses surgical treatment in relation to Chris. Although the author states at the beginning of the passage that some people "may desire hormone therapies or surgeries aimed at modifying their bodies so that they more closely align with their preferred gender identity," there is no "hint" by the author that surgery would be a useful treatment for Chris. The author instead discusses Chris's desire for hormone treatment, which is not a surgical procedure (as indicated by the quote referenced above, which refers to "hormone therapies" and "surgeries" as separate treatments). D is also incorrect; far from hinting that Chris's experience is due to a "personality defect," the author explicitly states that "basic defects in personality" are *not* involved. The correct answer is choice B. The notion that Chris's "uneasiness with his assigned sex" is influenced by the culture he lives in is definitely hinted at by the author. The entirety of paragraph 3 strongly argues this answer, beginning with the statement that "in this case, many psychologists may believe society is the culprit."

68. **C is correct.** What is the author's argument? This passage is *not* a completely objective representation of a psychological case study. The author's main argument is that "society is the culprit." Although the passage does not completely rule out "biochemical processes" as a possible cause, there is a strong emphasis on the involvement of societal and cultural factors. The hypothetical scenario of the effectiveness of antidepressant treatment, which alters biological functioning while leaving cultural gender norms intact, could indicate that biological factors play a larger role than is indicated by the author's argument. Since the new discovery is opposed to the author's argument, it does not confirm the argument and does affect it; choices A and B can be eliminated. The author's argument may be weakened by the scenario described in the question stem, but it is not disproved. For one thing, Chris only becomes "*somewhat* more comfortable." Furthermore, the fact that antidepressant treatment has an effect does not necessarily mean that Chris's discomfort was initially *caused* by biological factors. Social factors could still be the more significant cause. Thus choice D can be eliminated, and C is correct.

69. **B is correct.** Note that the correct answer must both be a passage "argument" and support the idea that "other cultures might not view Chris's experiences as 'disordered.'" Any answer choice that fails to meet one of these requirements is incorrect. Choice C can immediately be eliminated because the author argues that Chris is already well-adjusted; there is no reason to think that he would have been *more* well-adjusted in another culture. Unlike choice C, choice D is a passage argument, but it does not relate to the question that is being asked; in other words, it does not provide any insight into the views of other cultures. Choice D can be eliminated. Choosing between A and B may be more difficult. However, B is the better answer. The author argues that labeling influences perceptions of "abnormal" (i.e., disordered) behavior, and suggests that differences in labeling between cultures could influence how Chris's experience is perceived. Choice A could be tempting, but it does not describe a passage argument. Although the author implies that other cultures do not carry out this practice by saying that "many Western cultures" do so, this is a passage *implication*, not a passage argument. Furthermore, it is not as directly related to the question being asked as is choice B.

70. **D is correct.** This passage is not simply a descriptive case study. The author presents a particular viewpoint towards "our" society and its gender norms, presenting an unfavorable comparison to other cultures that may not be so restrictive. Since the author's view is clearly negative in some way, the answer choices can be narrowed down to C and D. "Distrustful" does not convey the strength of the author's negative attitude towards what he or she sarcastically terms as "our neatly constructed gender binary." Furthermore, "distrustful" simply is not as good a fit for the author's tone; who or what exactly would the author be said to "distrust?" Choice D is the better answer.

Passage II (Questions 71-77)

71. **B is correct.** The last paragraph of the passage explains that Dewey's theory focuses on norms and relationships between individuals. Considering the answer choices, you should think back to the beginning of the passage, which discusses "thick" politics, "thin" politics, classical liberalism, and instrumental rationality. The passage states that classical liberalism, which is a "thin" approach to politics and an example of instrumental rationality, is concerned only with individuals, not with their relationships to others or the societal norms they are expected to follow. For this reason, A, C, and D can all be eliminated. Remember that any time two or more MCAT® answers must all be correct if one of them is correct, they can all be eliminated. Dewey's approach more closely resembles a "thick" approach to politics, which considers the way people relate to each other within a society.

72. **A is correct.** This question, like most MCAT® questions, requires a thorough understanding of the author's main idea. The passage author argues that the "thin" politics of liberal democracies saps meaning from the world and leads to anomie. The author then considers some potential fixes for this problem, which the author believes is substantial. The entire argument is predicated on the idea that anomie is negative and harmful to societies, so the correct answer will likely focus on this point. D can be eliminated because John Dewey's arguments are not central to the author's argument—they simply represent one of multiple possible solutions to the problem. A, B, and C all focus on the relationship between anomie and society. If most democracies were not affected by anomie, the author's entire premise would be invalid, so C does not support the argument and is incorrect. Similarly, if societies with strong norms (the opposite of anomie) were more vulnerable to civil war and collapse, the idea of anomie being a societal harm is called into question, not supported; B can be eliminated. A correlation between anomie and societal collapse would provide strong evidence that the author's claims are true, making A the best answer.

73. **C is correct.** The "incoherent worldview" refers to Gellner's acceptance that scientific advancement and societal cohesion have different needs: science needs the Enlightenment-style approach in which no source of information is held as sacred, whereas societies need some privileged source of norms and traditions. The correct answer choice should refer to both of these ideas. A refers only to societal needs and B refers only to scientific needs, making both of these answers incorrect. Note that neither of these answer chocies are actually parts of Gellner's argument, another reason that they can be eliminated. D mentions both science and society, but claims that they have the same needs, which is the opposite of Gellner's incoherent worldview; D is incorrect. C correctly identifies the difference referred to in the question stem.

74. **A is correct.** The passage explains that Bellah believes a constitutional religion already exists because "the authority of political figures is historically based on something 'higher' than the self-interest of voters or politicians." Anything that challenges this reasoning could be a correct answer. Whether classical liberalism is a "thick" or "thin" approach to politics is irrelevant to this point, so B can be eliminated. Similarly, the current U.S. educational system is not relevant to the question, and C is incorrect. Note that these are both classic "round-about" answers; they include quotes and concepts from the passage that are meant to lure you into thinking they could be correct, but don't actually address the question. D is basically a rephrasing of Bellah's claim, which means it would SUPPORT rather than challenge his argument; D can be eliminated. Proof that societies do not draw political authority from some higher source directly contradicts Bellah's assertion, making A the correct answer.

75. **C is correct.** This question is asking you to link two key passage ideas. The correct answer must accurately describe both the author's view of a "thin" conception of politics and the nature of instrumental rationality. Recall that the passage defines instrumental rationality as being concerned only with the "means," not the "ends." A "thin" approach to politics is defined by its concern for only the rights of individuals, insisting that a State should do nothing more than establish rules to make competition fair. In other words, the "thin" approach concerns itself only with the "means" that individuals can take in pursuit of their interests, not the "ends" pursued. This relationship is explicitly stated by C, making it the correct answer. A and B are both characterizations of the "thick" approach, and are thus incorrect. While it could be true that the authors of the Constitution supported both concepts, it does not explain why one is an example of the other. For this reason, it is not a better answer than C, and can be eliminated.

76. **D is correct.** You can immediately eliminate C, since choices I and II are opposites and cannot both be correct. Recall from the passage that Gellner argued for separate treatment of scientific and societal needs. Gellner thinks that science "should not let religion interfere with serious cognitive and productive business", which makes answer choice I correct and II incorrect. Thus B can be eliminated. Choosing between A and D is a little bit more tricky. You may be tempted to discard choice III because it includes the word "cohesive," which seems contradictory to Gellner's concept of an "incoherent" worldview. However, an important part of Gellner's argument was the creation of societal cohesion through a set of cohesive norms (i.e., a constitutional religion) that would not overly interfere with scientific progress. This argument is accurately described by choice III. A can be eliminated, and D is the correct answer.

77. **B is correct.** Paragraph 2 explains that classical liberals were only concerned with establishing the "means" to allow individuals to pursue whatever "ends" they wanted, meaning they would not likely support using the State to promote any specific type of behavior (an "end"). Offering tax incentives to people who give money to charities can be seen as a way of encouraging an activity (charitable giving), and thus would not be supported by classical liberals, making A incorrect. A constitutional religion would similarly impose a set of beliefs and norms on the population, and would probably not find support among classical liberals; also recall that Gellner calls for a constitutional religion as a way to combat one of the problems arising from the liberal system. Thus D can be eliminated. Although classical liberals supported a very limited set of laws governing interactions, C is too extreme of an answer choice. How could the State ensure fair competition if *all* laws concerning intrapersonal interactions were abolished? A law preventing fraudulent investment practices would prevent the loss of property by the individuals giving their money to the bank, and would be in line with classical liberals' beliefs, according to the passage. For this reason, B is correct.

Passage III (Questions 78-84)

78. **C is correct.** The correct answer must be 1) a passage assertion that 2) would be weakened by the scenario posed in the question stem. Any answer choice that is not a passage assertion can be eliminated, and any that would be strengthened or unaffected can be eliminated. Choice A can be eliminated because it is not a passage assertion. Choice B is a passage assertion, but it is not weakened by the assumption in the question. The remarks have to do with the "tremendous passion" of Margaret's singing, not the "lyrics." This answer is not as responsive to the question as Answer C, which references "emotion" (i.e., passion). The passage established that Margaret was "the young woman of Faust's dreams" and asserted that her singing was "emotionless." If other critics thought that she sang with "tremendous passion," the assertion that her singing was emotionless would be weakened. Thus C is the best answer. Choice D is a passage assertion, since Margaret is said to be a commoner, but it is completely unrelated to the question stem. The passion of Margaret's singing has nothing to do with her social status. Thus D is incorrect.

79. **C is correct.** This question is best answered by process of elimination. Choice A is not indicated by passage information. You may have known before reading the passage that the Faust myth involves Faust losing his soul to the devil, but this is not referenced in the passage. Remember to leave prior knowledge behind when taking the CARS section! Choice B is not indicated by the passage; the country fair is referenced, but no comparison is made to the book. However, the broader statement of choice C is supported by passage information. Several references are made to differences between the opera and other interpretations of the Faust myth, including how "the book" offers a smoother transition to a particular scene ("the Witch's Sabbath on Walpurgis Night"). Choice D is arguable, but cannot be concluded as definitively as choice C. The author offers both positive and negative comments about the opera, and opens the passage by saying that "the New York City Opera production of 'Mephistopheles' deserves high marks for visual excellence." There is no way to draw a firm conclusion about whether or not the author ultimately enjoyed the performance.

80. **B is correct.** D can be eliminated immediately because no allusion to Scene III is made in the passage. Choice C must also be wrong because the author makes only one reference to Faust's singing, and it is not particularly complimentary: "Faust and Margaret sing very forgettable arias." There is no way to determine the author's feelings about Faust's singing as separate from Margaret's, and it seems likely that the author would not consider his singing to be an enhancement anyway. There is no evidence in the passage that the author thought the characterization of Mephisto was "poor." In fact, the author actually seems to have liked Mephisto's characterization. Process of elimination leaves B as the best answer. Prior to the point in the passage where Scene II is first mentioned, the author offers extensive praise of the opera. By contrast, the author is quite critical of Scene II, starting from the comment that "at this point, the play devolves into stock characters and slapstick."

81. **D is correct.** The passage starts with the author's high praise of the visual aspects of "Mephistopheles." There is perhaps no other aspect of the opera given such direct and unequivocal praise. The author's opinion of the music is unclear. The statement that the music was "only slightly corny" hardly rises to the level of the praise given to the opera's images; choice A can be eliminated. The author has many negative comments about "the singing of the opera," such as Margaret's "emotionless singing," so B is incorrect. Choice C is vague and is not supported by the passage. One could argue that the author greatly enjoyed the characterization of Mephisto, but this cannot be considered representative of the overall "plot." Compared to the evidence for choice A, choice C is unsupported.

82. **A is correct.** This question returns to the theme of differences between the opera and the original "Faust myth" or other versions of it. Also notice that the correct answer will include components that were only *suggested*, not necessarily stated, asserted, etc. You should evaluate choice III first, since it is included in two answer choices. This answer may seem attractive because of the passage statement that "this version presents temptation as essentially a wager, or struggle, between God and the Devil (which, at one time, was a remarkably blasphemous notion, as it contradicted the dogma that God is all-powerful over evil)." However, there is no reason to think that the phrase "at one time" refers to the "Faust myth." Thus choice III is wrong, and C and D can be eliminated. Choice I is clearly suggested by the author in the statement that "Faust and Margaret sing very forgettable arias about the supremacy of *feeling over reason*, a theme which is not really congruent with the Faust myth." The implication is that the Faust myth involved the supremacy of reason over feeling. Choice I is correct, making A the answer. You could also arrive at the correct answer by eliminating choice II. The passage does not suggest that Mephisto was "more evil" in the original Faust myth. The second paragraph describes the character of Mephisto in the operatic production and gives the impression that he has been portrayed/characterized differently in other versions, but does not make a direct comparison to his portrayal in the Faust myth. There is not enough passage information for choice II to be correct, confirming that only choice I is correct and choice A is the right answer.

83. **C is correct.** This question is unusual in that it involves a very specific piece of passage information. However, even without recalling or locating the exact reference in the passage, you can quickly narrow down the answers to two possibilities. Choice A can be eliminated because the visual imagery, although highly praised, was not linked in any way to the plot. Choice B can be eliminated because Faust's musings are not referenced as even being a part of the opera, let alone as a means of transmitting the plot. Between the two choices that remain, you may be tempted to choose D, since there is so much discussion of Mephisto in the passage. However, the passage focuses on the characterization of Mephisto and his actions within the opera; there is no indication that he relates directly to the audience in the manner described in the question stem. Just by this logic, you could arrive at choice C as the correct answer. You may recall from your first reading, or have time to go back to the passage and determine, that "a chorus presents the essential fundamental plot of Faust."

84. **D is correct.** The passage makes no attempt to consider whether Faust or the devil get the "better deal" from their bargain, so choices A and B can be eliminated. Both remaining answer choices relate to other versions of the myth. There is no basis in the passage to think that the devil made a bargain with Margaret in other versions of the story, so C is incorrect. However, the passage says that "In this version of Faust, it is Faust who seizes the devil's bargain." This statement "strongly implies" that the devil initiated the bargain in this version. In other versions, it may be Faust who bargains, making D the best answer.

EXPLANATIONS TO IN-CLASS EXAM FOR LECTURE 4

Passage I (Questions 85-91)

85. **C is correct.** The quickest way to answer questions like these is to first eliminate any answer choices you know are supported by evidence without going back to the passage. This approach will often get you all the way to the correct answer. The passage author gives an example of cancer patients to illustrate that it can be challenging for patients to make optimal decisions, so A is incorrect. The last paragraph gives an example of how a physician might talk to a patient to preserve their autonomy while still "nudging" them toward the best decision. This is evidence of D, which can also be eliminated. B is not supported by any passage evidence, but it is also not an idea advanced by the passage author. For this reason, it does not answer the question and is thus incorrect. It is important to read each question carefully. Although the author claims that advertising and medicine use "undeniably similar" techniques to coerce consumers to make certain choices, no evidence supporting this statement is provided, making C the correct answer.

86. **B is correct.** The author describes opt-out programs in support of the idea that "nominal freedom of choice" does not necessarily equal "effective freedom of choice." In other words, although people in an opt-out program appear to have the choice of whether or not to participate, the small percentage opting out indicates that they are not truly empowered to choose in practice. This explanation is summarized by B, which is the best answer. C is similar to B, but the wording is too extreme for a correct MCAT® answer. The author did not give an example of people with *no* freedom of choice, as indicated by the fact that some small percentage do opt out. They simply have *reduced* freedom of choice, and C is wrong. Choice A is incorrect for a different reason: rather than improving medical decision making, the author indicates that opt-out programs *restrict* decision making. This does not necessarily mean that the quality of decision making suffers, but there certainly is no indication that it improves. D is also incorrect; the author's point about the link between advertising and medicine comes later in the passage, and is not relevant to this example.

87. **D is correct.** Note that each answer choice has two parts, meaning the correct answer must satisfy two requirements: 1. It must answer the question accurately, and 2. Both parts of the answer choice must agree. The question stem gives an example of a potential application of medical paternalism that could save a large amount of money. Critics of medical paternalism would likely not support such a measure, and there is not enough information in the passage to indicate that any amount of monetary savings would be sufficient to justify medical paternalism. Based on passage information, the only thing that can be known for certain is that paternalism's critics oppose the philosophy because it hurts autonomy. Choices A and C can be eliminated. Choice B can be eliminated because the two parts of the answer do not logically agree: if the money saved IS significant enough to outweigh the cost of lost autonomy, there is no reason to oppose the measure. Process of elimination leaves D as the correct answer. The passage states that critics of paternalism oppose its exploitation of existing biases, but you did not need to remember that to answer the question.

88. **B is correct.** The passage establishes libertarian paternalism as a school of philosophical thought before describing the nudge techniques used by practitioners of this philosophy. In other words, nudge policies are one tool in the larger toolset of paternalism, making B the correct answer. Nudge policies are not used to fight libertarian paternalism according to the author, so answer choice A can be eliminated. There is a definite passage relationship between the two, so C is also incorrect. D is a good example of a "round-about" answer type: it uses information from the passage to make a true statement, but does not answer the question. Note that there is no mention of libertarian paternalism in choice D, so this answer choice cannot conceivably describe the relationship between nudge policies and libertarian paternalism!

89. **A is correct.** This question tests your knowledge of the author's stance on the passage topic. In the last sentence of the passage, the author proclaims that the "ideal" approach involves using nudge factors while promoting patient awareness. This indicates that the author is a proponent, at least to some degree, of medical paternalism. Based on the author's lack of a strongly opinionated tone, it is highly unlikely that he or she would argue for anything as extreme as refusing to write any prescriptions for the new drug or, conversely, prescribing it for every patient. Remember that answer choices using extreme wording like *all* or *under any circumstances* are usually not correct. This eliminates B and D. According to the author, giving patients access to all available information and letting them decide on their own leads to the problems that clinicians try to correct through tactics like nudge policies, so the author is unlikely to support this argument, and C is incorrect. Based on the author's stance on paternalism, he or she is likely to recommend that the clinician use a nudge technique to ensure that patients who do not need this new drug do not insist on it due to the variety of biases and other factors that unduly influence difficult medical decision making. This makes A the best answer.

90. **C is correct.** This question tests how well you understand the viewpoint of the opposition to nudge policies, which is a major idea of the passage. The critics explicitly refer to nudge policies as "manipulation," so A is a likely reason for their objection and can be eliminated. The passage author also refers specifically to critics decrying the limitations on freedom of choice that nudge policies impose, so D is incorrect. There is no mention of paternalism's critics questioning its effectiveness in the passage, and in fact the author mentions that it is effective. (Presumably, if nudge policies were ineffective, critics would not be particularly concerned about them!) For this reason, C is correct. Although the language of a "symptom of the problem" is not found in the passage, answer choice B lines up with the assertion that nudge policies exploit (utilize) biases rather than eliminating them. C is a better answer choice.

91. **A is correct.** This question stem requires careful reading. You are looking for the assumption that would most weaken the argument for paternalism if proven *false*. Disproving D would show that nudge techniques are effective at changing behavior, which strengthens the argument for paternalism; D can be eliminated. Similarly, proving that patients are not better decision makers than clinicians would only support the idea that clinicians need to steer patients toward the right decisions; B is incorrect. If, however, it was proven that clinicians are *not* better decision makers than patients, there would be no justification for giving clinicians the authority to "nudge" patients toward any decision. This would greatly weaken the argument for paternalism, making A correct. Disproving that *all* patients are poor medical decision makers would not necessarily weaken the case for paternalism; it could still be the case that *almost all* or *most* patients are poor medical decision makers and could benefit from medical paternalism. Choice A is thus a better answer than choice C.

92. **B is correct.** The correct answer to this question must satisfy two criteria: 1) It pertains to the information in paragraph 4, and 2) It is *implied* by the information in that paragraph. Saying that "the Health for All targets were always doomed to fail," although relevant to paragraph 4, goes way beyond the implications of the paragraph (and the passage in general), so choice A can be eliminated. Remember, a good MCAT® answer usually does not use extreme words like "always." Similarly, there is no mention in the passage of the popularity of Reagan's development policies in other countries. Although it seems likely that cutting foreign aid would be unpopular among the former recipients of that aid, this assumption requires outside knowledge, making this a classic "beyond" answer choice; choice C is incorrect. Choice B and D are similar answers. Note, however, that choice D is an absolute statement, whereas choice B contains softeners like "probably." For this reason, B is the better answer choice. The idea that selfishness could have contributed to declining aid is a major implication of the author's description of domestic support for Reagan's economic policies, making B the correct answer.

93. **D is correct.** This question requires an understanding of the main idea of the passage. The author's argument is that Malthus's theories about overpopulation leading to negative population health outcomes, which were once widely accepted, have now become taboo – even though they could explain many recent global developments. The idea that vaccines have been more beneficial than antibiotics does not affect the main idea. The author lists both of these as factors allowing large populations, but makes no distinction between them. This makes answer choice A incorrect. Although the scenario described by answer choice B would conflict with the author's statement that Malthus's ideas were initially widely accepted, the major arguments of the passage, which involve LATER views of Malthus's theories, would be unaffected; B can also be eliminated. The author would probably respond to choice C by arguing that the population has yet to exceed the Earth's carrying capacity. Although this answer choice is relevant to the main idea, it does not challenge or weaken it, and is thus incorrect. Evidence that population reduction is most likely to occur when population does *not* exceed resource capacity, however, would directly challenge the author's assertion that Malthusian "checks" are likely responsible for modern population reduction. This makes D correct.

94. **A is correct.** A good way to approach a question like this is to look for answers that can be eliminated because they deal with the main idea of the passage, which is typically well supported with examples. The author argues that huge advances in life expectancy in the 1970s undermined wariness about overpopulation. This is the "pernicious effect" referenced in D, which makes that assertion well supported by examples and thus incorrect. Looking at choice B, recall that this statement was the first sentence of a paragraph that then goes on to discuss several examples of countries in which life expectancy has fallen. B can be eliminated. C is slightly less relevant to the main idea, but looking back at paragraph 2 reveals the supporting example that "food production largely kept pace with the slowly growing global population" during the century after Malthus's death – C is incorrect. Although much support is provided for the claim that increased birth rates have been damaging to modern population health, there is none for the assertion that they have been disastrous for "many disciplines outside of public health." A is thus correct. The correct answer to this type of question will, like answer choice A, be a claim that the author states but then does not follow up with examples or evidence.

95. **C is correct.** Recall that rice was mentioned in the passage as one of the "new crop strains" of the 1970s. The author states that the success of these crop strains previously contributed to baseless optimism about the issue of overpopulation, rather than solving the problem. Thus the author would not view these crop strains as some panacea that allows for indefinite population expansion. For this reason answer choice A is incorrect. Note that choice A is also an absolute statement – a common characteristic of wrong CARS answers. C is a more nuanced statement that fits with the author's description of population growth in the 1970s, making it the correct answer. There is no reason to believe that the author would abandon his or her main idea because of this one new piece of evidence, so B can be eliminated. D describes the development of more prolific rice as a "positive check." Recall from the passage that positive checks are events that limit the population by causing deaths, such as war and famine. This is the opposite effect of that expected from the new rice strains, making D incorrect.

96. **D is correct.** This is one of the less common types of CARS questions; it tests a specific piece of passage information. If necessary, look back at the passage to remind yourself of what a "negative check" is. In the first paragraph, the author calls restrictions on marriage an example of a negative check. Given this information and the description of distinct "positive checks" as factors that limit the population by causing higher rates of death, you can infer that negative checks limit the population by lowering rates of birth. Of the answer choices, only growing birth control usage would decrease the population in this way, making D correct. Violence and famine are both examples of positive checks, meaning that B and C do not answer the question and can be eliminated. A higher vaccination rate is not a Malthusian check at all since it should allow for increased population growth, which makes choice A incorrect as well.

Even if you did not remember what a negative check was and did not have time to go back to the passage, you could still reason your way to the correct answer. B and C are similar enough that neither can be the correct answer. You should understand the general idea that "checks," both negative and positive, decrease the population. Between the answer choices that remain after eliminating B and C, only D will cause population decline.

97. **D is correct.** This is another question testing your knowledge of the main idea. Remember that the author's "point" is that Malthusian views on overpopulation are valuable but underused in today's global health theory. The idea that current population threats are the result of *excessive* foreign aid goes completely against the author's assertions concerning the policies of the Reagan administration, making choice A incorrect. Note that correct answers rarely contradict the author's viewpoint unless the question specifically asks for such an answer. The passage never makes any claims about the seriousness of population declines in other countries relative to each other, so B is beyond the scope of the passage and can be eliminated. While it is true that the author probably considers the Rwandan genocide and the AIDS crisis to be positive checks, his or her main point is that there is not enough acknowledgment of them as such, making C only half true. This is an example of an incorrect "feel-good" answer choice. Since Malthusian checks are consequences of overpopulation and are generally unacknowledged, according to the author, D is the better answer.

98. **B is correct.** A dissident is someone who opposes official policy, often of an authoritative state. The author is using the term here to allude to the overwhelming current lack of support for the "Malthusian view" discussed in the first paragraph. For this reason, C is incorrect – there is almost no current support for this important theory, according to the author. While many political dissidents are involved in military conflicts, there is no indication of one involving Maurice King, who is likely an academic, so choice A can be eliminated. All the information given indicates that the author agrees with King and is advocating for more consideration of his views, so D can also be eliminated. Quotation marks here are used to indicate irony: what was once an overwhelmingly accepted viewpoint (and one that the author claims is still valid) is now embraced by so few academics that they can be likened to dissidents fighting against an oppressive state.

Notice that although familiarity with the word "dissidents" is useful in answering this question, you could still find the correct answer if you didn't know the word. Looking back at the passage shows that the word "dissidents" is used to refer to people who consider overpopulation as a possible cause of population or life expectancy decline. There is no indication in the passage that such people would be involved in "military conflict," so choice A can be eliminated. B immediately looks like a good choice because it is in line with the major argument of the passage. C and D can both be eliminated because they are not consistent with passage information or the author's beliefs. There is NOT overwhelming support of Malthusian theory, and if there were, the author would not disapprove; C is wrong. Similarly, the author agrees with people like King who urge a reconsideration of Malthusian theory, so D can be eliminated.

Passage III (Questions 99-105)

99. **C is correct.** "These people" used in this context refers back to the discussion of local peoples that had been subordinated to the historical narratives of their conquerors. The first paragraph states that this population had especially strong feelings about promoting national pride and legitimizing their situation through the ability to define their own past. This idea is continued in paragraph two with the discussion of their hunger to establish their own cultural ancestry and culture-affirming archaeological practices. Choice A is incorrect because, in this case, the British were the conquerors, not the conquered. The Israelis described in choice D were not described as oppressed, but rather discussed in the context of an example of historical sites taking on new national importance. The Rhodesians in choice B do represent one group of formerly oppressed peoples who are described as hungering for new national identity. However, strictly speaking, the builders of the Great Zimbabwe were not oppressed by the British, but were rather the ancestors of the oppressed. Furthermore, the implications of "these people" as was used in the passage implies more general applicability to formerly oppressed people building new senses of national identities rather than being confined to a specific group.

100. **C is correct.** Choice A is supported by the example of the Israeli army recruits. B is supported by the example of the importance of recognizing the Great Zimbabwe as an African achievement. Choice D is explained in detail through the descriptions of how manipulation of archaeological interpretation can create a more valuable commodity for tourism. Choice C is mentioned in the passage, but the following information is more of a restatement than an explanation and not example is provided.

101. **D is correct.** A is incorrect because the passage actually seems to imply that financial gain (not political gain) is the main motivating force behind developing historical sites for tourism. The passage does discuss the importance of manipulating archaeology among formerly oppressed people to develop a sense of native identity, but there is no reason to assume that manipulation of archaeology is not equally important to supporting the hegemony of the oppressors. On the contrary, the rejection of the 'natives' by the British as possible builders of the Great Zimbabwe suggests that selective interpretation of archaeology was a force in supporting their oppression, making B incorrect. C is not discussed in the passage. D encompasses one of the main ideas of the passage and is supported with many specific examples that threaten objectivity (financial gain, political gain, creating national unity, etc.) making D the best answer.

102. **B is correct.** The tone of the passage is one of criticism toward biases and taking liberties when interpreting the past. The final paragraph of the passage strongly implies that archaeological research should be conducted in as an objective and scientific manner as possible. Choices A, C, and D all result in factual data, while choice B is based on subjective interpretation, which the author is more likely to discourage. Even without reading the article, it might be possible to identify B as the correct answer from the language of the answer choices. The three incorrect answer choices are very concrete in their language and goals whereas the term "speculation" in choice B implies a subjectivity that is unlike the others.

103. **C is correct.** In the passage, the appearance of archaeological artifacts on postage stamps and in souvenir shops is discussed in the context of peoples' hunger to establish their cultural heritage as legitimate. This should already give you a hint that C might be the correct answer. The relevant paragraph goes on to discuss the lengths societies are willing to go in using archaeology as propaganda to legitimize their existence in their current form including investing money, training local professionals and creation of archaeological infrastructure. All of these factors, along with the example of how the Israeli historical site becomes a national rallying place should give you a sense of the pride and unity that can be inspired by archaeology. The other three example choices, which sometimes use vocabulary from the passage, are not explicitly discussed by the author.

104. **B is correct.** The attendant temptations described in this section of the passage involve behaviors that use misrepresentation of archaeological knowledge to accomplish specific ideological and financial goals. Embellishing a story is analogous to unjustly glorifying the past or over-restoration of historical monuments, while publishing sensationalized stories is akin to "selling" a sensationalized version of history to affect beliefs and world view. Omitting sections from an interview is very like the passage's description of choosing only the "facts" that best support the chosen story. Only choice B seems out of step with the description of the temptations described in the passage, by not aiming to manipulate the story to suit the purposes of the author or publisher.

105. **A is correct.** This question can be a tricky one because all four possible answer choices are mentioned in the passage and represent opinions of the author. The key to selecting the best answer choice is to consider the context in which they were discussed. Choice B was discussed in the context of rebuilding national identity after a period of oppression; this does not seem particularly relevant to the hypothetical example of improvements before hosting the Olympics. Choice D is discussed toward the end of the passage as a transition into emphasizing the importance of relative objectivity (rather than subjective interpretation) in archaeology and does not relate to the question stem. Choice C is plausible in that the plans for beautification MIGHT demonstrate how the nation wants to be seen by the world, now that the spotlight of the Olympics is upon them. However, this point in the passage is brought up within the context of a discussion on the misuse of archaeology as propaganda, which is only tangentially related to the question. The description in the question stem of the over-development of historic sites most closely echoes discussion of exploiting archaeology for ideological and financial gain in the third paragraph of the passage. The likely influx of tourism that accompanies the Olympic games would fit nicely with this context and supports answer choice A as the best available answer to the question.

Photo Credits

Covers

Front cover, Coffee and glasses: © Examkrackers staff

Lecture i

Pg. 1, Herd of sheep scattered near mountain summit: © Horia Varlan/Flickr, adapted for use under the terms of the Creative Commons CC BY 2.0 license (http://creativecommons.org/licenses/by/2.0/legalcode)

Pg. 7, Teacher and students in math class: © Slobodan Vasic/iStockphoto.com

Pg. 9, Calculator: © Dana Kelley

Pg. 13, Abacus: © Michelle Gibson/iStockphoto.com

Pg. 13, Dice: © porcorex/iStockphoto.com

Pg. 14, Close-up of student solving a sum on the blackboard: © Jacob Wackerhausen/iStockphoto.com

Lecture ii

Pg. 30, Sir Isaac Newton Drawn by Wm. Derby and engraved (with permission) by W.J. Fry: Images from the History of Medicine (NLM)

Pg. 32, Young Woman Walking Dog: Amanda Mills/CDC Public Health Image Library

Lecture 1

Pg. 60, Professor reading book: © Grigory Bibikov/iStockphoto.com

Pg. 61, Students in study group: © Nikada/iStockphoto.com

Pg. 65, Clock: © deepblue4youi/Stockphoto.com

Lecture 2

Pg. 71, Keys to lock: © Thomas Vogel/iStockphoto.com

Pg.72, Hiker on summit: © Danny Warren/iStockphoto.com

Lecture 3

Pg. 85, Hammer on wood: © Dzmitri Mikhaltsow/iStockphoto.com

Pg. 86, Hourglass: © Alexander Shirokov/iStockphoto.com

Pg. 99, Thinking young woman: © DRBimages/iStockphoto.com

About the Author

Jonathan Orsay is uniquely qualified to write an MCAT® preparation book. He graduated on the Dean's list with a B.A. in History from Columbia University. While considering medical school, he sat for the real MCAT® three times from 1989 to 1996. He scored in the 90 percentiles on all sections before becoming an MCAT® instructor. He has lectured in MCAT® test preparation for thousands of hours and across the country. He has taught premeds from such prestigious Universities as Harvard and Columbia. He was the editor of one of the best selling MCAT® prep books in 1996 and again in 1997. He has written and published the following books and audio products in MCAT® preparation: "Examkrackers MCAT® Physics"; "Examkrackers MCAT® Chemistry"; "Examkrackers MCAT® Organic Chemistry"; "Examkrackers MCAT® Biology"; "Examkrackers MCAT® Verbal Reasoning & Math"; "Examkrackers 1001 questions in MCAT® Physics", "Examkrackers MCAT® Audio Osmosis with Jordan and Jon".

An Unedited Student Review of This Book

The following review of this book was written by Teri R—. from New York. Teri scored a 43 out of 45 possible points on the MCAT®. She is currently attending UCSF medical school, one of the most selective medical schools in the country.

"The Examkrackers MCAT® books are the best MCAT® prep materials I've seen-and I looked at many before deciding. The worst part about studying for the MCAT® is figuring out what you need to cover and getting the material organized. These books do all that for you so that you can spend your time learning. The books are well and carefully written, with great diagrams and really useful mnemonic tricks, so you don't waste time trying to figure out what the book is saying. They are concise enough that you can get through all of the subjects without cramming unnecessary details, and they really give you a strategy for the exam. The study questions in each section cover all the important concepts, and let you check your learning after each section. Alternating between reading and answering questions in MCAT® format really helps make the material stick, and means there are no surprises on the day of the exam-the exam format seems really familiar and this helps enormously with the anxiety. Basically, these books make it clear what you need to do to be completely prepared for the MCAT® and deliver it to you in a straightforward and easy-to-follow form. The mass of material you could study is overwhelming, so I decided to trust these books—I used nothing but the Examkrackers books in all subjects and got a 13-15 on Verbal, a 14 on Physical Sciences, and a 14 on Biological Sciences. Thanks to Jonathan Orsay and Examkrackers, I was admitted to all of my top-choice schools (Columbia, Cornell, Stanford, and UCSF). I will always be grateful. I could not recommend the Examkrackers books more strongly. Please contact me if you have any questions."

Sincerely,
Teri R—